Blue China

Blue China

Single Female Migration
to Colonial Australia

Jan Gothard

MELBOURNE UNIVERSITY PRESS

MELBOURNE UNIVERSITY PRESS
PO Box 278, Carlton South, Victoria 3053, Australia
info@mup.unimelb.edu.au
www.mup.com.au

First published 2001
Text © Jan Gothard 2001

Design and typography © Melbourne University Press 2001

Designed by Lauren Statham, Alice Graphics
Typeset by Syarikat Seng Teik Sdn. Bhd., Malaysia, in
10 point Meridien
Printed in Australia by RossCo Print

National Library of Australia Cataloguing-in-Publication entry

Gothard, Janice.
    Blue China: single female migration to colonial Australia.
    Bibliography.
    Includes index.
    ISBN 0 522 84958 X.
    1. Women immigrants—Australia—History. 2. Single
    women—Australia—History. 3. British—Australia—History.
    4. Working class women—Australia—History. 5. Women
    alien labor—Australia—History. 6. Australia—Emigration
    and Immigration—History. I. Title.
325.2410994

Contents

Preface

JUST DAYS AWAY from Hobart, Maria Luttman fell from the poop deck of the *Hooghly* into the cold waters of the Southern Ocean. The ship did not turn back. Julia Neagle joined her emigrant sister in Western Australia, married a convict from the Channel Islands and founded an Australian dynasty. Kate Teehan died in the Perth Hospital, hours after having set alight her kerosene-doused clothing. She had been in her new colonial home less than a week. Against official advice, Maggie Kelly worked in Boulder on the Western Australian goldfields, till she met and married an Irish miner there. She never told her strict Church of Scotland family that he was a Catholic. These tiny shards of narrative, pieced together with countless thousand others, make up the story of the migration of single working-class women to the Australian colonies.

Of course, every woman's experience of migration was unique. In the context which frames this book, each migrant's tale was also shaped by government policies informed by particular understandings of working-class femininity, of domestic service and of migration itself. Fundamental to my book is the belief that we need to understand the structures bearing upon women as immigrants, gendered structures which affected women differently from men, before a closer analysis of the characteristics and circumstances of large numbers of individual immigrants becomes meaningful.

Only by knowing the shape of the whole can we piece together the individual fragments of each woman's experience. How did Julia Neagle and others like her find out about opportunities in the colonies? What circumstances might have led to Maria Luttman's fatal fall? Why were Maggie Kelly and her contemporaries advised not to go to the goldfields? What safety nets were there to help a woman such as Kate Teehan—and why did they sometimes fail? With broad answers to such questions in mind, I look both at colonial immigration policies and practices aimed at single women and at how individual women experienced and responded to their circumstances.

Colonial government views on single female migration were shaped in large measure by a particular group of British women: not emigrants but middle-class women with a genuine concern for the protection of working-class women. Their interest, sometimes described as 'benevolent maternalism', translated into a threefold approach to migration. Careful selection of women who wished to emigrate, thorough protection in transit, and close follow-up and oversight after arrival as part of the colonial reception process, were all elements of this. While colonial governments thought first of the cost, British female emigrationists gave priority to emigrant women's welfare. In time, governments became convinced that the two ends could tie together. Protected migration, with due attention to all three stages of the process, would introduce to the colonies a group of well-selected and well-protected young women suitable for paid work in colonial households. Thereby governments could meet their responsibilities to colonists, to the new arrivals and to colonial coffers.

With this in mind, the theme that permeates this book is protection and control. While all assisted immigrants experienced some degree of government control, single women were subjected to the strictest regime. Control passed as 'protection', but it had many faces: protection of immigrant women from physical and moral danger, protection of the colonial government investment in domestic labour, protection of colonial homes from 'contamination' through contact with 'immoral' women. The three facets of the migration process—selection, shipboard protection and colonial reception—were intimately linked. I chart the implementation, practice and consequences of those processes from when women first put themselves forward as prospective emigrants until they finally passed into their employers' hands.

It is a truism in Australian history that single women were assisted to migrate to the colonies because of the disproportion of the sexes. Colonial governments are said to have wanted to introduce them to marriageable working-class men; conversely, single women are depicted as coming out to the colonies seeking husbands. Catherine Helen Spence's 1854 novel *Clara Morison*, with its detailed description of contemporary Adelaide, offers a telling counter to the view that single women were greatly outnumbered by desperate colonial bachelors. In the bush and the country, particularly at the time of the 1850s gold rushes in the eastern colonies, the imbalance of the sexes was very marked. But in the coastal towns and cities, where newcomers loved to cluster, the numbers of men and women were far more balanced.

Colonists clamoured for domestic servants (single women who ideally would stay that way, though of course many did not), not for wives. We do not know enough about domestic service in Australian society, nineteenth or twentieth, to judge how widely domestic servants were employed. However, in the space of half a century, colonial societies absorbed over ninety thousand domestic servants and the evidence suggests they could have used more. There are many questions to be considered about domestic service in colonial Australia, but there is no doubt that from the point of view of colonial governments and societies, women were assisted to migrate with a view to entering paid domestic service.

This book cannot explain why Kate Teehan killed herself. But it does offer an understanding of the processes by which single women crossed the ocean and sought new lives, of how and why they experienced the long transition from 'migrant' to 'colonial'.

Many people have given generously in helping me produce this book. Above all, I would like to acknowledge my partner Charlie Fox, critic, reader and friend. For years he and our three daughters, Katie, Madeleine and Erin, have been endlessly patient as this work unfolded, and I am indebted to all of them.

For a range of gifts, I would also like to mention with gratitude Maryon Allbrook, Anne Atkinson, Geoffrey Bolton, Joy Damousi, Rica Erickson, Joan Fox, Andrew Gill, Jay Ginn, David Gothard, Lois Gothard, Paula Hamilton, Lenore Layman, Anne McBride, Geoff Sherington, Dianne Snowden and Bogusia Wojiechowska Kibble. I must also record the particular generosity of the women of the Girls' Friendly Society around Australia for allowing me access to their archives.

Writing this history has involved poring over the intimate details of many immigrants' lives. Those who shared their family histories with me so willingly include: Alan Amery, Sydney; Mrs D. Ashworth, Tweed Heads; Mrs P. Beliveau, Kawana Waters; John Blundell, Orpington, Kent, UK; Dorothy Bryce, Toowoomba; Mrs G. Castleman, Canberra; Frances Chester, Hornsby; Marjorie Cole, Bayswater; Avis Davis, Allora; Betty Dennis, Warrnambool; Mrs Efford, Perth; Lottie Jenkins, Newcastle; Merna Kidgell, Pakenham; Marjorie King, Perth; Ruth Lanyon, Bendigo; Ellen Mahoney, Canberra; Noelene Montague, Launceston; Rosemary Sheens, Gorokan; Merle Storey, Perth; George Tanner, Goonellabah; Doreen Tomlinson, Roseville; Eileen Tucker, Perth; Doreen Turnbull, Wollongong; Mrs M. J. Vaughan, Hamilton South; and Trevor Williams, Whittlesea. I thank them all sincerely. Lyn Dale's sharing of her grandmother Maggie Kelly's journal, and Susan Groom's account of the 'four Julias' were recent unexpected and joyful bonuses.

Staff at Melbourne University Press have been patient and encouraging, as everyone said they would be. My thanks to Nerissa Greenfield, Margot Jones, Teresa Pitt and especially Jean Dunn.

The publication of this book has been assisted by a small publishing grant from the Centre for Research for Women, a joint facility of the four public universities in Western Australia, and a research grant from the Divisional Research Committee, Social Sciences, Murdoch University.

The list of my obligations goes on. I offer my thanks to all those people who have been supportive and interested and have provided hospitality and friendship over the years.

Jan Gothard
February 2001

Abbreviations

AOT	Archives Office of Tasmania
BLFES	British Ladies' Female Emigrants Society
BPP	*British Parliamentary Papers*
BWEA	[United] British Women's Emigration Association
CLEC	Colonial Land and Emigration Commissioners
CL&I	Crown Lands and Immigration Office, South Australia
CSO	Colonial Secretary's Office, Western Australia
EWJ	*English Woman's Journal*
EWR	*English Woman's Review*
FMCES	Female Middle-Class Emigration Society
GFS	Girls' Friendly Society
ML	Mitchell Library, State Library of New South Wales
NSW *VPLA*	New South Wales, *Votes and Proceedings of the Legislative Assembly*
PRO Kew	Public Record Office, Kew, UK
PROV	Public Record Office Victoria
Qld *JLC*	Queensland, *Journals of the Legislative Council*
Qld *VPLA*	Queensland, *Votes and Proceedings of the Legislative Assembly*
Qld *VPLC*	Queensland, *Votes and Proceedings of the Legislative Council*
QSA	Queensland State Archives
SA *PP*	South Australia, *Proceedings of Parliament*
SPCK	Society for Promoting Christian Knowledge
SPEW	Society for Promoting the Employment of Women
SRNSW	State Records New South Wales
SRSA	State Records South Australia
SROWA	State Records Office of Western Australia
TAS	Travellers' Aid Society
T *HAJ*	Tasmania, *House of Assembly Journals*

T *JPP*	Tasmania, *Journals and Papers of Parliament*
Vic *PP*	Victoria, *Papers Presented to Parliament*
WA *PD*	Western Australia, *Parliamentary Debates*
WA *VPLC*	Western Australia, *Votes and Proceedings of the Legislative Council*
WA *VPP*	Western Australia, *Votes and Proceedings of Parliament*
WES	Women's Emigration Society

Conversions

1 inch	2.54 centimetres
1 foot (12 inches)	30.5 centimetres
1 yard (3 feet)	0.91 metre
1 mile	1.61 kilometres

Currency

On 14 February 1966, Australian currency changed from pounds, shillings and pence (£, s, d) to dollars and cents at the rate of £1 = $2. Twelve pence made up one shilling and twenty shillings made up one pound. A guinea was a pound plus a shilling.

For my grandmother
Fanny Elizabeth (Bessie) Starkey
immigrant of 1911
and for all her descendants

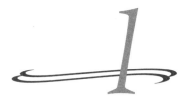

Emigrating Women

The emigration of men is a sort of automatic proceeding.
Men are more independent than women. They can transport
themselves with greater ease. They require no protection, and
accordingly they have been left—probably wisely—to their
own devices. But it is very different in the case of women.
There the emigration is, if possible, more desirable, and at the
same time it is attended with greater difficulties and even
with greater danger ... Women alone and unprotected cannot safely be sent great distances across the sea, to arrive in
strange lands where they have no friends or relatives to look
after them, and where they do not know how to act until
employment comes to them.

Joseph Chamberlain, 1901[1]

ON MAY DAY 1886, Hannah and Mary Wright made their
final visit to the graves of their parents. That Saturday
evening, farewelled by their brothers, they took the midnight
train to Kings Cross station in London. 'We are all to full to say
much', Hannah wrote of the parting, 'Yet we are hopeing to
meet again soon'. Mary was ill all the way down. A cab to Fen-
church Street station, a train to the emigrant lodging home on
the wharves at Blackwall, and the sisters found themselves
immersed in a new environment, preparing with their fellow

travellers for life in 'a Strange land'.[2] That night Hannah plaintively wrote up her first day's journal: 'and so ends our first Sunday away from home and without a home to go to'. The Wrights were bound for Queensland, just two amongst the twenty thousand single women given free and assisted passages by the Queensland colonial government in the 1880s.

Maggie Kelly had similarly poignant memories of her first night at the Emigrants' Home in Horseferry Road, London. She and her friend Lizzie Royle, both in service in Stockport, had elected to emigrate to Western Australia in 1900, at the tail end of the colony's 1890s programme to recruit single women:

> It seemed very strange all being strangers and sitting up in bed talking to each other as if we had known each other all our lives. They all seemed very nice. There were 10 girls in our room. One girl, Kitty Barber, started crying so of course I must go to pet her up a bit, and start crying myself, then one after another got out and joined in the chorus till we were all huddled up on the floor in our night dresses crying, and it was quite three in the morning before we were all in bed again. My bed was so hard I could not sleep.[3]

The hostel's ship-style bunk beds—'such funny beds one on top of the other'—were not designed to be comfortable nor to make the women feel at home. They were just a taste of things to come.

Between 1860 and 1900 close to ninety thousand single British women accepted an assisted passage to one of the six Australian colonies: 18 000 to New South Wales; 13 000 to Victoria; 9100 to South Australia; 46 000 to Queensland; 1700 to Western Australia; and 1600 to Tasmania.[4] They were part of a great nineteenth-century redistribution of people from the British Isles to distant parts of the Empire and to the United States. As a destination, the United States offered the British emigrant the advantage of proximity, which translated into cheaper passages and the possibility of a return home. To counter this, colonial governments across the globe sought to attract both the labour and capital they needed through assistance packages of land or subsidised fares. Without assistance the long sea voyage would have been prohibitively expensive for working-class people. In return, colonial governments intended that working-class women like the Wright sisters, Lizzie Royle and Maggie Kelly would solve the colonies' pressing 'domestic servant problem'.

The constant and unmet demand for satisfactory domestic servants characteristic of middle-class life in colonial Australia had long drawn comment from observers and visitors to the colonies. Despite a deal of debate in the colonial press, echoing similar discussions in Britain, there were only two possible solutions: encourage local young women to enter domestic service or import servants ready made. Local women were notoriously reluctant to enter domestic service, so colonists and their governments pursued the alternative. Single female domestic servants were the largest (and occasionally the only) category of labour given assistance with the cost of passage to the Australian colonies. No colony assisted female immigration for the entire time but single women were offered substantial levels of assistance from roughly 1860 to 1886 in New South Wales, the 1850s to 1873 in Victoria, 1850s to 1883 in South Australia, 1860 to 1900 in Queensland, from 1856 to 1863 and again in the early 1880s in Tasmania and, with different levels of intensity, from 1850 to 1900 in Western Australia. Single women had also been part of earlier schemes for populating white Australia. They were a focus of the earliest colonial assistance packages in the 1830s, and single orphan girls were also assisted to migrate to colonial destinations in the 1840s and 1850s. At all times, they were a critical requirement in terms of the productive and reproductive needs of Australia's colonial societies. The ninety thousand stories of the single women who migrated to colonial Australia between 1860 and 1900 collectively constitute a previously untold chapter in the history of British colonial and economic expansion.

A cheap passage in return for labour was an offer taken up by thousands of men and their families. For women, though, the exchange was not always straightforward. All assisted migrants were subject to routine examination in terms of health and character before they were permitted to embark, but for women this scrutiny went further. The Wright sisters, for example, travelled 'without natural protectors' and, as unaccompanied single women of working-class origin, they were subjected to rigorous controls on the passage out and even after their arrival in the colonies, until the colonial government had seen them safely into the hands of colonial employers or relatives. Though ignorant of this agenda, the Wrights' activities on the day of their arrival in London were already curtailed by it. They had hoped to visit a church to seek some spiritual comfort before the moment of departure but soon learned that single women were not permitted to leave the emigrant home after seven in the evening. They settled for an afternoon stroll instead.[5] Just as they would have been scrutinised before their acceptance for assisted passage, they were now subject to controls which would continue to shape their activities even after they disembarked in Brisbane. Had they emigrated to New South Wales two or three years earlier or to Western Australia a decade later, the relatively mild restrictions they faced migrating to Queensland would have been rather more rigorous. Single women's experience of this 'double control'[6] is a major focus of this book.

Though a good portion of this book is devoted to the passage to the colonies, emigration is more than simply the passage. Hannah and Mary Wright's emigration began long before their physical journey. Their decision to emigrate and the reasons behind it; completion of forms; successful application for passage; medical examination and search for appropriate referees: all are part of that story. In their case, we know that their brother Edward, and their cousins the Macfarlanes and David Wray Wright, were all Queensland residents anticipating their arrival, but we do not know whether they were 'sent for' by their relatives, or whether they themselves applied to the colonial government for an assisted passage. Even with the aid of family historians and genealogists, a biographical cameo such as the Wrights' only seldom becomes available to the migration researcher. Speculation is always part of the process of reconstructing emigrant stories. We know that Lizzie Royle and Maggie Kelly, typical of most nineteenth-century single female emigrants, had worked in domestic service. Perhaps an employer, a reader of one of the many middle-class women's journals which encouraged working-class emigration in the 1880s and 1890s, thought it in their employee's interests to emigrate, although the price of such advice was losing a servant. Travelling emigration lecturers visiting rural districts promised women such as Maggie and Lizzie the fulfilment of material dreams in a new country. The Wrights were regular church goers; they might have been members of the Girls' Friendly Society (GFS) and seen free passages to Queensland and Western Australia advertised in the GFS newsletter, *Friendly Leaves*. Perhaps the loss of the second of their parents was the catalyst which prompted Hannah and Mary, like many before them, to sever remaining family ties and try a new world. These questions prefigure the Wrights' night train trip to Kings Cross and, although this book cannot answer them all, countless other questions need to be asked about their experiences after arrival.

The availability of sources necessarily shapes the historian's approach. Letters and personal reminiscences are invaluable to the historian of migration but there is little doubt about their class and gender bias. Patrick O'Farrell, for example, found himself unable to take up the question of Irish female immigration because 'those Irishwomen who emigrated seem not to have been from the letter-writing classes'.[7] Consequently, in studies of migration which draw heavily on personal recollections and correspondence, both gender and class have become organising principles, although this is sometimes left unacknowledged.[8]

Much of what we know about the passage to the colonies comes from personal diaries written in the cabins of paying passengers.[9] Working-class journals are harder to find than those written by middle-class men, with those written by working-class women most scarce of all. Single women's illiteracy was not the reason for this, nor was shortage of numbers. Rather, we begin to find an explanation in their employment and social background. Andrew Hassam has accounted for the dearth of surviving journals written by working-class men in terms of occupation, mobility, and family circumstances, and these factors surely explain the absence of diaries written by working-class single women. Only more so, perhaps.

Emigrant diaries were traditionally written in the form of a letter home, addressed to a second person. Emigrationist Ellen Joyce advised 'her girls' to do just that: 'It is an excellent plan to take your envelopes ready addressed for home, and to write a journal of life on board ship, which you can post . . . when you land. Write small, as postage to England is sixpence'.[10]

Yet for many of the women who left Britain behind, ties with family had long been severed. Domestic service was a live-in occupation, which necessarily meant some loosening of familial bonds, and many female emigrants had spent years in paid domestic service before embarking for the colonies. Leaving a crowded rural family home for domestic employment, not even returning home for infrequent holidays because of considerations of space, was common amongst the domestic servants who comprised the bulk of colonial Australia's female immigrants. Many would not have kept in close touch with their families even while in Britain. In fact, isolation from home was one of the factors which made emigration an easier prospect. That first dislocating step away from the family home had already been made.

Statistical records are fragmentary, the amount of information required and preserved by each colony by no means uniform. But the remaining shipping lists reveal that for many women, the address they gave as their 'permanent home' was that of a previous employer, or else a landlady with whom they spent their holidays. Sometimes these people, their respectability assured by their stable address, acted as personal referee for the intending emigrant. As former employers or landladies, though, they were not necessarily the people for whom you would write a journal.

The physical difficulty of maintaining close contact with family in Britain, once a woman had entered domestic service, was another issue. Today we take for granted our ability to travel across countries and continents but, though we can understand readily enough the problems an emigrant might face if she wished to return home to Britain, it is easier to overlook difficulty with transport within Britain. After she was accepted for emigration to Western Australia in 1900, Maggie Kelly did not return to her widower father's home in Scotland to say her farewells (it was no longer *her* home). Many years later she told her daughter that she had not been able to bear the thought of that final parting but, more practically, distance and cost would also have been factors.[11] Maggie kept a diary but did not send it home to her father.

Life expectancies of working-class people in nineteenth century Britain were lower than today. Maggie's mother had died in 1892, aged just 48. Death hastened the breakup of the family and, as was the case with Hannah and Mary Wright, the death of a second parent was frequently a catalyst for emigration. A relatively high proportion of single women who chose to emigrate had already lost one or both parents. Of 77 of the 79 single women who sailed for New South Wales on board the *Dunbar Castle* in 1871, 30 had two parents still alive, 26 had lost one parent and 21 had lost both.[12] Only 13 of the 34 single women travelling to New South Wales in 1870 on the *Sobraon* had both parents still living; 11 had no remaining parents and 10 had lost one.[13] On the *Hawkesbury*, which reached Sydney on 5 March 1871, 18 of the 58 single women had lost one parent and 12 had lost both.[14] Perhaps it is not so surprising that relatively few single women wrote diaries which have survived. Those diaries that were written, if kept in the colonies, would have been baggage to carry from one domestic employer to another till a woman found her own permanent home in marriage; or if journals were sent back, they might well have gone to friends or relatives who themselves had no settled family home. Sisters or female cousins were all possible recipients of journals. But these were the very women who so often followed the adventurous pioneer out to the colonies. So the chances of working-class women's journals surviving were even more remote than for those sent back to the well-rooted middle-class families of the cabin passengers. All these factors made the preservation of letters and journals more precarious and the infrequent surviving journal such as Hannah Wright's or Maggie Kelly's infinitely precious.

For that reason, the three hundred or so middle-class women who migrated to Australia in the 1860s and 1870s as governesses, through the Female Middle-Class Emigration Society, have been proportionally over-represented in the literature on female migration. Many of these 'emigrant gentlewomen' left lucid and literate accounts of their experiences. Further, the British women behind the work were very visible in Britain, their self-sought prominence necessary to attract the funds required to finance their cause.[15] Given how scarce emigrant letters are, particularly those written by female emigrants, emphasising the experiences of this particular category of middle-class female emigrants is understandable. Unfortunately, this emphasis has rendered working-class emigrant women less visible than middle-class women, as a perusal of many texts on nineteenth-century migration will confirm. Yet their voices have not been altogether lost. There are always other sources, as every genealogist knows. And, 'Precisely because Australian migration required extraordinary governmental intervention and human engineering ... it was more selective and *better documented* than most other mass movements of the time'.[16]

Though first-hand accounts are scarce, the range of well-documented sources concerning aspects of migration specific to single women can be overwhelming. Of all the emigrants assisted by colonial governments, single working-class women, 'doubly controlled' by immigration authorities, are perhaps even more visible in government archives and official records than working-class immigrant men. Further, if diaries written by single working-class women are themselves rare, a different style of journal can provide an immensely rich vein of material on the experiences of single women travelling steerage. Read 'against the grain', the journals and reports written by the shipboard matrons appointed by colonial governments to look after single immigrant women, still remain a largely untapped resource.

Despite this, immigrant women's lives and experiences have been largely overlooked or dismissed from the historical record. The work of Caroline Chisholm, 'the immigrant's friend', has been relatively well documented,[17] but immigrant women themselves (those Chisholm helped in the 1830s and 1840s and the many thousands who came in later decades), have too often been presented simply as migrants' wives or as wives-in-waiting. They have been caricatured as inefficient workers or as prostitutes; their economic role as domestic servants, although substantial, has been overlooked or trivialised, and their unique experiences have been very largely ignored. In Australia, the study of convict women is a burgeoning field, with recent work by Joy Damousi, Deborah Oxley, Kay Daniels and Dianne Snowden, and older texts such as Portia Robinson's, now revamping overly simplistic dismissals of convict women as whores and reprobates. Nearly four times as many working-class women emigrated to colonial Australia as were sent out as convicts. Though the process of recovery of immigrant women has begun through the pioneering work of Jim Hammerton on middle-class women, and more recent work by Paula Hamilton, Emma Curtin, Nicole McLennan and Margrette Kleinig, historians have not yet done comparable justice to immigrant women's experiences.[18]

Disproportion of the sexes

One theme which has characterised past discussion of single female migration to colonial Australia has been the notion of the demographic imbalance of the sexes. Like nineteenth-century British government officials who monitored colonial immigration policy, some historians of migration have been over-influenced by the idea of population imbalance as a motivating factor behind the granting of government assistance to female emigrants. A demographic explanation of colonial assistance policies, moreover, always stemmed more from a British perception of colonial need than colonial readings of the same circumstances. The British Colonial Office's Colonial Land and Emigration Commissioners (CLEC), who managed colonial emigration and land policies from the 1840s, saw the apparent disproportion of the sexes in the colonies, with women significantly outnumbered by men, as a primary reason to encourage female migration. British concern with colonial sex ratios were also overlain with notions of Britain's own 'redundant' middle-class women. Despite the class differences, solving the 'problem' of England's redundant women by shipping off the excess to mate with working-class colonial men had an 'appealing symmetry'[19] about it for British government policy makers, but the appeal was largely lost on both the colonists and prospective middle-class emigrants.

In an earlier period, the rhetoric of sexual, hence social, balance had been explicitly used to justify British-directed and British-funded policies of assisting female migration. A poster from the 1830s was forthcoming about British government intentions, namely encouraging the emigration of 'SINGLE WOMEN to the AUSTRALIAN colonies with the view of reducing the great disparity which exists there between the sexes and of improving their social condition'.[20] We can see the same formula at work in Western Australia in the 1850s and 1860s, at a time when the British Treasury was responsible for female emigration to the newly convict-receiving society. (*Male* convict-receiving, that is: Western Australia received no women convicts, but was sent single female immigrants at British government expense instead, as part of the agreed convict transportation package.) But this was not the case once control of colonial emigration and responsibility for payment shifted to colonial hands.[21] In the other colonies as colonial governments one by one implemented their own policies of immigration, they specifically rejected such population-based arguments. While single British women were implored to try the Canadian frontier where they would quickly find themselves husbands, that style of entreaty was completely absent from the advertising circulated by Australian colonial governments.[22]

NEW SOUTH WALES.

GOVERNMENT EMIGRATION
TO
SYDNEY.

PASSAGES in Ships of the highest class are granted by the Agent-General for New South Wales to eligible applicants, such as Farmers, Agricultural and other Labourers, suitable classes of Mechanics, and Female Domestic Servants, at the following Rates, inclusive of Bedding and Mess Utensils:—

Married Couples not exceeding 40 years of age, **£6** each couple.

Children of 3 and under 14 years of age . . **£1** each.

Single Men . . . . **£4** each.

Female Domestic Servants (who may obtain high wages, and for whom there is a great demand in the Colony) . . . **£2** each.

LAND IN NEW SOUTH WALES MAY BE ACQUIRED ON VERY FAVOURABLE TERMS.

For further particulars apply personally or by letter to

THE EMIGRATION DEPARTMENT,

NEW SOUTH WALES GOVERNMENT OFFICES, 5 WESTMINSTER CHAMBERS, LONDON, S.W.

OR TO THE LOCAL AGENT :—

Poster to attract prospective assisted emigrants to New South Wales, c. 1883 (State Records New South Wales).

Colonial governments recognised that one essential factor in encouraging the growth of families and population in the colonies was the availability of household help, and so they responded to the demands of the colonists for domestic servants. Women who could not fit into that one existing gap in the paid female labour market were neither wanted nor needed. They were certainly not given assisted passages.

Nonetheless, ideas about sexual imbalance have continued to overshadow this evidence and have lent undue historical weight to the British perspective on the colonial need for female immigrants. The CLEC always represented the masculinity of the colonies as a matter of social concern and so too did other British commentators, to the point where colonists became very weary of the 'demographic balance' argument, conceived in ignorance of colonial conditions and constantly foisted upon them by British interests. In 1892, in response to the London *Evening Standard*'s suggestion that 'surplus' single females should be shipped out to Australia, the *Bulletin* responded tiredly, 'When any country contains two women to every three men, it has as many as can be sufficiently provided for . . . There is no room in Australia for the superfluous women of England'.[23]

Of course many, even most, immigrant women married, and their marriages worsened the domestic service problem in two ways: by reducing the number of women available for hire and by creating new families and potentially increasing demand for servants. The immigration of single women had its own multiplier effect on demand, as colonial immigration officials were well aware: 'female domestic servants of every description . . . *must* be an increasing requirement from the fact of so many who yearly marry and become themselves employers'.[24] Although not all working-class families could aspire to employ a servant, some certainly did.

Assumptions about the importance of the sex ratio to colonial assistance schemes, shared by British government agencies and historians alike, take the motives of single emigrant women themselves for granted.[25] The complement to the argument that colonial governments introduced women to marry them off is the view that women emigrated *in order* to be married off. This caricature was common in both Britain and the colonies. Yet others writing outside the colonial and imperial context suggest that employment, not the availability of single men, was a key factor in stimulating the mobility of single working women. Work on domestic service in nineteenth-century France and Britain confirms this view of women workers, with domestics a particularly migratory group.[26] This view is reinforced by personal accounts which depict life in domestic service as a series of relocations throughout a working life.[27] Such analyses reveal that 'the history of domestic service in the nineteenth century is the story of urban migration'.[28] It should come as no surprise then, that women emigrating to the Australian colonies chose to stay in the larger towns and cities where employment in domestic service was readily available, rather than heading for rural locations where far more single men, prospective marriage partners, were available. Married country women desperate for servants were well aware of that, and passed their message of complaint on to immigration authorities. In some cases they were listened to, and new arrivals were denied the option of staying in town. Despite the 'lure' of single men, compulsion was sometimes the only way to get immigrant domestic servants to move inland.

This book also explores the roles played by middle-class women in promoting and directing almost all aspects of female migration. Much of this philanthropic work, which has been characterised as 'benevolent maternalism', was undertaken by both British and colonial women in Britain and the colonies in an effort to protect colonial homes by safeguarding the women who would work in them. The nineteenth-century bourgeois ideology of femininity represented women within the home as a civilising force, exerting a beneficial influence on society as a whole. Women as paid domestic workers within colonial homes fitted neatly and conveniently within the terms of this discourse. Further, time spent working as a servant, practising domestic skills under the eye of a middle-class mistress, was deemed ideal training for prospective wives and mothers of the working class.

Middle-class women played another role in this story of protected migration, as paid and professional shipboard matrons. In some ways, however, their paid work represented a paradox. At a time when 'femininity' was understood in terms of home and hearth, the spectacle of middle-class women embracing travelling careers spanning oceans seems strangely out of place. The role of the shipboard matron was at once both intimately tied to prevailing understandings of women's need for protection, and at odds with it. As this book shows, this contradiction was played out at length in incidents and inquiries over the decades.

Forms of assistance

In understanding female immigration, sometimes the type of assistance which enabled a woman to come out to the colonies was important in determining the amount of time she spent in the government's hands and the extent of control exerted over her. Basically, two mechanisms or forms of assistance were available: nomination and selection. Nomination schemes, sometimes called passage warrant or remittance schemes in different colonies, generally operated on the basis of a colonial resident 'naming' or sponsoring a British friend or relative for emigration. They were the precursor of our contemporary family reunion schemes. When applying to bring out a friend, the sponsor would deposit some proportion of the fare, usually a pound or so in the case of single women, to secure the nominee's passage. The colonial government then met the remaining costs of the immigrant's passage.

Selection schemes involved prospective emigrants in Britain exercising the initiative by approaching colonial representatives and being 'selected' or approved by colonial authorities for a reduced-cost or free passage to the colony. They also involved the colonial government in a wide-scale process of recruitment and advertising. Domestic servants, sometimes alongside agricultural workers but other times taking precedence, were always particularly sought by colonial selection agents.

In theory at least, selection policies gave the colonial authorities who financed immigration a much greater control over the composition of the immigrant population. Such policies were used chiefly to introduce the occupational groups the colonists required. They had other advantages over nomination, too. Selection policies did enable some small manipulation of the colonial sex ratio, though this was never as significant an issue as British interests thought it should be. Female selection policies in Victoria in the 1850s, for example, and in Western Australia in the 1890s, were explicitly linked by policy makers with the numbers of unassisted male immigrants pouring into those colonies in search of gold, although the outcome was recognised as being of marginal demographic significance. Men would come without encouragement if the lure were strong enough; women needed financial assistance. Even so, prospective wives were not wanted as much as servants, and goldminers were no keener to have women around them at the diggings than were the colonies' itinerant (and usually single) male rural workers.

Selection policies could also be used to control the proportion of English, Scottish and Irish introduced. The clannish Irish were the group most likely to make use of nomination policies, and so colonies such as New South Wales, which generally placed a greater emphasis on nomination, found that they were introducing more Irish than some colonists wanted. By pursuing selection policies, colonial governments could elect to focus on particular geographical regions as a source of supply and ignore others.

Nomination policies had different advantages for colonial governments. Based on the idea of 'family reunion', they were sometimes seen as encouraging a more settled population, since people coming out to friends would, it was thought, be less likely to leave the colony. One of the chief fears for colonial governments was that their assistance packages would be used to subsidise the introduction of people who would simply disappear to greener pastures, over the border to Queensland or across the Strait to Victoria. Some colonies refused to assist the immigration of applicants with relatives in neighbouring colonies. Having a family or network of friends in the colony also suggested that immigrants would not need to fall back on the government for support if employment were slow to come. This was particularly important for single women. Nominated women generally went straight off with their friends, whereas selected women spent some brief days in the immigrants' depot, at government expense, before taking up a job in domestic service. Although demand almost invariably outstripped supply, colonial immigration authorities were always keen to see immigrants off their hands as soon as possible. The downside of this was, nominated women did not usually enter the domestic servant market as quickly as colonists would have wished, preferring to spend some time with their friends first.

The other issue which affected a colony's choice of nomination over selection was female morality. There were suggestions throughout this period that the very act of emigrating 'without natural protectors' made a single woman's character questionable. To critics of selected female migration, migration within a family group or, failing that, migrating to join family members already resident in the colony, seemed preferable. The carefully established strategies for shipboard protection were partly designed to eliminate colonial fears about the contaminating effects of the shipboard passage. In some colonial eyes they also encouraged a 'better type' of single woman—one who would not otherwise contemplate the passage—to apply for emigration. Ultimately colonial governments had to be practical in their choice of immigration policies. 'The difficulty is we want single domestic female servants & do not want the others', one Colonial Secretary noted in 1896 in response to the suggestion that Western Australia revert to a programme of assisting families.[29] In each colony, different variations of policy were implemented to enable immigration authorities to juggle competing elements of cost, responsibility for care and employers' demands for domestic servants.

Before beginning this account of the process of migration, a point about the language of migration is relevant. Nowadays we use the verb 'to emigrate' as an intransitive verb; we might say, 'she emigrates' or 'they emigrated'. However, in the language of nineteenth-century female migration the verb was frequently used transitively, giving the common usage, 'they emigrated the women'. 'Emigrating' thus becomes something which can be 'done' to someone else. The *Oxford English Dictionary* attributes early usage to Maria Rye, a well-known mid-nineteenth century British emigrationist active in the field of both female and child migration. The transitive use denotes the taking away of agency from people who were 'emigrated'; they become the objects of the actions rather than its subjects. A usage evidently confined to single women and children, it indicates the way in which the organisations and authorities which promoted female emigration, such as governments and private philanthropic organisations, understood emigrant women. Like children, they were considered people without agency, whose lives and actions could and should be controlled by others.

This book is largely the product of records generated by those who sought, without malice and with the best intentions, to take away the agency of emigrating women. Their attitude is captured in the words of one Canadian emigrationist, who wrote in the 1880s, 'Woman, it has been said, is like blue china, very valuable when sound, but very worthless when damaged or broken'.[30] If blue china needs protection to retain its value in some markets, the patina of experience can add worth of a different kind. Most immigrant women came to Australia to improve their circumstances and as such they made the most of the opportunities available to them. Predictably, there is substantial evidence of negotiation of control. Theirs is not a story about broken vessels and neither is this book. Just as they used government-provided funds to travel to the colonies, immigrant women found their own uses for the systems established to control them.

Manchester Cottons and Bermondsey Boots

IN LATE 1855, Ellen Door and her sister applied to emigrate to New South Wales to join their aunt and cousin in Sydney. An experienced domestic servant, Ellen had spent the last three years working in Cork for a master cooper named Sheehan and another three in the household of Mr Clark, a draper. She could cook, do general household work and milk. Both she and her sister were accepted for a free passage. By February 1856 she found herself not in Sydney but in Adelaide, appearing before a South Australian Select Committee inquiry, in the extraordinary position of having to justify her presence in the colony which had paid her passage. She explained to the Select Committee into excessive female immigration how, while she and her sister were in Plymouth preparing for embarkation, 'I was kept back because there was not room for me in the *Cressy*, and I was sent out here in the *Australia* . . . I cried a great deal and said I would rather return home than be separated from my sister'.[1] But no one was moved by her tears and the sisters were separated.

Frances McDowell had a different background from Ellen Door's but was equally unhappy about where she ultimately found herself. In Dublin Frances had taught in an industrial school and 'was induced by the published statements to think that I might do well here', she told the Adelaide Select Committee inquiry. She had originally applied for a passage to Melbourne, although her colonial destination had largely been a

18

matter of indifference to her. She had no friends in any of the colonies and she had not objected when she was peremptorily despatched to Adelaide. Now though, she agreed before the Select Committee, her coming to the colony had been 'indeed a mad proceeding'. Twelve months after arrival she still had no work.

Jane Higgins had also wished to go to Melbourne, though she did not object to Adelaide, largely because she thought objecting would be a waste of time. She was a housemaid from County Kildare and an experienced dressmaker, and chose to emigrate 'because other girls were coming, and in the hope of bettering myself'. Ellen Neal had decided to emigrate because she had friends doing well in Sydney and 'thought it was a good country'. She had elected to go to Melbourne but thought nothing of a change of destination because 'a passenger told me that Melbourne was only a day's walk from Adelaide'. We don't know whether the passenger's geography was as poor as Ellen's or whether it was a fine joke at the Cork girl's expense, but in any case she embarked for Adelaide on the *Octavia*.

Mary Fitzgerald had an uncle in Melbourne and applied to go there to join him but then was told she would be sent to Adelaide. Although she 'expressed great disappointment to the person in charge at Plymouth, . . . thought it was useless to make any objection'. She told the Select Committee that she 'had no clear knowledge of the distance between Adelaide and Melbourne, and . . . was under the impression that the Commissioners were bound to send me on from Adelaide to the place I applied to be sent to'. Margaret Duggan and her brother applied for passages together for Melbourne. He was sent there but she was sent to Adelaide. When she objected, she 'was told it would be for my advantage, that he might, by being before me, have a place ready for me'. The authorities in Britain 'promised to write to the Commissioners here [in Adelaide], to have me sent on to Melbourne'.

Anastatia Collins' parents had contributed towards her passage to Melbourne, where she had friends, and were unhappy to find her sailing orders were for Adelaide. So they went to the person they had paid and were told, Anastatia reported, 'it would be quite easy for me to get from Adelaide to Melbourne'. Two dozen other female immigrants told the Select Committee similar stories.[2]

The inquiry was conducted to account for the large number of unemployed single immigrant women in Adelaide in the mid-1850s. Such terms of reference were extremely unusual. All colonial inquiries into immigration in later decades highlighted a shortage of female immigrants and domestic servants rather than an excess. This was the case even at times of depression, when the immigration of men and their families sometimes contributed to local unemployment. It was unusual, yes; but it illuminated themes which underpinned existing relations between the colonies and British government authorities in the immigration field and was fundamental in shaping colonial attitudes towards female immigration for the next several decades.

Much of the South Australian inquiry focused on the inability of the colonists to employ the very large numbers of single women sent out. The inquiry blamed this on poor selection, meaning in this case, lack of appropriate occupational skills. Certainly many of the women had little experience of paid domestic labour. The Select Committee also highlighted 'individual acts of injustice' perpetrated on the women themselves. The chief complaint was that women had been despatched to South Australia against their will, a fact made even worse for the colonists because they had to pay for it. On one apparently typical day, 19 February 1856, a survey of the single women waiting at the Adelaide Depot, unemployed and on government rations, indicated 'that, of 311 immigrants, 100 had applied for passages to Melbourne, five for Geelong, and forty-eight for Sydney—leaving 158 only as having applied for Adelaide'.

This situation occurred while selection for South Australia was still in the hands of the British government's Colonial Land and Emigration Commissioners (CLEC). Many immigrant women were questioned before the Select Committee and their answers confirmed the colonial authorities' belief that the CLEC had neglected their responsibilities towards both the women and the colonists who financed their immigration. That finding hastened the transfer of responsibility from the CLEC to the colony's own appointed agents. Over the next several years all the mainland colonies but Western Australia went down the same path. (Distrustful from the first of British intentions in populating the colonies, the Tasmanians had never used the CLEC.) The South Australian government went even further, introducing a policy of proportional assistance, with assistance limited to the proportions of English, Scots and Irish in the British population.[3] Many of the unemployed women were Irish, a factor which had contributed to their unpopularity. With the future interests of colonists thus 'protected', the issue of female immigrants deceived by selection agents and despatching officers was quietly ignored.

One of the many noteworthy features of this inquiry was that it provided an important first-hand record of immigrant motivation. Getting on, bettering oneself, and the anticipation of enhanced employment prospects were major reasons. So too was joining family or accompanying a friend. Advertising seems to have been reasonably successful in promoting an idea of Australia and emigration, but less so in creating a specific colonial destination. Some women alluded to the impact of published advertising material but in most cases this seemed unrelated to the colony which had paid for it. Friends doing well, letters home, and money sent back for passages all seemed to be important factors, with knowledge of localities almost universally vague even amongst those with colonial friends and relatives.

Advertising directed at selecting women for assisted passages almost always followed the same lines. In the 1860s prospective emigrants were advised that 'Female Domestic Servants, who really understand their business, are in great demand in Australia, and are sure to obtain immediate employment at good Wages'.[4] Thirty years later the same carrots were being proffered, with advertisements universally suggesting that 'situations and work are abundant at good wages'.[5] Although colonial specifications for single women eligible for assistance were seldom

uniform, assistance was offered almost exclusively to one category of female worker, the domestic servant. The colonists
wanted neither the specialist cook nor the ladies' maid, but
all-round domestics, 'such as have a knowledge of good plain
cookery, or have either been engaged in or would easily adapt
themselves to general domestic service'.[6] The women were to
be single; they were generally to be aged under thirty-five;
sober, industrious, of good moral character; and free from physical and mental 'defects'. Selected emigrants at least were
expected to be accustomed to working for wages and to intend
doing so in the colonies. Single women with illegitimate children, or those described as 'habitually on parish relief', were
ineligible.[7]

Women younger than eighteen or older than thirty-five were
sometimes accepted, and so too were widows with no children
under sixteen. Annie Hurn, for example. Born Annie Maria
Woodlake and brought up in a London Foundling Hospital, she
was assisted to emigrate in early 1894. She could cook, wash,
iron, do housework and needlework, and came with good references. With her husband dead, emigration might well have
seemed an attractive option to orphan Annie Hurn, who was
only 23 when she was selected for a passage to Western
Australia.[8]

Regulations relating to women eligible to be nominated were
usually less strict, since the onus of care and support was on the
nominating relative. In some cases, though, a colonial government did not trust families to ensure that nominated relatives
could find employment or independence. In the 1890s the
Western Australian government supplemented its selection
programme with the nomination of single women but, though
the cost of nominating was quite high at half the usual fare (a
nominated passage cost £7 10s on a sailing vessel and £10 7s by
Orient steamer), colonists could still only nominate women
qualified as domestic servants.[9] Henry Payton, a Perth tailor
whose wife kept a few boarders, applied to nominate his sister
Mabel, a 25-year-old single woman from Ealing, London, but
the application was rejected, government officials noting that

'we do not I should say want to import Governesses or Book-keepers', Mabel Payton's areas of expertise.[10] In 1891, Bishop Parry successfully nominated four Sisters of Mercy to take charge of the Girls' Orphanage in connection with the Perth House of Mercy, but three years later Bishop Gibney's request to introduce young women from Miss Corless' Nurses Training Institution in Dublin was rejected, on the grounds that 'there is no doubt that the want of nurses is at times greatly felt in Perth, but it is questionable whether there is regular work all the year around that can be depended upon'.[11] In Western Australia at least, even for nominated immigrants, gender alone was insufficient qualification for an assisted passage. The ability to find guaranteed work was imperative. On the other hand nationality was no barrier and H. Hoost of Coolgardie was permitted to nominate two housemaids from Sweden, providing their passage was first paid to England.[12]

We know relatively little about the motives of immigrant women as a whole, but we know even less about nominated immigrants than selected women. They appear less often in government records because of their particular status as the responsibility of their families. There is little doubt though, that nomination regulations were used, directly and indirectly, to improve the material circumstances of family members at home in Britain. In May 1893, Rose Gilbert, who had emigrated with her sister some years previously, was unsuccessful in bringing out her parents and younger brothers to Western Australia, but Ellen Heywood was more successful in nominating her sister. Ellen, who had come out on the *Gulf of Martaban* and was in service with Mrs Chipper of Hay Street, Perth, wrote in her application for assistance, 'I have made up my mind to stay in the Colony but if not I intend going back, sometime next Winter I would like my sister to be here with me, & my parents are willing to let her come if I will nominate her'.[13] Former immigrant Margaret Howard, in service with the Congdons in Fremantle, successfully requested a passage for her sister, and William Henderson of Karridale nominated his two sisters from London.[14]

One young immigrant, whom we know only as Frank, wrote home to his mother in 1861:

> I have just received Mary's letter and it gives me great pleasure to hear that I shall soon have one of you out here at last for I was beginning to think that I should never be able to get money enough together to send for you the way things are getting on here lately with me at least however when Mary arrives I think it will make a difference for surely between us we can soon raise enough and she'll have a better chance than I will I believe I have only had one weeks work since I wrote to you last . . .
>
> If the ship sailed when Mary mentioned in her letter I expect she'll be here in about five weeks that is if she comes here to Melbourne at all for she might go to any other port on the coast as well as here but which ever way it is I'm afraid she'll have to go to a situation when she comes because I dont suppose I shall have any money . . . however there are plenty of respectable and comfortable places about Melbourne so I dont think that Mary can go so very far wrong for two or three months and during that time she can be earning a knowledge of the town very likely and the different houses and tailors shops.[15]

The letter indicates how precarious the immigration network was, with colonists seldom knowing when or even where other family members might disembark. This was a particular problem in Victoria and Queensland with their chains of ports, and in those colonies which pursued policies of forced distribution of single women. Had Mary set off for Melbourne in 1856, she too might have ended up in Adelaide like Anastatia Collins and Ellen Neal, her expectant brother none the wiser.

Frank's letter also underlines the casual nature of the labour market for many unskilled male workers, a situation which prevailed throughout the eastern colonies' so-called 'long boom' of the 1860s to 1890s. Single women working in colonial domestic service, though earning less than men, often found it easier to nominate a sister or female friend, someone who could secure employment and accommodation as a domestic servant immediately on arrival. We don't yet know enough to suggest whether men or women used the nomination regulations more frequently but certainly single women were often the initiators of chain immigration under nomination regulations.

If the system backfired or if the family did not accept its responsibility, the government was sometimes slow to fill the breach, and it was the new arrival who suffered. For that reason labour agent Mary Anne Pawsey, appearing before a New South Wales inquiry into immigration in 1870, condemned the system of nominated immigration then operating in the colony under the name of assisted immigration:

> Many were brought out under that system who were quite incapable of doing any work whatever … In fact, I could point to two or three, who are now in the poorhouse, that came out in that way … Many of them spoke to me in such a way as this:—"My sister had no right to bring me out here; I never as much as washed my own pocket-handkerchief; I thought I was coming to independence here." I am sure many of the unfortunate girls on the streets at night were brought out in that way … They are not able to earn their living because they have never been taught service.[16]

As colonial arrangements with the British government and the Colonial Office shifted over the years, so too did the processes and patterns of applying for emigration. In the 1850s the London-based Colonial Land and Emigration Commissioners (CLEC) acted as agents selecting assisted emigrants for all the mainland colonies. Emigrants knew them as the Park Street Commissioners, and genealogists searching shipping lists will sometimes find their relatives listed amongst the 'Park Street selections'. In later decades, colonial governments appointed their own selection and emigration agents but, even after selection passed entirely into colonial hands, the CLEC still retained responsibility for details of the despatch of some of the vessels carrying single women. After 1873, when the administration of the British Government's Passenger Acts was transferred from the CLEC to the Board of Trade, the CLEC's activities were wound up.[17] In any case, by this time all the CLEC's responsibilities for the selection and despatch of emigrants had ceased, as colonial-assisted migration had either been suspended, as in New South Wales, Victoria and South Australia, or taken on entirely by colonial agents.

Colonial governments had always suspected that if control of selection passed out of colonial hands, their funds would be spent on the introduction of women the colonists did not want and could not use. In 1855, at the time of their inquiry into excessive female immigration, the South Australian government offered up to 300 of their unwanted single women to the Tasmanian colonial government, at the cost of their introduction from Britain. The Tasmanians declined the offer, on the grounds that women not good enough for South Australia were certainly not good enough for Tasmania.[18] Yet other factors, invariably financial, sometimes prevailed over the desire for colonial control of selection. The following year, the Tasmanian colonial government permitted colonists who introduced domestic servants from Victoria to claim the cost of their passage from the mainland, although the practice was discontinued when the Victorian government objected to the women introduced at the expense of their land funds being filched.[19]

Nor were colonial suspicions about the character, morality or origins of female immigrants entirely abandoned when colonial agents controlled their own selection. Selections of some of the women who emigrated to Queensland in 1879 were described as 'most ill-advised', comprising 'young girls of 15 or 16 years of age . . . sent from Industrial Schools, and accepted as domestic servants'. Colonists also suspected even their own appointed Agent-General of 'beating-up recruits from Workhouses and Reformatories'. Increasing the pool of prospective emigrants was one thing, but 'selection must not . . . be made in the shape of recruits from institutions of this kind', the Queensland colonial secretary insisted.[20]

Even when not using the CLEC, colonists were still heavily dependent on British selection agents. Though paid by the colonists, their motives were always suspect. Above all, colonists were suspicious of workhouse immigration, characterised by John Dunmore Lang as 'shovelling out paupers'. In 1860 the Tasmanian Board of Immigration advised its selection committee in Britain to exercise great care in its choice of single women emigrants:

> It is of great consequence that none but first class Immigrants should be engaged; great expense being incurred in intro-ducing them, exceeding £21 a head, and if such a class as those from Reformatories are to be sent out, the Board here might as well at once avail themselves of the services of [the] Land + Emigration Commissioners.[21]

Hobart's *Mercury* similarly recorded in 1860, 'England has been accustomed from the first to make of her colonial empire . . . an outlet for more than one "social evil"'.[22] This was part of a particularly Tasmanian distrust of the intentions of both the British government and British philanthropists.

Colonial officials constantly suspected the CLEC of promoting British over colonial interests, by reducing Britain's population of 'redundant' or unemployed women through colonial-funded programmes of assisted migration. Similarly, philanthropists were suspected—often with justification—of seeing the colonies as suitable places of reform for their 'hopeless cases'. Baroness Burdett Coutts and Charles Dickens, for example, through their work with former women prisoners at Urania Cottage in London's Shepherds Bush, were intent on assisting the emi-gration of precisely the women the colonists wanted least.[23] The Tasmanian female selection committee in Britain was also cau-tioned in 1860 to 'beware of Houses of Refuge & Reformatories, and distressed Needlewomen, they are dear as a gift, and our board are positive in their injunction that not one is to be engaged, so let Mrs. Sydney [sic] Herbert expend her efforts on other Colonies'.[24] Sidney Herbert and his wife's philanthropic work in the 1850s emigrating 'distressed Needlewomen', as unemployable in the colonies as in urban Britain, was well known.[25]

In 1879, G. P. Merrick, the prison chaplain at Westminster Prison, wrote to the *Daily News* calling for the establishment of an emigration fund to benefit women prisoners who, on release, 'will have neither character, money, employment, friends, nor home to fall back upon, and who, either from their repeated convictions, the nature of their offences, or from the fact, perhaps, of their being deserted wives, are not eligible for the ordinary Homes and Refuges which abound in the metropolis and elsewhere'.[26] To the colonists few women could have appeared less attractive. While colonial assistance was denied to women where such a background was known or suspected, colonial governments could do little to prevent the introduction of 'undesirable' women whose passage was paid by benefactors.

Both mindful and resentful of colonial suspicions, the CLEC sought to avoid accusations of putting British before colonial interests. In 1855, when British philanthropist John Leyland suggested to the CLEC that the British government might emigrate to the colonies a number of 'the unfortunate class of females who walk the streets of Liverpool at night, who may evince a disposition to reform their lives', he was advised that the CLEC spent colonial money in strict accordance with the wishes of the colonial legislatures and that 'such women would be very unwillingly received, and that they would by no means enjoy any peculiarly good prospects of earning an honest subsistence or of becoming respectably settled in life in the colonies'.[27] However, the colonists retained grave suspicions about CLEC motives.

From time to time, and almost invariably in the occasional government inquiries into assisted immigration, single women immigrants were identified as a source of prostitutes. Over the years, the women from a number of different vessels acquired unsavoury reputations immediately on arrival because of allegations about 'irregularities' on board and a breakdown in shipboard controls: the *Princess Royal* to Van Diemens Land in 1832, the *Lady Kennaway* to New South Wales in 1854, the *Emma Eugenia* to Western Australia in 1858, and the *Isles of the South* to Tasmania in 1860, for example. And there were occasional selection agents dismissed because too many of 'their' women proved disreputable or immoral. Prostitutes have traditionally come from the ranks of working-class women; single immigrant women, with fewer sources of family support in the colonies, may well have contributed disproportionately to their number. That said, there was no occasion in the second half of the century where so strong a link was established between single female immigrants and prostitution that it demanded major government intervention. The words of one witness at a government inquiry in 1877 were found convincing:

> There is no doubt, I believe, that scarcely an immigrant ship arrives in South Australia, but unfortunately the single women furnish an addition to the prostitution of the country; but not to anything like the extent that is popularly supposed. I believe the statements which are sometimes made to be a gross libel. There are individual cases no doubt; but nothing like what is supposed by some people.[28]

Over this same period, New Zealand colonial authorities focused much more strongly on alleged links between working-class female immigration and prostitution, which emerged in their Contagious Diseases Acts. In the Australian context, however, links between prostitution and immigrant experience, though often suspected, were less clearly drawn.[29]

Both the CLEC and colonial agents selected emigrants in a similar fashion. Single women were selected through a network of local selection agents spread across Britain who were responsible either to the CLEC or to representatives of the colonies, usually Agents-General or Crown Agents located in London. Selection agents were generally the first point of contact for the prospective emigrant. Their duties included screening local working-class applicants for assisted and free passages, and circulating information concerning colonial prospects. They comprised a range of backgrounds: clergymen and their wives, professional men, commissioned officers of the forces, merchants, gentlemen and servants' registry office keepers.[30] Some specialised in selecting particular occupations. Of eighty-eight agents used by the CLEC in 1865, for instance, nineteen selected only female domestic servants. Mrs Mary-Ann Fox of Clapham, Miss M. Smith of Pimlico, and Mrs Mary Anne Kingsland of Croydon, were among the five women agents who specialised in the selection of women.[31]

Most of these agents dealt with all the colonies currently recruiting, and their enthusiasm for one colony over another was frequently in proportion to their commission. In 1877, the South Australian emigration lecturer R. J. Day reported on one revealing conversation he'd had, incognito, with the Worcester selection agents, the Stanleys:

> They knew nothing about South Australia, and didn't advocate it at all as a field for emigration. She said they wanted a good class of servants themselves; and from her description you would have thought South Australia one of the most frightful countries on the face of the earth.[32]

Day found South Australia's prospects no better when viewed from Leicester. Most agents worked for several colonies—the Stanleys also worked for Tasmania and Canada—and unless an emigrant had a fixed idea about destination, perhaps because of friends or family members, agents and the size of the commission they were paid played a significant role in determining the migrant's ultimate destination.

The colonies were also publicised by travelling lecturers, especially in the rural districts, through the circulation of cheap literature, and by advertising in appropriate papers and journals. As well as helping to detach working-class people from their local roots, advertising also promoted the colonies for people of capital. At different times New South Wales, which usually concentrated more on nomination than selection policies, and Queensland, with its emphasis on land grants, both invested heavily in advertising to attract capital to their shores.

As well, raising the colony's profile helped reduce the significant attrition rate amongst both selected and nominated migrants. The number of 'no show-ers', those who failed to take up the offer of passage after arrangements had been made, was always high. The rate was generally worse amongst nominated emigrants; in New South Wales in the 1860s, for instance, about one-fifth of all nominated emigrants failed to embark because of a change of heart. Selected emigrants had taken the emigration initiative themselves and were more likely to follow through; but nominated people 'called for' by colonial kin sometimes ultimately preferred not to heed the call.[33]

More trustworthy than British agents but generally less successful were unpaid colonial visitors to Britain. In 1863, Tasmanian colonists Duncan McPherson and his wife were requested to select fifty single domestic servants in Britain for emigration to the colony, although apparently failed to do so.[34] The Reverend E. Wilson of Rockhampton gave twenty lectures on Queensland in Scotland in 1897, and George McLennan and his daughter, a teacher at the government school in Townsville, spent forty-four days distributing emigration literature and talking to people in the Scottish agricultural districts.[35] Shipping lines which served the Australian colonies also provided free publicity through advertising material and placards distributed to selection agents and their own advertisements in the local press. More important perhaps were 'letters from relatives and friends in the Colony, whose accounts and advice are considered and accepted as disinterested and trustworthy by the laboring classes here'.[36] 'Individual testimony', it was always said, was 'the soul of colonisation'.[37] Some of those letters found their way into publications circulated in Britain. However, while letters home were often critically important in promoting a particular colony, they could equally act as deterrents. In the 1890s, once assistance to Queensland resumed as the economy moved out of depression, emigration agents complained of 'the almost constant stream of warning letters from residents in Australia, cautioning people not to migrate there under any circumstances . . . For every one published many similar are received by private persons who circulate the information, and thus as against your desire for a larger population, we have to reckon with "the foes of one's own household"'.[38]

Publicity gave the prospect of emigration wider currency amongst the working-class population but material considerations had a greater impact in determining the emigrant's choice of destination. North America was attractive, more accessible and cheaper, and so it drew the bulk of the nineteenth-century British diaspora. Against this, however, the availability of assisted, even free, passages, to the Australian colonies made emigration a possibility for women who could not afford the more desirable North American destinations. Unquestionably, the availability of government-assisted passages meant that the Australian colonies attracted the least wealthy emigrants. Consequently, incentives to emigrate were largely couched in material terms of good wages and future prospects.

Immigrant women made rational economic choices about emigration. Colonial agents selected women; but women also selected colonies, and cost was a pre-eminent factor in that decision.[39] Domestic servants were offered the best concessions and the cheapest passages of any emigrant group, as a consequence both of colonial demand for their labour and the lower wages women earned. In the 1850s, the CLEC covered the cost of travel to the port of embarkation for female emigrants. In addition, they maintained single women at the emigrants depot before departure if the women were out of work. Some were destitute awaiting embarkation.[40] Certainly the Victorian government, and probably others, made it a rule to maintain young single women emigrants who had given up their jobs before embarkation, recognising that leaving employment meant loss of accommodation. Sometimes women faced considerable difficulties making embarkation and resignation coincide. In the 1860s, the South Australian government offered domestics transport to their port of embarkation as well as a free passage.[41] In the late 1870s the shipping firm which selected female immigrants for Western Australia successfully convinced the colonial authorities to subsidise the cost of ship's kit and transit to port in cases where it was needed, particularly among single women. Arguing in the language most likely to appeal to the colonial government, that of financial self-interest, the shippers suggested they could subsequently attract 'a more desirable class of Emigrants, especially females, none of whom would be in a position to leave the Colony, at all events, till they had remained a sufficient length of time to earn the means to move elsewhere'.[42]

Emigrant destinations, however, were more than just a matter of finance. While emigrants were often very ignorant about colonial assistance packages and conditions, gossip about attractive and unattractive destinations circulated fairly readily within informal migrant networks. Unfavourable conditions of passage and the restrictions attached to assistance packages were part of that. Further, colonial governments found it hard to accept that the women they most wanted because of their excellent skills would generally stay on in their good jobs in Britain. Consequently the women who emigrated frequently didn't have the level of employment qualifications the colonists sought.

Immigrants were particularly put off by restrictions imposed on their activities after arrival. The Victorian Agent-General complained bitterly in 1871 that the colony's assistance policies seriously hampered his ability to attract the women the colonists wanted since, under the regulations, single women were bound to go anywhere within the colony the government directed them. Further, applicants with relatives in Victoria or the neighbouring colonies of South Australia, New South Wales or Tasmania, were henceforth ineligible for selected passage assistance.[43] Four young women selected for the *Corona*, which sailed from Plymouth early in 1870, were caught up in this new Victorian policy and no doubt their stories circulated widely. When questioned at the Plymouth depot before embarkation, Anne McManus, Mary Ann Carrow (or Nuncarrow), Lucy Talbot and Mary Ann Roades had all freely admitted that they had relatives in Victoria, though none had mentioned this on the application form.[44] Under the new regulations, all those women were prohibited from taking up their passage unless their relatives in the colony nominated them and paid a deposit on their behalf. On the verge of departure, the unfortunate young women found themselves in an impossible situation.

Anne McManus wrote, 'I am to be sent from here almost immediately and have no money whatever and feel greatly distressed not knowing what to do', and requested that at the very least the agent return her to her home in Enniskillen.[45] Mary Ann Carrow protested that she had not known she had an uncle living in the colonies until after she had applied for passage and begged the Agent-General to believe that 'I do not know him he will not do anything'.[46] Similarly Mary Ann Roades had no real knowledge of the friends living in Adelaide and had not heard of them for years till her mother had mentioned them casually just before her departure. She too wrote:

> On being questioned by the Commissioner I considered it my duty to speak the truth and said I had friends, I beg to tell you Sir that I have not the slightest intention of joining these friends that I do not know anything of them, If sent I shall go to Victoria with the intention of taking a situation in that Colony, and if allowed to proceed, I trust and will endeavour that you shall have no cause to regret sending me.[47]

The letters had the desired effect and the women were granted their passage. But politics played a greater role to charity or justice in that decision. The Agent-General wrote:

> Considering that it would not only be dangerous to turn out four young women without friends or money in a seaport town, but that the fact when known might make it very difficult for me to carry out the instructions of the government, to increase the number of single women selected, I suffered them to go at the last moment, upon condition that they should satisfy the despatching officer that they had not wilfully attempted to deceive, and that they should sign an agreement to take service in Victoria and remain there.[48]

The selection criteria were informed by a discourse of working-class femininity which suggested that working-class women who were to be employed in middle-class colonial homes had to meet certain criteria: morality, and knowledge of household skills. Employment references could be fabricated or misleading and the motives of those supplying references were often dubious. But certainly, morality was the more important factor. Domestic skill could be learned or acquired in the colonies; morality, once lost, was beyond recall. Although neither was self-evident, morality was even harder to judge and selection agents were expected to be absolutely scrupulous in assessing that aspect of an applicant.

For that reason, as well as the amount paid to agents, conditions of payment for selecting single women differed too. Agents received half their commission when single women sailed and half once a colonial report confirmed the selected women's 'suitability'. This portion could be withheld if the immigrant were found objectionable 'on the ground of character, incompetence in her calling, or of any other ineligibility'. In practice though, while a woman's lack of employment skills was a matter of concern to the colonists, that was seldom more than a short-term obstacle to employment and the selection agents involved generally incurred no financial penalty. Morality was scrutinised more closely. Unlike their attitude to married immigrants and single men, colonial authorities considered a single woman's character and morality a legitimate subject for investigation. Her behaviour was always closely watched, both on the passage out and after arrival.

Withholding a portion of selection agents' fees or cancelling agencies were the only ways colonial governments could police selection agents. In 1883 the emigration agent for South Australia stopped working with local agent Mr Tebbut after colonial authorities complained about his selection of female domestics for the *Arthurstone*.[49] In 1876, another South Australian agent Miss Fowler had lost her position for similar reasons.[50] If, as occasionally happened, a single woman died on the passage out, the second half of an agent's commission would still be paid unless the ship's surgeon reported unfavourably on the woman's moral character.[51] Agents were financially accountable for what they were commissioned to police, female morality and character, but even they were not held responsible for acts of God.

Female emigrationist Maria Rye once pointed out that colonial governments ordered batches of immigrant women from Britain in a manner 'as peremptory and as defined as that of any Melbourne merchant writing to the corresponding house in London, about Manchester cottons or Bermondsey boots'[52] and the image is an apt one. If the goods, after scrutiny, weren't satisfactory, governments felt entitled to fine the suppliers. Returning to sender was more difficult, but where the goods were fatally flawed, even that was sometimes a possibility.

Every stage of the screening process was fraught with difficulties: for selection agents at the local level, for emigration authorities in London and of course for the applicants. As the first step towards acceptance for an assisted passage, each applicant completed a form detailing age and occupation. This had to be signed by a number of referees, including the local minister and doctor, and the woman's most recent employer. The process was not always simple. Some doctors, for example, charged a fee of up to five shillings to sign such a form, an amount well beyond the resources of most domestics.[53] The selection agent also had to confirm with referees that the applicant was of 'sound character' and of 'sober industrious habits'. Single women unaccompanied by married relatives, applying through the CLEC for passages to Victoria or New South Wales, required a special examination, being personally quizzed concerning their employment qualifications and moral character.[54] In 1885 the Agent-General for Queensland, Sir James Garrick, noted that 'Every care has been taken in the selection of the single women by a careful examination of their certificates of character, and by the issue of a confidential circular to their late employers'.[55]

Even so, the system was not foolproof. 'Character flaws' were not always detected, personal references sometimes unreliable. Local referees frequently acted in terms of their own interests: omitting to point out traits which would be a barrier to emigration; refusing to recommend a worthy candidate. In 1857, following the South Australian inquiry into female immigration, the CLEC defended the selection of women they had despatched to the colony by protesting that they had carried out every part of the selection process thoroughly. 'We cannot believe that a large number of the Magistrates and Clergy of Ireland could have been guilty . . . of testifying to untruth', they declared, but the evidence—the lack of employment experience of many of the Irish women sent to the colony—seemed compelling.[56] Twenty years later, South Australia's emigration lecturer R. J. Day reported that 'The ministers said they did not mind signing for indifferent persons so as to get rid of them, but it was very unreasonable to suppose that they would sign to get rid of the best male and female servants in the place'.[57]

Maria Rye, who selected single women for both the Queensland and the Victorian governments in the 1860s, made a stronger statement to readers of *The Times* in 1867:

> Three only out of my 90 girls in [the *Red Jacket*] are reported as persons of bad character (and I have to thank Birmingham for two of these), as I find by looking over my books that in all three cases I have had evidently false characters given me. I should like it to be distinctly understood that for the future I shall, in similar cases, publish the names of the girls and of all persons wilfully misleading me on this subject. I do not surely ask too much when I ask for honest answers to plain questions. With fair play, and the moral support of truthfulness in referees, this work may continue, prosper, and be a blessing to thousands of struggling women; but if employers will falsify facts to suit their own selfish purposes, the sooner I end my labours the better.[58]

In their references, employers went well beyond comment on a woman's employment skills, clearly believing themselves both qualified and obligated to discuss a female domestic's 'character'. Many reveal the currency of the view that single women emigrated with marriage in mind, and that this was both the colonial expectation and objective. Employers therefore commented on a woman's morality and qualifications with a view to this future occupation as much as further paid domestic employment. Mrs L. Palmer, for example, who had employed Elizabeth Jeffreys as a domestic for 14 months in the early 1890s, stated that 'While with me she appeared rather inclined to flirt but probably in the Colonies she would soon get married & settle down a steady & industrious wife'.[59]

After completed forms were submitted, central authorities advised intending emigrants if they had been approved and it could be further weeks before the date of passage was confirmed. In a village or small town especially, a prospective emigrant was subject to great pressures over this period, since everyone would be aware of her intentions, and the likelihood that an applicant would change her mind was quite high. Employers might remonstrate with a domestic servant, or else throw her out and seek a replacement, leaving her both unemployed and homeless pending departure. The waiting period was certainly an unwelcome trial and, as agent Day noted in 1877, 'Many of these laboring classes have not 5s. or 10s. to call their own; and if they have to wait for three or four weeks before embarking they may as well give up all idea of emigrating'.[60] This was a particular ordeal for single women.

If the selection process 'broke down', colonial governments faced two problems: financial responsibility and public accountability. Nomination policies shifted some of the responsibilities to colonial nominators, but once a colonial government had assisted the migration of a selected single woman who, for some reason, proved unemployable, it was morally responsible for her care if she needed medical or welfare assistance. In the case of single female immigrants, unemployment and a consequent need for government aid usually stemmed from the most exceptional circumstances. In the prevailing climate of high demand for domestics, it could also indicate a problem with selection. Before the South Australian Select Committee on Immigration in 1877, William Hunt suggested it was common for male immigrants and their families to resort to the destitute asylum for support because of unemployment but could give very few examples of single women in the same circumstances. Seasonal cycles in the rural labour market, with men needed for the harvest then laid off, were particularly obvious in South Australia but demand in the domestic labour market generally remained consistently high across the seasons. Hunt was able to describe the 'glaring case of a woman, who evidently must have obtained a passage as a domestic servant':

> She is a widow; and if she is a day old, she cannot be less than
> 60 years of age. I won't say she is too infirm to work, but she
> is quite unfit to take labor as a servant; and she really has

done nothing. Mr. Solomon [of the Destitute Board] . . . came to the conclusion, that since, to a certain extent, her friends assisted to bring her here, they were responsible for her support; and, very properly, he declined to give her relief.[61]

However, relatively few single women immigrants sought relief from the destitute asylum. When they did, it was often the result of pregnancies which had commenced before departure for the colony. Pregnancy, a temporary complaint, was not grounds for repatriation but there were other cases where more permanent conditions led colonial authorities to favour that solution. Women with a permanent disability, such as Alice Newman,[62] unable to work because of her bad legs, or Annie Wilson who was virtually blind,[63] were sent back home. So too were Bessie Dunn, Catherine Casey and Mary Stanley, all judged to be insane after arrival in Western Australia.[64] The question of repatriation was often complicated, however, by the expense: was the cost of supporting a permanent burden greater than the cost of sending a woman back? And who should pay? In 1868, single female Catherine Hennessy, who emigrated to Western Australia on the *Strathmore*, had exhibited 'alarming' behaviour on the passage out and on arrival was unfit for service. The CLEC refused to take responsibility, arguing that this was clearly a cost the colonists could be expected to bear, in return for British government funding of Western Australian migration.[65] Fortunately Hennessy eventually found work as a domestic.[66]

Governments were quick to make use of other sources of funds, and would sometimes contact friends at home for financial assistance for a return fare. Frances Adge, who arrived in Tasmania in 1885, had Girls' Friendly Society connections and in this case the local GFS raised funds on her behalf.[67]

Ideally, the selection process should have prevented people with limited employment prospects from the misfortune of a fruitless passage. While the financial cost was generally borne by the colonists, the personal cost borne by the unemployed immigrant was considerable. Wide spread and lasting unemployment amongst female immigrants, however, was rare. Even the women who were the subject of the South Australian inquiry in the 1850s eventually found employment, in other colonies if not in South Australia.

Over the years, though there were always complaints about single women's lack of suitable employment experience, colonists dealt with this by paying new arrivals less than the going wage rate. Most investigations into breakdowns in the selection system stemmed from physical and mental health problems, pregnancy and 'immorality'. In Victoria in 1869 an inquiry investigated the backgrounds of three single women selected by the CLEC. Ann Pike and Ellen Heather were pregnant on arrival in the colony. The third, Kate Baker, was said to suffer so badly from offensive breath that she was impossible to employ. All three had furnished adequate employment and medical references, Baker being described as 'the very girl to please the Melbourne people—not too rough or too smooth'. Walcott of the CLEC justified the selection of these women in terms of their satisfactory references and added by way of consolation to the frugal Victorian government that, as all had applied direct to the CLEC office, no agency fees were payable.[68] This begs the question of what happened to those three women.

Maria Johnston, despatched to Queensland on the ship *Elizabeth Ann Bright* in 1864, was found to be 'of unsound mind'. As it later turned out, she had previously been an inmate of a lunatic asylum. Her case attracted some publicity in the colonial press, with the relevant selection agent branded by the government as 'culpably negligent'.[69] In 1870, Queensland Agent-General John Douglas conducted inquiries into the 'characters' (that is, morality) of five young women from the *Indus*, all of whom were assessed as 'unacceptable'.[70] Follow-up inquiries revealed no anomalies in the selection process and, although Douglas asserted he would prevent it happening again, there was little he could do.

Government authorities themselves were not above misleading prospective emigrants, particularly in the matter of wages, but they were quick enough to prevent their agents profiting from emigrant ignorance at government expense. Local agents were paid by the governments they were working for, either through the CLEC or through the colony's Agent-General. They were not entitled to receive any further fee from the prospective applicant.[71] Though we don't know how widespread this practice was, there's no doubt that some agents used the emigrants' ignorance of procedures to increase their cut. In 1869, seven young Irish women from County Clare were nominated by various friends and relatives resident in Victoria, with arrangements left in the hands of agent Mrs Anne Madders of Ennistymon. The cost of their passages was covered by deposits made in the colony by the relatives nominating them. Yet Madders charged these women an additional sum, despatching them to the CLEC as though they were selected emigrants and therefore liable to make a contribution towards their passages.[72] As was usual with small local agencies, Madders was not a direct agent of the CLEC but worked through Denis Brennan, the CLEC's Cork agent, who declared that 'if the statement of these young women be true, I think, for the protection of the Public, as well as for the duly appointed Agents, the party concerned ought to be prosecuted—& I will give you every assistance in my power in the matter'.[73] Brennan's record was already under scrutiny. He'd been responsible for the unfortunate selection of Catherine Hennessy in 1868 and, although exonerated in that instance, thirty-two out of fifty-one of his female applicants for assisted passage had already been rejected by the CLEC and this final incident cost him his agency.[74]

Colonial perceptions of single female immigrants were always fluid and changed with colonial circumstances. Consequently the two goals of selection—broadening the pool of applicants while keeping out the women the colonists did not want—involved constant renegotiation. Irish women were a prime example. In the 1850s, the high proportion of Irish amongst the CLEC's selections sent out to South Australia, New South Wales and Victoria stirred up enormous bitterness amongst colonists and colonial governments, with the consequent desire to control the regional mix amongst selected immigrants instrumental in colonial governments taking on greater control of selection.

With economic conditions in Britain, and particularly in Ireland, improving from the 1850s, the CLEC continually complained about the great difficulty of finding the numbers of single women the colonies requested. The number of Irish emigrating declined dramatically from 1852 to 1855. More constant employment and better wages became available and, in the south-eastern counties of Ireland in particular, domestic servants were increasingly able to find good employment. However, prospects still remained limited for less skilled Irish workers, particularly in the south-western province of Munster.[75] While the CLEC failed to find as many trained domestics as the colonists requested from England and Scotland, their selection agents could still find numbers of untrained women in Ireland, 'where large numbers of women are anxious to emigrate, who are used to farm work, and, though not so tidy or instructed as might be wished, have been frequently described as ready to learn and of remarkably good moral character'.[76]

The government of South Australia disagreed, preferring to receive no women at all than the untrained inexperienced Irish women the colony had received in the mid-1850s. By 1865, of the eighty-eight agents used by the CLEC, fewer than half a dozen were located in Ireland.[77] The remainder were spread across England, Scotland and Wales. Nomination could also be used to favour regions other than Ireland. Following South Australia's lead a decade earlier, New South Wales introduced a policy in 1869 of permitting the nomination of only a limited number of Irish, in proportion to the existing population.

Western Australian colonists were more receptive to Irish women. Certainly in the 1850s the colony, an unattractive destination for all types of labour, was desperately short of domestic servants. Although other accounts temper his enthusiasm and account a little, according to Governor Kennedy the first parties of Irish women the CLEC despatched to the colony were, 'universally well spoken of as a useful and well-conducted class'.[78] Various methods of inducing more women to emigrate were suggested by the Western Australian immigration authorities, including payment of a small bonus to each woman although, as the CLEC reported back, 'Sensible and respectable English women will chose their destination because it is the best and not in order to obtain an immediate gift of one or two pounds, and for the Irish the inducement is unnecessary'.[79] So the CLEC and the local immigration agent agreed that Irish women would do. Throughout the 1850s the CLEC continued to recruit in Ireland, regularly despatching parties of fifty to a hundred Irish single women to Western Australia.

For the Western Australians the alternative to Irish women was generally even less attractive. Like Tasmania before it, Western Australia was quick to see itself as a dumping ground for vulnerable women the British government did not want. They were right to be suspicious. In 1863 for instance, when conditions in Lancashire were poor, the Duke of Newcastle approached all the Australian colonies to accept unemployed female cotton weavers as prospective immigrants. None responded favourably, although all but Western Australia were happy to accept other single women qualified in domestic service. Western Australia alone reported few employment prospects for any immigrants.[80] Yet it was to Western Australia that the CLEC sent fifty young female Lancashire cotton weavers as part of the sixty-seven single women sent out to the colony that year. By their own report the CLEC were vindicated—all found employment. But the colony's wishes were clearly secondary to the priorities of the British authorities who controlled the emigration purse strings.

Despite denying the practice, the CLEC also despatched workhouse women to Western Australia in the 1850s. The CLEC particularly favoured Cork Union women; local poor law inspectors said they were domestic servants, thrown out of employment and onto the Union in large numbers by the massive emigration of local small farmers and tradespeople. The poor law authorities enabled many of these young women to emigrate to the closer destination of British North America at parish expense but the much more expensive passage to Australia was a prohibitive drain on parish resources, with Australian colonial governments refusing to grant assistance.[81] Western Australian colonists had less choice. The virtual prohibition against selected Irish women in other colonies had increased the demand in the east for English and Scottish emigrants so, in order to leaven their heavily Irish selection for Western Australia with at least a few English women, the CLEC turned to London workhouses. In justifying this action, which they knew would be unacceptable to the colonists, the Commissioners asserted that the workhouse women were 'respectable Women who might properly be sent to Westn Australia at the expense not of the Colony but of the Imperial Govt'.[82]

The arrival of the *Emma Eugenia* in mid-1858 brought the practice to an end. Though there were dissenting voices, colonial immigration officials reported that the English workhouse women on board 'were of a most objectionable class, and behaved disgracefully during the voyage'. Twenty-four were said to be as bad as possible, with at least eighteen thought to be prostitutes.[83] As a result, the Secretary of State directed that the experiment of selecting women from English workhouses cease; Irish women were to be sent instead.[84]

Despite widespread comments about their incompetence and unsuitable employment backgrounds, the Irish single women also had a reputation for chastity and morality not always lost on the colonists. Other colonies too occasionally regarded parts of Ireland, if not its workhouses, as a preferred source of immigrants. In 1874 Queensland Agent-General Richard Daintree reported with enthusiasm that the number of single Irish women recruited was increasing. Somewhat unrealistically, Daintree believed that women from Ireland's agricultural districts would be admirably suited for domestic work with rural families but in practice they were no more keen 'to go bush' than other immigrants.[85] As historian Patrick O'Farrell has noted, 'In the cities Irish women tended to stay, not merely for social preference, but because these were the locations of their employment in domestic service'.[86] In this, the Irish were no different from English and Scottish women. And despite earlier displays of anti-Irish prejudice, the Victorian authorities also requested in 1870 that women be selected not only from the rural districts of

England and Scotland, but 'more especially the Northern and Midland counties of Ireland. The experience of girls from the North of Ireland, who are also preferred by employers here is that they are strong, willing and civil and apt to learn & generally turn out well'.[87] (The Catholic south-western province of Munster was not seen as a desirable recruiting ground.) Victorian authorities also recommended the despatch of an occasional vessel from Belfast, 'which is nearly as central as Plymouth'.[88]

The shift in favour of *some* Irish women was related to two factors: growing recognition that the best-qualified working women in Britain found little to attract them to the colonies; and increased colonial emphasis on the morality of women immigrants and their ability to learn. But it happened to coincide with an even greater contraction in the Irish supply. One of the unusual characteristics of Irish emigration in the second half of the nineteenth century was what David Fitzpatrick has called the 'uniquely ordinary balance' of the sexes.[89] By the 1890s, the balance of the sexes in the emigrant Irish population was even more unusual, with the number of women emigrating exceeding the number of men.[90] Single Irish women were a very migratory group; by the end of the century though, there was little likelihood of encouraging many to emigrate to Australia because of the competing attractions of North America and because local demand had risen so much. Ireland became a particularly barren recruiting field. The local press refused to print details of anything savouring of emigration, and in this they had the support of the local bishop and clergy. [91]

Colonial attitudes to Scottish immigrants were also fluid. In the 1850s, some of the island women sent out to the colonies, particularly to Victoria, under the auspices of the Highland and Island Emigration Society had been rejected by the colonists because of the extreme poverty of their background and their total inexperience in domestic service.[92] Rye would later describe these Islanders as 'half-savage and wholly untaught', 'born and bred in peat huts' and knowing 'nothing of the requirements or even decencies of civilized life'.[93] The islands such as Skye were not generally regarded as a suitable field for recruitment because of their poverty and the traditional crofter lifestyle. Crofters were said to be so deeply attached to family and soil that relocation was virtually impossible:

> [the] home feeling . . . so strong among them that they prefer their sons and daughters to hire out for the fishing season, the former manning the boats and the latter to assist in the fish-curing establishments, rather than send them to service, as this gives them the opportunity of spending the winters together.[94]

Single women from these communities could generally only be induced to emigrate as members of a family.[95] On the other hand, the daughters and sons of island tradesmen had often trained as domestics or farm labourers in the larger farms of the district and, as Queensland's agent Fleming noted in 1887, it was 'seldom that any party of emigrants does not include a few persons of this class'.[96]

Other social factors also seemed to promote female migration from the area. Ardent opponent of Irish immigration John Dunmore Lang argued that the high fatality rate amongst the young men of the Orkneys and the Shetlands, and the consequent high proportion of women in the island population, made the islands a fertile recruiting ground.[97] New South Wales labour agent Mary Anne Pawsey, herself a Scot, also recommended the rural areas of Scotland as a good recruiting ground for single women, although she warned against recruiting in Glasgow as the women there were 'not of the class that would suit the Colony'.[98]

From time to time colonies targeted other rural areas. In 1865 South Australia's Plymouth agent, James Wilcocks, suggested recruiting young women from Cornwall in preference to Irish women. Cornish mining men had already been successfully employed in South Australia's mines and Wilcocks believed the idea of rejoining their countrymen would make the normally sedentary Cornish women more amenable to the prospect.[99] Sometimes influential local people took on the task of stimulating regional emigration. Agents who hoped to benefit from this claimed the practice was designed 'not merely as a means of getting rid of undesirable neighbours, but for the advantage of the Emigrants themselves'[1] but motives were not always transparent. The Highland and Island Emigration Society, for example, was explicitly developed to facilitate highland clearances in the 1850s. In 1871, the Countess of Portsmouth wrote from North Devon to the Victorian Agent-General:

> I have found a certain hankering after emigration among our women here but with such a timidity about it that after sitting with me and talking it over backwards and forwards it ends in nothing but I have just seen two more who say they think if more companions from the same district will go that they will be inspired with greater courage. I know of no part of England where it is so desirable for women to emigrate . . . I have seen several whom I believe will be able to bring me good Characters from their employers, strong, sturdy, working girls from 18 upwards who are just the kind I imagine likely to do well.[2]

Certainly, once the first migrant left a district, others soon followed.

The desire for experienced domestics also had to be balanced against the fear of urban contagion.[3] The common progression for domestic servants might be a shift from a first position in a rural location to a more skilled and better paid situation in town. Women who had already moved on from their first situation were generally more accessible to the lure of emigration.[4] Yet in spite of their greater experience, such women carried with them a reputation for being less tractable, less deferential and in many cases even tarnished by urban contact.

Though desirable, rural recruiting was not always practical. Colonial recruiting and selection agents were spread across the British countryside but, although they were heavily canvassed, the agricultural districts were not necessarily the most fruitful source of female emigrants. Agents faced extreme difficulty in encouraging people to break the ties and associations of their rural homes. The Queensland agent for Scotland, George Wight, observed in 1876:

> Notwithstanding all our efforts . . . to teach and impress the purely agricultural population, the agents in large towns, such as Glasgow, Edinburgh, Dundee, &c., will always furnish the major portion of our emigration . . . for those towns have attracted, and are still attracting large numbers annually from the agricultural districts, of the men and women who make the best colonists, and who are the more easily induced to emigrate because of having already loosened themselves from their natal homes.

Wight added that, 'When the immigration from the country to the towns has resulted in deterioration of character, which sometimes happens, such persons are not admissible as emigrants, as a matter of course'.[5] Thus Wight reflected the agent's dilemma, the nub of the selection issue. The towns proved most fruitful in terms of the numbers of emigrants the colonists wanted and in many cases their employment experience, but the 'quality' of those emigrants—their character and morality—was allegedly more open to question.

Ultimately control of selection was vested in the colonies' Agents-General, located in London, and these men often found that their task of inspecting the selected emigrants conflicted with the colonists' desire for women recruited away from major towns. In 1866, Queensland's Agent-General Henry Jordan was severely criticised by his colony for the poor quality of immigrants he had despatched, and he complained bitterly that the price of his obtaining a large number of emigrants was his inability to retain personal control over policing their quality.[6] The difficulty of the task of the Agents-General was exacerbated when women were recruited in rural districts. In 1870 with colonial finances in mind, Victorian Agent-General Verdon planned to increase the number of women selected from the London area, enabling both a personal inspection of the women and a saving on agents' fees if the women applied directly to the Agent-General. He argued that 'it would be more injurious to the best interests of the Colony, to send out a large number of unfit persons, than to send an insufficient number, whose character and fitness have been ascertained'.[7] This did not meet with colonial approval. Single female domestics selected from London had by report of their employers been largely selected from the East End and were said to be 'impertinent & slovenly' as well as unskilled and prone to 'disorderly living'. Thus Verdon was directed to refocus his interest on the rural counties of England and Scotland, but especially Ireland.[8]

Meeting the dual aims of selection was a constant problem for colonial emigration authorities in Britain, particularly in view of the constant demand for experienced domestics and associated high wages offered in Britain. For well-qualified women migration offered little in terms of immediate financial benefits, but ultimately, domestic skills could be learnt. So authorities in Britain placed greater emphasis on the character of their female emigrants as a way of playing down their inexperience. The South Australian agent reported in 1863 that 'good moral character, good health, with a willing and cheerful disposition, are qualities which go a great way towards making a good servant, who though not otherwise particularly skilful or clever, will generally be found to satisfy the reasonable expectations of their employers'.[9] Similarly the Queensland Agent-General reported of the women despatched in 1887 that 'Care has been taken in every case to inquire into the characters of the girls, and it is therefore hoped that all those who have been sent— although they may not be experienced domestic servants—yet are certainly capable of becoming serviceable colonists'.[10]

Selection agents had little real choice about the occupational experience of the women they sent out. At the same time, domestic skill was seen as readily, even 'naturally' acquired and, perhaps for that reason, was valued less highly than the skills of male labourers. Female morality was regarded rather differently. It could not be acquired, nor recovered once lost. In a comment typical of the many made before inquiries and select committees into immigration, Caroline Stapley, matron of the Adelaide Servants' Home, complained in 1877, 'For the sake of getting a fee [selection agents] accept whatever offers; and there certainly is not sufficient attention paid to the character of those who are sent out'.[11]

This obsession with female immigrants' morality can be attributed to a concern about immigrant women as the mothers of the next generation, but it was an even more immediate concern to the employers in whose homes the domestics would live. The particular nature of live-in domestic service, the intimacy between employer and employee, was fundamental to the drive for careful selection and close guardianship of women emigrants. After all, employers played a part in controlling the process through offering or withholding employment.

Implementing government selection policies involved a complex juggling of the competing ends of selection. The ability of selection agents to satisfy colonial authorities was limited by a number of factors, including competition among colonies, changing colonial definitions of acceptability, and the different agenda and priorities of British selection agents and British government authorities themselves. Ultimately, the two goals of selection could have been satisfactorily reconciled only given an endless pool of women from which prospective emigrants could be selected. Such a supply did not exist. Colonial dissatisfaction with the results of selection policies failed to take into account that only a limited number of single women were prepared or interested in the prospect of emigration. In that sense, the limits on government agents' ability to select were determined by the women themselves.

'A reward for good conduct, not banishment for bad'

Ellen Joyce and the parable of the lettuces

I had just written the word 'Emigration' at the top of my paper when my little visitor, Ella Brandon, came to ask me to bring my writing out into the summer-house, that I might be near to her whilst she planted her garden . . . and so it came to pass that I heard my little friend have her first lesson in gardening.

'Andrew, are you ready? What will you give me first? I want lots of flowers to make my garden pretty.'

'Well, Missy, I ain't justly ready yet awhile, for I must plant out my young lettuces to-day, they are all drawing up and spoiling; but if you really want to learn from the beginning, you come along wi' me, and I'll larn you.'

The child walked deftly down the furrow between the carrots and the parsnips, till old Andrew began his work amongst the lettuces. He pulled one here and another there, and slid his trowel in and out, and filled his large garden-basket.

'Andrew, isn't it very cruel of you to take them away from their brothers and sisters, and cousins and friends?' asked Ella, with a tone of pity.

'Cruel! bless you no, Missy!' he answered. 'I've let them stop in the nursery-ground far too long already. They would never come to any good here. They would all run up like hop-poles, and die at the root if they stayed here much longer. There is not strength enough in the ground to feed all these plants in this bit of ground; and as for being lonely, why just you see what a lot of them I am taking in this load! Lettuces are not any better for being crowded together than people. It stifles them at starting.'

Ella was half-convinced by the old man's words.

'Have you got a nice place to put them in, Andrew, not too far off?'

'Bless your little heart!' he cried, straightening himself, and brushing his strong grizzly hair back, as he drew his brawny arm across his forehead. 'Why, they're like my children to me. I'm always getting ground ready for putting out my plants. Their place has been waiting for them for ever so long. It's sunny and airy, and about the nicest place in the garden.'

'Oh! do take this one, if it's such a nice place,' cried the child, catching some of his enthusiasm.

'No, he will come to no good. He sprouted up as if he was better than his brothers. He would fall over on one side or the other if he was left to stand alone. He has always been propped up by his neighbours. Now, here is one might do. He's had a very rough time of it on the outside edge, where the east wind comes. He had to do all he knew to keep on living at all. He can bear a rough thing or two. He shall have his chance.'

The old man paused, and was moving off, when Ella exclaimed, 'Mayn't this little one go? It looks as if it wanted a change. Please, Andrew.'

'Ah, no; that's a sour-tempered one. Look how jagged and short its leaves are! Those twisty-looking plants are just like cross-grained men, they won't thrive on the sweetest ground.' And Andrew nearly trod down that ill-favoured lettuce with his great boot.

'Give it one chance more, it does look so unhappy,' pleaded the little gardener.

'Well, well, just to please you; and it may do better in the old place now it has more room. I don't believe it had fair play before, the young plants were so thick they almost pushed each other out of the ground.'

Then the old gardener took up his load and the child followed him, and their voices floated away in the light summer air . . .

I could have no better illustration of my subject, emigration, than the first principles of gardening:

Transplant from England because of overcrowding.

Plant out in better ground, where there is room for all.

Send friends together for company.

Advise those to go who have shown hardihood and fortitude here, and rest assured that you are doing best for those who stay behind as well as for those who go.

Ellen Joyce,
'Letters on Emigration', 1883[1]

COLONIAL GOVERNMENTS and the CLEC were not the only promoters of female emigration. There were other agents and organisations in Britain, women like Ellen Joyce, working to a rather different agenda. Most justified their work not in terms of the colonial shortage of domestic servants which, after all, simply replicated Britain's own servant problem, but with reference to the needs of Britain's working women themselves. Like British government authorities, they were aware of Britain's apparently 'excessive' number of unemployed single women, but they sought to match British women with colonial employment openings rather than husbands. In that sense their interests dovetailed with those of the colonists.

The 'problem' of Britain's redundant women had been raised most prominently in an article written in the 1860s by W. R. Greg.[2] Greg's emphasis was on the middle-class woman 'failed in business' because she neglected to find a husband but feminists and other social activists understood the problem in terms of employment. The argument remained in circulation in Britain throughout this period. In 1894, a promotional article for female emigration pointed to the most recent British census, showing an excess of 600 000 women over men in the population of

Great Britain and Ireland, but added, 'For a girl who relies merely on her feminine attractions, and emigrates in search of a husband, the prospect is the worst that can be imagined'.[3] Sometimes working alone, sometimes in tandem with colonial partners or government agents, middle-class women took up the cause of filling colonial employment opportunities as a perceived cure for 'redundancy' at home.

The ideas of many British emigrationists emerged from a climate of concern with local employment opportunities for women. The background to the formation of the Female Middle-Class Emigration Society (FMCES), the progeny of Maria Rye and Jane Lewin and the Langham Place feminists who founded the Society for Promoting the Employment of Women (SPEW), has been well covered by writers such as A. J. Hammerton and Patricia Clarke.[4] What is less well known is that as the emigration of middle-class women foundered because of lack of funds, some of the most prominent female emigrationists redirected their interests towards promoting the government-funded emigration of working-class women.

From the 1860s a number of influential British women's publications promoted the paired themes of employment and emigration. Through the pages of the *English Woman's Journal (EWJ)*, the Society for Promoting the Employment of Women began its task of publicising the colonies as a place where impoverished middle-class women could find work as governesses. (The journal and the SPEW shared a home at 12 Portugal Street in London with both the FMCES and the National Association for the Promotion of Social Science, which was also co-opted into publicising the cause of female migration; so the Portugal Street premises became a convivial centre for the task of promoting female emigration.)[5] For middle-class women who wanted to find work, though, the colonial employment field was even more barren than the British, with demand quickly satisfied. Whereas in Britain the SPEW had sought new employment opportunities for women beyond the traditional 'governessing' role, promoters of female employment soon recognised that even fewer avenues were open to women in the younger societies of colonial Australia. But the feminists behind middle-class female migration were practical above all. Recognising that the demand for female labour in the colonies was in domestic service, some of them began to promote the notion of paid domestic service for middle-class women, a suggestion made more palatable by the location of the work, far from Britain. Indeed the feminist platform had always been one of training middle-class women for whatever befell them. Middle-class women, they argued, could make excellent 'superior' servants if properly prepared; in the colonies they could attain the independence denied them in Britain.

Over the next decades, this discourse of respectable middle-class domestic employment continued to permeate the pages of the *English Woman's Journal* and subsequently the *Englishwoman's Review*, which came to replace the *EWJ* as a forum for the views of the SPEW. Some were swayed by such ideas. Rosamond Smith and Isabella Maugham were two educated women who took advantage of free passages to emigrate to Queensland in the early 1860s; and there were others. Like the governesses sponsored by the FMCES, they also sent back letters to those who had helped them and some were published in the pages of the *EWJ*. The colonial authorities kept no records of the class of the women they despatched to work in colonial kitchens so we have few details of middle-class women who sought 'independence' and respectability working in colonial homes. We do know, though, their number was small, their fate uncertain. And like many of the governesses, they too found colonial life and society hard. Florence Hill, a well-connected English philanthropist visiting Australia to collect information on philanthropic work there, wrote home in 1873 to the *EWR*, 'I much fear ... that women above the hard-working servant class are practically as "redundant" here as at home. I am amazed by the number of unmarried women of the middle class, many of whom have a hard struggle to maintain themselves'.[6] The work continued slowly.

Perhaps the most important of the later journals promoting emigration was Louisa Hubbard's *Woman's Gazette*. This journal had been established in 1875 as a vehicle for regular presentation of information relating to women's employment, especially that of educated women, and, to reflect that focus, in January 1880 its name was changed to *Work and Leisure*. Though not directly connected with SPEW or the *EWR*, they had many philosophies and principles in common, not least the belief that 'early training and deliberate preparation for work' were essential prerequisites for working women of all classes.[7] Through its pages, Hubbard promoted the notion of emigration as offering advantages to both working-class and middle-class women who sought work. It improved prospects for the women who left and, by lessening competition, increased the opportunities available to those remaining. In May 1877, in its first foray into the emigration field, the *Woman's Gazette* published a letter which repeated the suggestion, by then well-worn, that emigration was the answer to the alleged 'problem' of the excessive number of women in Britain and which blamed the British government for neglecting an obvious way to reduce dangerous overpopulation in England.[8] Throughout this period the British government had refused to encourage emigration in any form, despite the issue being raised in parliament on a number of occasions. In response, the Agent-General for South Australia wrote to the journal, advising that the colony's government was currently offering free passages to 'thoroughly good female domestic servants'.[9] Recognising the significance of this practical and concrete form of assistance (one never made available to middle-class women at any stage in the history of female migration), the journal consequently began to highlight the availability of these and other passages for working-class women, although it consistently maintained its interest in middle-class emigration.

Caroline Blanchard was a woman with extensive practical migration experience and in 1876, as 'Carina', she began to write a regular emigration column for the journal. She had previously acted as selection agent for the New Zealand colonies and in the

1860s had accompanied a party of free women emigrants to that country, as shipboard matron.[10] When she took up Carina's pen she was already working with Queensland government representative Thomas Archer on the biggest ever programme to despatch single women to an Australian colony. *Woman's Gazette* served as a useful platform for her work. She also volunteered to give personal advice to prospective emigrants from the *Gazette*'s office at 42 Somerset Street, Portman Square in London, which effectively became an information office for women's emigration for the next few years.[11]

Although the free and assisted passages then available through Queensland, South Australia and New South Wales were all aimed at working-class women, the prospect of middle-class women taking them up was not abandoned. In January 1880, a new emigration society was born designed primarily to assist middle-class women to emigrate, either as governesses or helpers in households. The Women's Emigration Society (WES) set out to operate along similar lines to the FMCES (by that stage languishing for lack of applicants and any driving organisation), the difference being, as the new society's rules stated, that not just middle-class women but women 'in all ranks of life whose character and health are good' were to be assisted. Unlike the FMCES, which had always rejected the idea of government passages and domestic service for the women it sponsored, the WES and Caroline Blanchard worked directly with colonial governments offering assisted passages. Together they were an important vehicle for promoting colonial emigration schemes.[12]

Yet from its inception there were divisions within the new society. Some were to do with the debate over whether financial assistance towards the cost of passage should be in the form of a loan or a gift. Purists regarded any 'gift' of funds as pauperising; reducing the recipient to an object of philanthropy; unseemly and demeaning when offered to middle-class women, no matter how 'distressed'. The gift of charity was to be bestowed on members of a 'lower' class, not on one's own.

Equally divisive, and equally immersed in issues of maintaining class and status, was the question of whether middle-class women, educated 'gentlewomen' who aspired to become governesses in the colonies, should first qualify themselves in domestic service. With WES loan funds depleted, taking up free passages as domestic servants was effectively the only emigration option available to impoverished British women of any class; yet to many this remained unacceptable. The schism was great enough to split the society. An acerbic exchange in *The Times* in late 1883 between committee stalwarts and those who were already abandoning the WES ship heralded the end of the society's useful life. Adelaide Ross, a mainstay of the female migration movement from its outset and a practical and visible worker in the WES's East End branch, wrote, 'One of the indirect uses of the society, in its original idea, was to re-assert the dignity of labour and to do away with the miserable class distinctions which cause such irreparable mischief at home'. As the other employment areas where women could participate were so oversubscribed, Ross argued that women ought to think about countries where domestic service was valued, pocketing 'the foolish pride which makes [a woman] prefer a lily-white hand to real happiness'.[13]

Another of the same mind added:

> Become domestic servants? Aye, domestic servants if you will with a certainty of immediate, happy, and highly remunerative employment. But remember that in a colony a young woman, like a young man, is respected for what she is, and not for any pretensions based upon some far removed family connexion; for what she can do well rather [than] for that which she might fancy she would like to do.[14]

Colonial commentators too argued for the dignity of all women's labour, paid and unpaid. In her reminiscences of South Australian life, republished in the *Women's Gazette* for the interest of her feminist readers, Catherine Helen Spence applauded the self-respect of the female worker. Far from decrying the fact that middle-class colonial women devoted their time to housework rather than art and charity, thereby making themselves the objects of both the pity and derision of visiting observers, Spence argued that 'the happier community is that where there is a fair share of work and the rewards of work for everybody', and that 'in spite of all sentimental objections our colonial experience proves that the useful woman was quite as affectionate a wife and mother as the useless one'.[15] Spence's views, however, were well ahead of mainstream colonial sentiment and, while Adelaide Ross and others like her took advantage of government assistance for the people they helped, middle-class women continued largely to reject the discourse of genteel domestic service, no matter how remote the setting.

Colonial governments too, with their emphasis on attracting 'a better type', reinforced class differences through the process of migration. The Queensland government's Immigration Act of 1882 institutionalised the widely held belief in the superiority of the self-funding emigrant. In addition to free, assisted and nominated passages, the Act established what became known as 'seventeenth clause' passages. Under this scheme, the impecunious but status-sensitive who objected to travelling on emigrant vessels, even as full-paying passengers, could be despatched on private vessels.[16] On these vessels, passengers paid £5 for privilege of the roughest accommodation in steerage, and £15 for the second cabin. The Queensland government paid the shipping company £10 'bounty' for every individual introduced, and left most aspects of selection and despatch of passengers in the shipping company's hands.[17]

Both the Queensland government's offer of free passages and its emphasis on a 'better type' suited the dual interests of the women's emigration societies. In 1882 Queensland's Agent-General Archer attended a meeting of a women's emigration society organised by Lady Strangford and Caroline Blanchard, aimed at promoting the emigration of women of 'a superior class'; and, through her emigration column in *Woman's Gazette* and later *Work and Leisure*, Blanchard frequently drew the colony's new bounty or seventeenth clause emigration to the attention of those interested in female middle-class emigration.[18]

But the relationship between the societies and the government was not always mutually satisfying. In 1886, Archer was advised by Queensland's immigration agent:

> I would respectfully suggest more care in London as regards the references of single women sent up by the 'Ladies' Emigration Society' and other philanthropically inclined persons, for there can be no doubt that in their anxiety to give 'ne'er do weels' a fresh start in the new country, where they hope the people may turn from their erring ways, these well-intentioned but not well-informed societies quite lose sight of what is due to the people in the Colony, by whom they desire their protegees shall be received and treated as respectable.[19]

General indifference to selection was always a corollary of bounty-type systems of migration, with a prospective traveller's ability to find £5 or so and the desire not to travel on government emigrant vessels sufficient qualification. Yet Queensland representatives were vigilant enough when directly confronted with the issue of the immigration of 'undesirables'. Archer was aghast when the Local Government Board (previously the Poor Law Board) attempted to negotiate for some of its people to emigrate as bounty passengers, with their portion of the fare to be covered by the State-Aided Emigration Committee. The object of the seventeenth clause would be defeated, he argued, if any proportion of the fare, ideally produced through 'industry and frugality', were provided by charitable funds.[20] Clearly the Queensland authorities believed the women's societies were attempting much the same sort of sleight of hand through the seventeenth clause regulations, introducing apparently 'respectable' women who would not have passed close colonial scrutiny.

The public perception that their work was 'charitable' was a perennial bugbear faced by female emigrationists. While the organisers of most of the female emigration societies specifically denied the charge of charity in their work and insisted that they were vigilant in demanding high standards of character and morality, some philanthropists certainly perceived the colonies

as a place of redemption for 'fallen women'. Distancing themselves from any suggestion of philanthropic intent was a major
public relations exercise for female emigration societies and
their representatives from the 1860s into the new century. It
was a problem they shared with all British-based emigration
agents working for colonial authorities.[21]

Despite Archer's contacts with female emigration societies,
the widely-disseminated knowledge of the bounty system and
its evident popularity amongst those who could contribute
substantially towards their fare, relatively few single women
came forward as bounty emigrants.[22] In 1883, for example, 3770
domestic servants were despatched to Queensland as assisted,
free and remittance passengers, but only 179 went out under
the seventeenth clause.[23] So the government continued to give
high priority to the selection of domestic servants for free passages, to supplement the numbers of women nominated from
the colony. The agency and support of prominent and well-
connected emigrationists such as Caroline Blanchard, Adelaide
Ross and Ellen Joyce of Winchester who, like Blanchard, also
acted as Queensland government selection agent,[24] helped direct
a huge number of working-class women to Queensland that
decade.

Alongside Jane Lewin, her fellow co-founder of the FMCES,
Maria Rye is probably the individual most associated with
middle-class female emigration. Even in the 1860s though,
when the FMCES was at its most influential, Rye devoted a great
deal of energy to working-class emigration before changing tack
in her later years to focus on child migration to Canada, which
was to become her life work. She was always quick to spot an
opportunity or create an opening and worked closely with two
Australian colonial governments to further working-class female
emigration. Neither of these arrangements was long lasting or
particularly satisfactory and, as was the case when Rye became
involved in emigration to New Zealand, led to ultimate estrange-
ment between Rye and the various governments.[25] Rye was an
assertive, even acerbic woman, with no inclination to adopt the
pliant passivity more often expected of a young single Victorian

woman. For that reason, she was frequently unpopular with the men she dealt with, who were apparently more comfortable with deferential than defiant femininity. In her work with women she was tireless and unstinting, demanding of those she worked with the same energy and devotion she herself gave to the task. She was seldom satisfied, almost invariably critical, but her primary focus remained the well-being of the women she was assisting.

From the outset, Rye and the activities of the FMCES received extensive coverage in the press.[26] Much positive publicity was driven by Rye herself, who used *The Times* as a personal bulletin board for her emigration activities over the next decades, although others also used the columns of *The Times* to criticise her.

In the early 1860s, Queensland agent Henry Jordan was in London seeking workers for his colony, newly separated from New South Wales and eager to supplement its population. Rye saw an opportunity here for some of the working-class women she was then championing, young women who were not necessarily experienced as domestics but were desperate for work. Their number may well have included some of those few middle-class women who were prepared to take up domestic service.

Initially Jordan was reluctant to grant passages to any of these women but his inability to provide Queensland colonists with the number of domestic servants they wanted forced him into a more lenient interpretation of the regulations. In theory women selected for free passage required employment references. By July 1862, two months after first meeting Rye, he decided to offer free passages to some of Rye's women if they could provide statements from their parents testifying to their ability to perform domestic duties, as well as a certificate from a magistrate or minister guaranteeing the parents' respectability.[27] One hundred of Rye's women sailed for Queensland on 12 August. In September that year Jordan gave a lecture in Cork on the subject of female emigration to Queensland.[28] The following month he advised the colonial secretary that he would offer free passages to young women, 'whose *fitness* as domestic Servants is properly ascertained' and who were sponsored by Rye. Subsequently he began negotiations through Rye and the FMCES to despatch working-class women from Cork.[29] Rye was less successful in her other negotiations with the Queensland agent. She had long been keen to see some of Britain's unemployed factory workers despatched, women who, by virtue of their former occupations, were effectively barred from selection. Here Rye attempted to use her connections to overcome Jordan's objections. One was former Queenslander Matthew Marsh, one-time member for New England of the New South Wales Legislative Council and member of the House of Commons from 1857. A strong supporter of Moreton Bay separatism, Marsh acted as representative in England for the Queensland government, and was the principal commissioner for Queensland at the London Exhibition in 1862.[30] On Rye's behalf Marsh pressed Jordan to accept a number of these female factory workers for free passage:

> I think the factory girls would be rather an acquisition to the colony. They have all industrious habits. They are not the worst of their class, which we all know must to a certain extent be the case with some others as for instance good servants can always get places and indeed as I know from experience are not very easily got.[31]

And if the colonial government objected to offering the women free passages, Marsh himself offered to provide the fares which, under the complicated system of land orders then in operation in Queensland, would have made him eligible for land grants.[32]

As we have already seen, a background in factory work was the least desirable qualification any single woman could have offered the colonists and, while Jordan was expected to be careful about the experience and morality of the female domestics he himself selected for passage, he had to be even more cautious about bending the regulations relating to 'eligible' emigrants on whose behalf land orders were issued. Marsh's proposition was rejected outright. He replied to Marsh:

You can have little idea of the great difficulty I have experienced in preventing the violation of this rule and I am convinced that its strict observance is essential to the successful working of this part of our land-order system. Otherwise Speculators + Shippers would at once rush at this trade and inundate the Colony at the expense of our land fund with the most worthless Class of persons. With all my care, this irregularity has not been entirely prevented and in dealing with those who have ignored this requirement the Government would be greatly embarrassed could it be shewn that I had in a single instance overridden it myself.[33]

As well as Rye, others interested in female emigration saw the possibilities in Queensland's new emigration schemes, and in 1862 Jordan was also approached by the National Female Emigration Society. As he had done with Rye's women, he eventually decided that women who could provide a certificate attesting to some domestic ability might conveniently top up shortfalls in numbers of single females, but he remained wary of the motives of this basically philanthropic organisation: 'The classes of young women suffering most in England would be chiefly such as would be most incapable as Servants, and unsuited to the Colonies'.[34]

Jordan also made a sidelong pass at Marsh in a letter home to the Queensland authorities, in which he reiterated the colonial response to the British notion of a colonial imbalance of the sexes: 'An idea prevails that the dearth of labor and of females makes almost anything acceptable, and this is too often encouraged by gentlemen who have been resident in Australia themselves, but have no idea of it as a home for themselves, or their families'.[35] The embattled Jordan, who later resigned after savage local criticism of his role in Queensland's sorry emigration schemes of the 1860s, was outraged at these attempts to usurp his control of emigration. Even if the women found domestic employment in Queensland, as did the fifty women cotton weavers the CLEC sent, unwanted, from Lancashire to Western Australia the following year, Jordan was aware that he would still be held responsible for granting free passages to people the colonists would regard as quite unsuitable.[36] Jordan was directly accountable to the colonial authorities, wheras most selection agents understood their accountability to cease once prospective emigrants had been passed into the hands of the colonial authorities responsible for passage arrangements. The attitude of the female emigrationists was different yet again. Rye viewed migration as giving British women who deserved it an opportunity to experience a new and better life. In theory at least, her women were carefully chosen for this colonial life and, as an appropriate response, she believed they should be well catered for, both in transit and after arrival. Other women emigrationists shared this point of view.

Women emigrationists also shared a belief that colonial governments were largely indifferent to issues of responsibility other than to the servant-employing colonists. In a bid to force the colonial governments into a measure of compliance, some entered into arrangements with colonial women to oversee and protect immigrant women after arrival. Rye, as did Caroline Blanchard and Ellen Joyce in later years, took the process further. She herself had escorted a large party of single women domestics to New Zealand in 1863 and, following that trip, had journeyed on to the Australian colonies to examine conditions for the reception of single working-class women who had emigrated to the colonies.[37] The time she spent there enabled her to establish a new selection arrangement with the Victorian colonial government but it also caused a rift in her relationship with Queensland immigration authorities and certainly would have destroyed any wish on her part to select for the colony again.

Rye arrived in Queensland in 1865 in time to hear the outcome of the Select Committee inquiry into the passage of the notorious *Commodore Perry*, whose chief officer was found guilty of drunkenness and violent behaviour towards the single women.[38] That was bad enough; but Rye's concerns were directed more at Dr Luce, the ship's surgeon-superintendent. As Rye saw it, Luce's failure to report the chief officer had effectively condoned his behaviour; yet despite this failure, Luce was not to be dismissed from the emigration service. Consequently, the target for her criticism became the Select Committee inquiry itself. Not content with protesting before Queensland authorities, she directed the matter back to the CLEC in London. Clearly what she had seen in Brisbane convinced her that those in authority in Queensland were indifferent to matters of female safety, both physical and moral. She relayed to the CLEC her allegations about further incidents ignored by Queensland authorities:

> That in the *Wansfell* on her last trip, a young woman . . . was entrapped one evening into the 2nd Cabin by a party of young men 8 in number, who made her stupid with drink and then, after ill-using her all night, kicked her out quite naked in the morning, when she was found insensible by the Mate. This girl died in the Hospital at Brisbane 2 days after her arrival at Port.[39]

She had also been told of another incident on the *Flying Cloud*. On that vessel, which had arrived in Brisbane in early 1865, a young single woman named Annie Doyle had been hurt in an accident in which a ship's boat laden with potatoes crashed to the deck. One man was killed, and a woman and a second man were also injured. Doyle's jaw had been broken in five places, her teeth smashed and her arm, shoulder and ribs broken. She was lamed for life. In neither case, Rye claimed, had there been an inquiry; nor had she been able to obtain any compensation for Doyle.[40] She also raised the matter in the British press, which did nothing to improve Queensland's worsening competitive position with regard to immigration, as the colony's economic conditions deteriorated.

Subsequent inquiries in the colony found little or no evidence to support Rye's charges; and indeed her allegations about the ill-treatment of female immigrants elsewhere were sometimes highly coloured and equally lacking in corroborative evidence.[41] However, her accusations had the effect of bringing her clearly to the attention of the CLEC: as a critic and no doubt a prospective troublemaker. For Rye's work, her notoriety was to prove untimely.

From Queensland Rye travelled south, arriving in Victoria to find immigration arrangements there in a state of flux. In the early 1860s, government-assisted emigration to Victoria had been conducted through a number of different channels, with the CLEC and private shipping companies both playing a role in despatching selected and nominated emigrants to the colony. This arrangement had provoked bitterness and friction between the Victorian authorities and the CLEC, largely relating to what the CLEC saw as the inadequate shipboard protection given to single women, who comprised the great majority of Victoria's assisted migrants at that stage. From 1866, partly in response to criticism of shipboard protection but also because CLEC passages could be obtained more cheaply, the colony returned the transportation of single female emigration entirely to the CLEC, as had been the case before 1861.[42] By the time this occurred, the eastern colonies generally languished under regional depression with consequent unemployment and a general fall in the level of migration from 1865 levels.[43] Yet as the constancy of demand for female immigrant domestics over this fifty-year period shows, while demand for male workers might wax and wane the demand for domestic servants was never tied so directly to cycles of boom and bust, nor even seasonal fluctuations. Despite unemployment in the male labour market, demand for women workers remained consistently high, even urgent, and the government was keen to guarantee supply. On the day before her departure from Victoria, Rye was appointed to select female emigrants in Britain for the Victorian government.[44] While it is not clear whether Rye or the Victorian government initiated the arrangement, it seems unlikely that Rye waited to be approached.

Returning to Britain in June 1866, Rye immediately set out to implement her new commission, and her first vessel left for Melbourne within weeks. Rye heralded the vessel's August departure with the announcement that the women, on arrival in Victoria, would all be maintained in excellent barracks, free of charge, until work was found for them, and that she 'had every confidence in the master and mistress of the barracks'.[45]

So compelling was Rye that she managed to convince even the CLEC, to their chagrin, that she had been given complete authority to select single women, with the CLEC responsible only for arranging shipping contracts:

> We understand . . . that as soon as Miss Rye commences her operations the whole of the selecting business is to pass into her hands[,] that we are not to interfere with her discretion, &, in short, that we are to cease to take any part in it, or to be responsible in any way for the quantity or quality of the emigration.[46]

However, either Victorian government policy changed or a misunderstanding was clarified and both the CLEC and Rye, in uncomfortable tandem, selected women.[47]

Initially, Rye's selected women were all to be despatched through the CLEC, but this arrangement was guaranteed to exacerbate existing strains between the CLEC and the colonial government.[48] Rye had always been a firm believer in the principle that female emigration should be dealt with by women and doubtless expressed her views on the matter to the (male) CLEC and their (male) staff. Writing in 1897, Edwin Pratt attributed her appointment by the Victorian government directly to her allegation that the CLEC had mishandled the selection of single women. Many more, she argued, were willing to emigrate if dealt with correctly, and such assertions may have confirmed the Victorian government's own suspicions that the CLEC mishandled their role. According to Pratt:

> [the CLEC's selection of women for Victoria] was left mainly in the hands of a staff of young men clerks, before whom the women had to go to make their applications, and some of these clerks possessed a sense of humour which led them to address to the candidates such remarks as, 'Going out to get a husband?' It amused the young men, but annoyed the young

women; and Miss Rye suggested that it would be better if the selection of the emigrants were put into the hands of women.[49]

Her penchant for publicity did not help. Rye took it upon herself to publicise her own work, with the departure of her parties of female emigrants for Victoria always heralded by reports in *The Times*,[50] and she was no less reticent about publicising her complaints. Understandably, Rye's repeated references to the despatch of 'her' ships to Victoria in the letter columns of *The Times*, would have infuriated the CLEC who were also selecting single women for part of this period and who, for the entire period, remained responsible for fitting out and despatching Victoria's emigrant vessels. For whatever reason, the CLEC were not pleased at sharing responsibility with her.

The *Underley* was one of the earlier vessels carrying Rye's emigrants. A new iron ship owned by the White Star Company, she left Liverpool in late December 1865 bound for Melbourne. It was her first passage and carried '93 single women and ten families for Miss Rye', in addition of course to the emigrant women selected by the CLEC and the nominated emigrants (known as passage warrant holders), who continued to make up the bulk of the emigrants at this period. *The Times*, in an article headed simply 'Miss Rye's Emigrants', further asserted:

> The girls going out in the Underley are said to be superior to even those going out in the Red Jacket, which possibly may be accounted for by the fact, now getting well understood, that Miss Rye is determined to make emigration, as far as she is concerned, a reward for good conduct, and not banishment for bad behaviour.[51]

Rye selected 189 women for despatch on CLEC vessels in the latter months of 1866 but the CLEC still selected the majority.[52] In fact, the shipping lists for these vessels clearly indicated women who were part of Rye's selection and those who had been selected through the Park Street Commissioners. With both the CLEC and Rye eager to prove the superiority of their own selections, listing responsibility for selections may have been one way in which the CLEC attempted to shore up its position against colonial criticism about both quality and quantity. Yet the CLEC were pessimistic about the continuing success of the arrangement with Rye, pointing to 'the increasing rates of wages in this Country, & the strong competition of other Colonies for the same class of Emigts.'[53] as 'impediments' to success, and further noting that 'the fact of two authorities being in the labour market seeking simultaneously the same class of Emigrants will add to the difficulty of the operation of each'.[54]

Certainly the new arrangements did not greatly improve the supply, but this was at least partly the fault of the Victorian government itself. Despite the government's evident concern with the shortage of female domestics (the government requested that the CLEC select and despatch 150 single women per month, in addition to married couples and nominated emigrants), it neglected to send sufficient funds. This delay was beyond the Victorian government's control, stemming from a problem with the passage of supply in the colony, but it took relations with the CLEC to a new low. Only six emigrant vessels (including the *Underley*) arrived in Victoria in 1867 carrying selected single women.[55]

On board the *Atalanta*, which arrived in July 1867, were ninety single women selected by Rye and a further seventy-six selected by the CLEC. Mary Casey was one of the twenty Irish women amongst Rye's selection; she was twenty-three years old, a general servant, and was hired out at eight shillings a week to a Brighton householder just eight days after disembarking at Hobson's Bay. Rye had also selected the McKenzie family, comprising the mother Mary and her four daughters. The widowed 41-year-old was described as a nurse, her four daughters as nurse maids. All went to separate employers, 13-year-old Victoria and 11-year-old Susanna for just three shillings and four shillings a week each. Normally too young for an assisted passage as 'single women', they had been permitted to embark, ironically, to keep the family intact. Amongst the CLEC selection was Eliza Kingston, a 29-year-old dressmaker, who could read and write and, unlike most of her fellow Irish, was Anglican. She was engaged for the very good salary of £30. Twenty-eight year old Englishwoman Caroline Reid took a position as a general servant in St Kilda.[56] Like most of the selected single women arriving in Victoria in the 1860s, all the women from the *Atalanta* found employment very shortly after arrival. More would have been equally well received. The CLEC had selected only 475 single women, and Rye 266, of a total of 3335 emigrants despatched that year.[57] (The remainder were predominantly nominated emigrants and there were a few married couples selected to accompany the single women. Of course, a proportion of the nominated emigrants were also single women.) Neither Rye nor the CLEC sent out as many single women as the Victorians had hoped for. Yet despite the CLEC's better success rate, the Victorian immigration authorities were somehow persuaded to pass selection of female emigrants entirely to Rye. They evidently thought she could serve them better if given a freer rein and reduced competition.

The new arrangement seemed designed to strengthen Rye's hand but it still left her dependent on the CLEC for all passage arrangements. The system broke down rapidly. This was partly for reasons familiar to all those involved in selecting and despatching emigrants to the colonies but CLEC sour grapes also played a role. In January 1868 the CLEC advised the Victorian authorities that, immediately they had the money, they would contract for a vessel for Rye's exclusive use, providing she had sufficient single women to fill it. The CLEC were well aware of how unlikely this was, and how difficult it would be for Rye to meet the shippers' contractual requirements. For such a lengthy passage, as the CLEC pointed out, the vessel had to be capable of carrying perhaps 300 adults or more. Rye would therefore need to have at least 250 single women waiting to embark, as well as a dozen families, before she could call on the CLEC to charter a ship. This was far more than she had ever previously mustered. Obtaining the vessel by public tender, and fitting it out to CLEC standards, would take at least six weeks. As the CLEC well recognised and pointed out to the Victorian authorities:

> the length of time that must elapse in procuring so large a number of young women ... cannot fail to add prejudicially to Miss Rye's success, by producing a large defection amongst this particular class of candidates who are naturally impatient of delay and frequently change their minds if exposed to it.[58]

If the ship sailed short of emigrants, then the colonial government would have to bear the cost of the shortfall. Contracting for a vessel to carry a smaller number of emigrants would increase risks to passenger comfort and health, lead to increased passage costs and in any case would probably not much lessen the rate of defaulters.[59]

Though the CLEC were unhelpful, they had a point based on long experience contracting and fitting out vessels to carry emigrants to the colonies. The result was that the system of female selection operating through Rye became unworkable and had to be abandoned. Rye ceased to work for the colonial government and further selection of single women by the CLEC also ceased, though they despatched nominated emigrants for a further eighteen months.

At the turn of the decade selection of single women for emigration of Victoria was revived briefly, under a colonial agent, but only a few hundred more selected women were despatched before assisted emigration was withdrawn entirely in the early 1870s. Under the new Victorian regulations of 1871, nominated emigrants continued to trickle in till the end of the decade, but that was effectively the end of government-assisted emigration to Victoria that century.[60] Rye henceforth turned her face across the Atlantic. Shortly afterwards readers of *The Times* learnt of her efforts to despatch young working-class women to Canada, with the links between Rye and the Australasian colonies now permanently severed.[61]

One of the hallmarks of Rye's work was her attempt to oversee all aspects of the migration process. While she took personal responsibility for overseeing the selection of her emigrants, she also had a hand in managing shipboard protection arrangements; and of course her trips to the Australasian colonies gave her the first-hand knowledge available to few other emigrationists, of reception facilities in the Australian colonies. Her personal philosophy was always that emigration should be regarded as a reward, not as exile. Consequently she vehemently opposed any suggestion that she would knowingly, even deliberately, despatch women who were not fit to emigrate, a position she continued to argue in her Canadian work:

> I feel that I am continually disappointing my correspondents and offending friends by refusing these cases, but no work is worth doing that is not done conscientiously, and I will not —I dare not—spend any time in passing bad people from one port to another. One would think, to hear the way some people talk, that the Atlantic waves were the waters of regeneration, and that bad habits, bad principles, bad lives would all be eradicated by a sea voyage. I say that occasionally I have taken such cases in hand and sent them abroad, given them the one chance more, and that the result in all cases has been a perfect failure, and that it is wiser, safer, and kinder to take poor, friendless women, or orphan girls, whose only misfortune is their poverty; and that by selecting only from this class of people I do a far greater good ultimately, even to the mother country, than if I shipped off every wretched case that was or could be brought to me.[62]

Only the best need apply. The corollary was, being of good character, women selected for emigration had a right to expect proper treatment, care and protection after arrival. These two principles, fundamental to women emigrationists such as Rye who rejected suggestions of 'philanthropy' or charity in their work, were also implicit in the migration work of women in the Australian colonies. Working alongside colonial governments, they sought to feminise the process of receiving well-selected emigrant women and providing them with adequate support after arrival.

Similar ideas were fundamental to the most important of the British female emigration societies in the nineteenth century, the United British Women's Emigration Association (ultimately known as BWEA). Whereas Rye's approach derived from her assertive feminist beliefs, the BWEA's stemmed from the evangelical Christianity of the early organisers and the broader climate of interest in emigration which flourished in Britain from the early 1880s.

In 1878, the Anglican Church's Lambeth Conference had publicly addressed the question of emigration, not as a means of supporting or encouraging it but in terms of the Church's concern with the spiritual welfare of its own members, and indeed with the body of the Church itself. Emigrant Anglicans, particularly those going to North America, were too often lost to the Church. Yet despite the recommendations of the Conference, few systematic contacts were established between the Church in Britain and in the colonies, prompting the Archbishop of Canterbury to write a letter on the Church and emigration published in *The Times* in December 1881. At a time of bitter winter cold and social discontent, Archbishop Tait's statement urged the Anglican Church to take a more active interest in emigration, through the publication and distribution of cheap literature on the colonies and the colonial clergy, the establishment of support networks in the colonies for new arrivals, and the provision of commendatory letters, to be carried by emigrants to colonial clergy.[63] Tait died shortly afterwards but his successor, Archbishop Benson, was keen to support his initiative and, even more than Tait, spoke publicly on the subject, earning him condemnation from working-class representatives for what was regarded as his collusion in the process of shipping off Britain's 'restless classes'. In response to his appearance at a large meeting organised by the State-Directed Emigration Society, for instance, a working-class publication noted it was 'a curious thing that the Archbishop of Canterbury, who drew £13 000 a year, should go to the Mansion House and speak in favour of emigration'.[64]

The Church's actions also sparked the growth of a rash of new emigration societies. Many existing and new emigration organisations sought Benson's patronage: the Central Emigration Society (an offshoot of the Charity Organisation Society), the Church of England Emigration Association, the Church Colonisation and Land Society and the National Association for Promoting State-Directed Emigration. Yet though Benson was approached for nominal sponsorship by these and other organisations, he refused, perhaps wary of further alienating his working-class membership.[65] The Church's role was, after all, not to promote emigration but to prevent the loss of its membership should they choose to emigrate.

For female emigrationists, the Church's interest in emigration had two by-products. The middle-class emigration work of the Women's Emigration Society (WES), by this stage already foundering, was almost totally eclipsed by this ground swell of interest in working-class emigration, though the society tried unsuccessfully to interest Benson in their cause, and from that time the society ceased to be a real player in female emigration. It was officially wound up in 1894, at the instigation of the Charity Organisation Society, but by then had been dormant for some years.[66] Simultaneously, another Anglican group maximised the opportunities of the moment. Working not for middle-class women but for its own working-class membership, the Girls' Friendly Society created an Emigration Department. At the helm from its inception was Mrs Ellen Joyce. The widow of an Anglican clergyman and the mother of another, she was a strongly religious woman in the Evangelical tradition. Although Caroline Chisholm and Maria Rye are both better known, undoubtedly she was the most significant single influence on British female emigration practices up until World War I.

Through the GFS Emigration Department, Joyce drew on the resources of a number of other similar organisations for working-class women, such as the Young Women's Christian Association (YWCA) and the Metropolitan Association for Befriending Young Servants (MABYS), as well as the newly established Emigration Department of the Society for Promoting Christian Knowledge (SPCK). Simultaneously, she began to promote female emigration in larger spheres and by the late 1880s, under Joyce, the society which was to become best known as the BWEA had emerged as the major private vehicle for female emigration.[67] Loosely organised in 1884 into the

United Englishwomen's Emigration Register, Joyce and a number of other women emigrationists soon formed the United Englishwomen's Emigration Association, which became from 1888 the United British Women's Emigration Association. From 1901 to 1919, the organisation was known as the British Women's Emigration Association.

Alongside Joyce, other early members of the BWEA such as Adelaide Ross and Mrs Walter Browne already had extensive experience in female emigration through the various manifestations of the Women's Emigration Society. Jane Stuart Wortley, the BWEA's first president, had been involved in female emigration even longer than most, having served as a member of Sidney Herbert's Committee to emigrate distressed needlewomen in the 1850s. These women brought together decades of practical experience in emigration work and a determination not to be side-tracked by the political issues which had riven the Women's Emigration Society. They also combined an interest in middle-class emigration with the recognition that the opportunities for female emigration lay in making use of the schemes designed to promote working-class emigration.

The BWEA continued and perfected many of the traditions long associated with women's emigration work, both in Britain and the colonies. One was their commitment to seeing the process of female emigration kept largely in women's hands. Rye had objected to men intervening in female emigration at a personal level, and the BWEA equally rejected the impropriety of single women having to outline their qualifications to men whom they considered unqualified or socially inferior: perhaps a mere junior clerk in the absence of the Agent-General. The BWEA's organisation of women workers offered an alternative. Through its network of middle-class women spread across Britain, the Association publicised the availability of free and assisted passages to the colonies and helped working-class women to take advantage of these offers. It enabled prospective emigrant women to find out as much as they needed to know about the process of emigration—whom to contact, how to complete forms, the differences between colonies, what assistance was available—without tramping from one Agent-General to another, or running the potentially embarrassing gauntlet of the young male clerks at the British government's newly opened Emigrants' Information Office. (Though the British government did not itself promote emigration, it had opened this central office in London where colonies and dominions promoting emigration could circulate their publicity material.)

Like the WES before it, the BWEA did not offer financial assistance to working-class women. It always sought to avoid any suggestion that it did so since, even amongst middle-class supporters of emigration, there was still some ambivalence about seeing the British supply of domestic servants reduced, and the BWEA was of course dependent on public subscription for its survival.[68] The British were experiencing their own 'servant problem'. Relaying information was one thing, actively financing emigration quite another. Consequently the working-class women who were offered advice and guidance through these organisations, and who subsequently emigrated, did so through the various colonial governments which offered assisted passages.

While their impact is hard to measure numerically, the influence of women's societies from the 1880s was substantial. Their strength lay in their widespread publicity networks. Though BWEA headquarters were in London, Ellen Joyce operated from her home in Winchester, and the BWEA and GFS network right across Britain enabled direct access to emigration information. While the colonies' appointed agents and lecturers sought to attract both male and female emigrants, travelling lecturers generally focused on rural opportunities such as land grants and cheap land, which were designed to appeal to men. Recruitment initiatives based on public rural meetings chaired by and largely directed at men were masculine in approach and virtually impossible for women in service to attend, if they did not coincide with the occasional evening off. Women's societies did not generally lecture directly to prospective emigrants. Instead they sought the help of an unofficial network of individual middle-class women, through the pages of a range of journals, to reach out indirectly to working-class women. Certainly the magazines of the GFS and the YWCA were far more likely to find their way into the hands of domestics than were the publications favoured by the colonial governments. And as Mrs Walter Browne said in the middle-class *Englishwoman's Review*, the other style of publication favoured by female emigrationists, 'No girls are likely to read this paper, but I trust that some of those who do read it, will tell them of the life which awaits them in new countries'.[69]

The BWEA also retained an interest in the emigration of educated women and was keen to advise on the possibilities of non-domestic openings in the colonies, dominions and, later, the Australian States. Though this work had started earlier, a specialised offshoot of the BWEA known as the Colonial Intelligence League was formed in 1911 to focus primarily on the emigration of educated and professionally-trained young women within the Empire. However, although the BWEA would assist any woman who had the means who wanted to emigrate, perhaps to join family or friends or to go to employment, the main thrust of its Australian work was to assist the emigration of women entering domestic service.

By the mid-1880s, only New South Wales, Queensland and Western Australia still offered assistance, and that decade Joyce was active in facilitating the emigration of single women to New South Wales, particularly through her GFS contacts there. She also attempted to improve the support available to GFS women going out to Queensland through the BWEA, through the appointment of individual GFS mentors, although this met with only limited success. The following decade, she and the BWEA became effectively the sole agents for the Western Australian government's new programme of recruiting single women. She was responsible for selecting and despatching small parties of single women, up to fifty in each, on one or two vessels every year from 1889 to 1901. Although the numbers were fewer than one thousand, this was one of the BWEA's most successful ventures in directly assisting working-class emigration. It is also a scheme about which we know a great deal and from the outset it bore Ellen Joyce's personal stamp.

In Western Australia the assistance programme had its genesis in the 1880s, when the newly appointed Immigration Board considered ways to increase the number of single female immigrants then arriving in the colony. At that stage the colony had a system of nomination in place but the number of nominated single women was low. So nomination was supplemented with a scheme to despatch parties of domestics from Ireland, twenty women in each group, three times annually. Even that did not produce enough single women and consequently Ellen Barlee, sister of the former Western Australian Colonial Secretary, was asked to make a one-off selection of about thirty domestic servants to bolster the numbers coming out through the Crown Agent. She had previously selected single women for both South Australia and Western Australia.[70] Despite the colonial depression of 1887–88, the demand for domestics remained relatively high and the numbers arriving inadequate: 'The labour market is fairly supplied; but constant inquiries are made for female domestic servants, who appear to be very scarce, and suitable persons are reported as not obtainable'.[71]

Of eighty-eight nominations approved in the colony in 1888, only seventeen were for domestics. The need to finance a broader selection programme was critical, and so the Board of Immigration decided to send for another selection of sixty. This was increased to one hundred three months later.[72] Aged between sixteen and thirty, the women were to be 'carefully selected both with regard to character health and capabilities', and country women would have preference.[73] The piece-meal approach previously adopted was abandoned and the government turned to an organisation with a wider sphere of influence in Britain than Ellen Barlee, entering into a systematic arrangement with the BWEA. As a result, parties of about fifty women each were despatched twice annually to the colony over the next decade. Although agencies in Dundee and Edinburgh sent a few individuals and some other women went direct through the Agent-General's office, almost the entire responsibility of overseeing the selection of these women was vested in Ellen Joyce.

The first eighty-five women despatched under the new scheme arrived in 1889 on board the *Nairnshire* and the SS *Wilcannia*. Immediately a few of the women experienced problems, possibly relating to the emigration authorities' failure to inform them appropriately about their conditions of passage, although the BWEA is also implicated here. Alice Wright and Elizabeth Hancock from the *Nairnshire* both applied to leave the colony shortly after arrival, but this was a breach of their agreement with the Western Australian government, which stipulated that in return for a free passage they would remain in the colony as domestic servants for twelve months after arrival. However, they were permitted to move on after repayment of £15 passage money each, although it's not clear how long it took them to provide this amount, a considerable sum of money.[74]

More important for immigration authorities than the disinclination of these two women to stay was the success of all the other women in finding work. This and the colony's gold-flushed prosperity, which only added to the clamour for domestic assistance, persuaded the Board to continue the arrangment with Joyce.

Once news of the scheme circulated amongst local householders, the imminent arrival of every boatload of female immigrants provoked a flood of applications for domestic servants, directed both at government immigration authorities and at Mrs Salter, the GFS associate in Perth who kept Joyce in touch with local immigration matters. Colonists' requests to be provided with an immigrant crowded the in-trays at the Colonial Secretary's Office.[75] Many were written in response to news and letters from Britain. The papers of the GFS, *Friendly Work* and *Friendly Leaves*, in which Ellen Joyce had a regular emigration feature, were a particularly effective means of reaching the domestic servants the Australian colonists most wished to attract. The BWEA also featured in dozens of articles in the

British press in the 1880s and 1890s publicising its work: *The Times, Daily News, Daily Telegraph, Standard, Manchester Guardian* and *Cassell's Saturday Journal* for instance, as well as *The Queen, The Lady's Newspaper, Home Sweet Home* and *Our Paper,* the paper of the YWCA. As well, the scheme was publicised through the colony's Agent-General and the British government's Emigrants' Information Office.

From the colonial point of view, the arrangement with the BWEA seemed to work outstandingly, with boatloads of seemingly well-selected immigrant women arriving regularly in the colony to public acclaim. Inevitably, however, no matter how closely Joyce scrutinised her applicants, not all ultimately lived up to her standards. In 1893 Alice Hamilton, a hospital nurse assistant from New Cross, London, arrived in the colony pregnant. Joyce was very grieved at the news, for she herself had seen Hamilton's references and they had been good; and the evident surprise and humiliation of Hamilton's friend, who had travelled out with her, seemed to testify that this was 'out of character'. Salter, from the GFS, offered to provide Hamilton with some personal support, and we know no more of her fate.[76] She was by no means the first single woman who, facing an unwanted pregnancy in Britain, sought self-exile in the colonies.

The *Gulf of Siam,* which reached the colony late in 1894, carried several women who, though selected according to the usual procedures, turned out badly in colonial eyes. Two sisters (the daughters of a dissenting minister and thus, Joyce later concluded with Anglican assuredness, 'unused to self discipline'), had originally asserted their intention to enter domestic service but were apparently found quite unfit for it, being 'most insubordinate and offensive'.[77] Another woman, a young widow who had seemed respectable, turned out 'infamous and abandoned'.

Yet early perceptions were sometimes misleading, with immigrant women often settling down to official and colonial satisfaction despite an unpropitious start or poor shipboard reports.[78] These same *Gulf of Siam* women had travelled out with a relatively inexperienced matron (an unusual occurrence for BWEA parties), and the normal tensions of the passage had been exacerbated by the outbreak of a fire on board which burned, barely under control, for five days.[79] Salter later informed Joyce that many of those women were of a 'superior class' and added that those from the previous vessel were also doing better than shipboard reports might have suggested.[80]

Joyce herself played a significant role in personally scrutinising all applications and meeting as many of the women as possible. She was also prepared to tighten up selection procedures where she could. From 1894, all members of her Western Australian parties were compelled to sign a set of rules agreeing to submit to the matron's authority on board, and the period at the emigrants' home before embarking was also probationary, serving sometimes to detect an 'undisciplined' emigrant. This was no empty threat and more than one single woman was rejected after scrutiny at the BWEA home at 53 Horseferry Road, Westminster, or at the Blackwall Emigrants' Home, where the Western Australian parties assembled before departure.[81] Joyce herself tried to visit all BWEA parties before embarkation and, one way or another, she usually made quite an impression. 'Mrs Joyce came in the afternoon, didn't like her —too showy', Margaret Kelly recalled of their encounter at Horseferry Road in 1900.[82]

From the moment of the arrival of the *Nairnshire* and the SS *Wilcannia,* Ellen Joyce began to assert her authority over the programme.[83] One of the keystones of the BWEA approach was to link the process of selection in Britain with the reception of single immigrants in the colonies. Middle-class women in Western Australia, such as Mrs Parry, the wife of Bishop Parry, and Mrs Salter of the Girls' Friendly Society, provided what Joyce saw as 'that personal + individual interest in the young women which must always be woman's part of the work'.[84] However, though the BWEA saw this local care as indispensable, it was still viewed as secondary to the government's responsibilities. Appropriate reception was part of the government's obligation towards the women introduced and those who had sent them, in the BWEA view, and was a complement to careful selection and protection. Thus a satisfactory reception procedure became the linchpin to the emigration process. This cut both ways. Joyce and the BWEA believed that close policing of emigrant women was justified in fairness to colonial authorities, who paid for migrant women with both domestic skills and proven good character. Hence the women's acceptance of the controls Joyce imposed became a mark of their good character. In return Joyce argued that, since the women she despatched *were* of good character, they deserved the best protection the colony could offer. Without it, Mrs Joyce refused to select domestic servants for the colony. She policed the activities of the colonial government as closely as she policed the women she despatched.

As far as Joyce was concerned, depot facilities were inadequate. In the colony, a local Anglican minister had complained to the Board of Immigration about lack of proper supervision of the single women on arrival at the Fremantle barracks, and in Britain Mrs Joyce heard reports of 'girls . . . allowed to go about the town or receive outsiders at the Depot'.[85] At her request, Western Australia's Governor Sir William Robinson undertook to have the colony's reception arrangements improved and a new depot established in Perth. Robinson also suggested that the matrons who supervised the women on board ship remain with them after they had been transferred to the depot, as much to deflect the suggestion that trouble only occurred once the immigrants were entirely in the hands of the colonial government, as to continue their supervision.[86] This simply duplicated Mrs Joyce's own stipulation.[87]

Joyce also began to influence colonial conditions of domestic employment. In February 1891 she argued that new arrivals should not work in public houses straight out of the depot since only those 'used to the ways of the Country . . . [were] able to insist upon their self respect being preserved' in such jobs.[88] It took some time before this ruling was fully effective. In December 1891, in spite of Mrs Joyce, immigration agent William Dale recommended a single female immigrant as cook for Mrs Bell of the Railway Hotel in Katanning.[89] The following year immigrant Martha Scammett was engaged by Mrs O'Connell of Fremantle, but was in fact passed on to work with Mrs Armstrong of Armitage's Hotel. Once they realised this, immigration authorities told Martha that if she wished, she could return to the depot and a new post would be found for her.[90] Similarly in March 1894, Dale was forced to make 'private and confidential' inquiries concerning Mrs Connor, wife of the Member of Parliament for Wyndham, who had engaged Lilly Gardner from the *Port Victor*. Authorities suspected she intended taking Lilly back to Wyndham to work in Connor's hotel.[91] Ellen Joyce's wishes were becoming commands.

Joyce also insisted that the government use a BWEA-appointed matron to oversee parties of emigrant women. Mary Pittman Monk, one of the BWEA's longest serving and most highly regarded matrons, escorted almost every Western Australian party despatched in the 1890s, giving a uniformity and coherence to shipboard protection not achieved under any other colony's assistance programme. Having effective control of both selection and shipboard protection, and through personal intervention and the use of GFS intermediaries in the colony, Joyce and the BWEA were enabled to implement the three aspects of emigration which they saw as fundamental to their notion of 'protected emigration'.

The women who sailed for Western Australia through the BWEA were asked to write back about their experiences and many did so. Some were critical and, although we cannot now know if the most critical letters were suppressed, the open publication of these letters serves to reinforce the BWEA's assertions that it always sought to place a reasonably balanced picture of emigration before British women. It's also possible, of course, that women most disaffected with the BWEA process would not have bothered to write. Most writers mentioned the level of wages and their general satisfaction with their new life. 'F.W.' wrote from Perth in 1896:

> I have a very nice place indeed, very comfortable; I am general, those seem the best places to me. It is not a hard place, no washing, and I am getting £2.10s. a month. I am

quite satisfied, and I feel very thankful that I came. I think if the English girls knew more about it, there would be more wanting to come out.[92]

In its recruiting material, the BWEA also stressed the idea that paid domestic service involved no social degradation and that such work was conducted in a more egalitarian atmosphere in the colonies than in Britain. With young women in Britain increasingly rejecting domestic service as an occupation because, amongst other things, they considered it demeaning, this message was now addressed as much to the young working-class woman as the distressed gentlewoman of an earlier era, teetering on the brink of abandoning her class.[93] One letter from 'H.R.' in Western Australia reiterated this theme, in combination with others also dear to BWEA hearts: fair wages for hard work, lower wages for inexperience, comfortable and familial working conditions, and a gradual reversal of an initial dislike of the new colony:

> After I arrived in W.A., I was engaged as nursemaid to four children, which I grew to be very fond of. I had 30s. to start with, and after a few months was raised to 35s. I stayed there 13 months to the day, and now I am living as housemaid in an hotel, but am thankful to say I have nothing at all to do with the bar, my work is all upstairs work, and I am also glad to say that Mrs. S——is not like a mistress but a mother to me, and they never look down on their servants. My first place was not up to much, but I did my best to please them and to stay my twelve months . . . When I came to Mrs. S.'s I had to come for 30s. a month because I did not know how to wash and iron, but she has taught me how to do it, so I am getting on nicely. I do not dislike W.A. at all now, but did not like it at first.[94]

Letters published by an organisation which had a stake in favourable publicity cannot be accepted uncritically as an accurate measure of immigrant satisfaction. Nonetheless the range of evidence available suggests that the recruitment procedures of the BWEA were less likely to mislead prospective emigrants about colonial conditions than were the government selection processes. All literature aimed at recruiting female emigrants, including BWEA material, focused on the ready availability of domestic employment in the colonies and the greatly improved material conditions of life. More particularly though, women's societies emphasised the need to work hard and the value of training and experience. Most promotional articles mentioned the possibility of earning high wages while simultaneously pointing out that things other than money were also important. An article in *The Queen* in 1890, on the work of the British Women's Emigration Association, typically combined hyperbole and cold water:

> In the colonies the whole scale of remuneration is higher . . . In Victoria girls who would earn from £12 to £20 here, can there obtain from £25 to £35, and experienced cooks even better pay than that. Melbourne and Adelaide are veritable servants' paradises. It is not uncommon for well-trained domestics in those cities to be offered £35 and £45 per annum. Prizes such as these do not, of course, fall to the lot of the inferior servant; but for her, provided she is strong and willing, there is always a plentiful choice of places where the wages are much more than enough for her simple needs, and where the conditions of life are not so restricted as they would be in England.[95]

At the same time, publicity coming directly from the BWEA suggested that wages were more likely to be in the vicinity of £2 a month.[96]

In the tradition of Maria Rye, the BWEA saw its role in the selection procedure as two-way: it protected the colony, by sending out only the type of women the BWEA believed the colonists wanted, and it protected emigrant women themselves by attempting to prepare them for the new life they would face. As one woman wrote in 1896 of the work of the BWEA, 'It sometimes comes out that an applicant is quite unfit for Emigration . . . A grumbling spirit may be observed, a crabbed or an over enthusiastic temper is found . . . Then she is refused, or kindly advised not to go'.[97]

If making an inquiry was the first step towards immigration, there was plenty of room for reversing one's steps. Many a woman changed her mind; most did so before receiving their papers, but some after. Attrition had always been a problem. Miss Gladys Lefroy, the honorary secretary of the BWEA, said in an interview in 1895, 'The number of applicants has been very large indeed, but we invariably find that many drop off, either because they cannot answer the searching questions we put to them, or because "mother has a cold" or because their heart fails them'.[98] The BWEA selection process was a genuinely critical one which might result in either approval or rejection. In 1896, the BWEA received 2282 applications from women contemplating emigration and conducted 1902 interviews, but only 441 women emigrated.[99] That reflects the number of passages available but also indicates the possibility of 'picking and choosing'.

There were critics of the BWEA and its work. Agent-General for Western Australia Sir Malcolm Fraser worked closely with Joyce in Britain and, perhaps for that reason, was not entirely happy with the colony's arrangements. He would have borne much of the burden whenever the all-seeing Joyce was dissatisfied with any aspect of colonial procedures. He also tapped into that deep vein of criticism about the propriety of a scheme which despatched to the colony young single women with no ties. His preference was for young women and girls in family units, an argument long promoted by those who favoured nomination policies over selection. Though his criticisms went unheeded, the scheme did not long outlast Fraser, who was replaced in London in mid-1898. Late the following year, the new Agent-General received instructions for a further party of fifty domestics but, though a party was selected, most vessels had by then been commandeered by the imperial government for South African war service. The prospective emigrants, of course, as working women, could not be kept in limbo awaiting departure because of their need to give notice to employers.[1] Two parties of women accompanied by Mary Monk sailed in 1900, Maggie Kelly and Lizzie Royle on board the *Banffshire* amongst them. But with the sailing of the SS *Perthshire* in May 1901, also under Monk, that particular emigration programme and the BWEA's direct involvement in Western Australia's female migration history came to an end.

As a means of selecting women, the relationship between the Western Australian authorities and the BWEA had proved excellent. But over the decade, Joyce's insistence on overseeing matters which the government thought outside her realm had begun to prove unpalatable. Like Rye, Joyce's 'feminised', totalising approach to migration had always gone well beyond her original sphere of selection, at least as the government understood it. We shall see more of her intervention in immigrant employment and accommodation in a later chapter. Both Rye and the BWEA shared a belief in what we would now term a holistic approach to emigration, which saw the three aspects of the process—selection, shipboard protection and careful reception—as intimately connected. It was this which tended to differentiate the approach of private female emigrationists from the colonial governments. By adopting different strategies from Rye's energetic and confrontational individualism, ultimately the BWEA was probably more successful in encouraging colonial governments to provide the sort of protection and care which it thought appropriate. Its philosophy of 'benevolent maternalism', underpinning the practice of 'protected emigration', significantly shaped many aspects of assisted female migration to the Australian colonies to the end of the nineteenth century. There is no doubt, however, that Joyce's insistence that migration was an integrated process, coupled with her determination that colonial authorities recognise their responsibilities towards well-selected and worthy young women, was instrumental in the government's decision not to use the BWEA again.

'A season of industry'

There is a certain class of girls who lose their heads the moment they enter a railway station. One of them was found the other day standing by a train, without the most remotest idea as to where she wished to go. Directions and advice are wasted upon them; the only thing to be done is to put them and their luggage into a carriage, and then when they arrive at their destination, take them out again.[1]

TOWARDS THE END of the nineteenth century, a number of British organisations such as the National Vigilance Association with its interest in the white slave trade, and the Travellers' Aid Society (TAS), began to look very seriously at the issue of women travellers at risk. Travellers' Aid work developed from the Young Women's Christian Association's concern with the needs of 'unprotected' female travellers, particularly working-class women, within Britain. Understandings of the need for protection were class-specific as well as gender-based; there was a very real fear amongst middle-class female philanthropists that women of 'a certain class', unprotected and alone in an unfamiliar environment, were at grave moral and physical risk. Such notions had underpinned and shaped the activities of female emigrationists for almost half a century.

When government-assisted emigrants sailed to the Australian colonies, they generally travelled in organised government parties on contracted ships. As part of the offer of assistance made to both male and female emigrants, colonial governments acknowledged a degree of responsibility for their well-being in transit to their new homes. Conditions of emigrant passage from Britain were governed primarily by the Passenger Acts of 1855, and colonial government contracts with the shipping companies which carried their prospective fellow colonists stipulated appropriate safety standards, sound and plentiful food and fresh water, and adequate shipboard ventilation and hygiene. The British emigrant diaspora to the Australasian colonies was one of the world's most closely regulated and safest population movements.

While the physical aspects of the passage were similar for male and female emigrants, protecting assisted female emigrants went beyond a concern with material well-being. Selected and nominated women alike travelling 'without natural protectors', that is, without male family members, required moral care, a perception of emigrant women's needs shared by both imperial and colonial government authorities and the middle-class British and colonial women who helped shape the implementation of government policies.

Middle-class women perceived their own needs rather differently and again, this perception was shared by British and colonial government migration authorities. In 1879, Caroline Blanchard had highlighted the cheap 'seventeenth clause' passages then being offered by the Queensland government: reduced cost fares which enabled travellers to go out as 'passengers' rather than 'emigrants'. The distinction was a significant social one not lost on the impoverished but proud middle-class women who were the target for many of the earlier female emigration societies. Blanchard wrote with approval of women who had not 'shrunk' from sharing the accommodation of the ordinary emigrant vessel for the benefit of a free passage. Yet she was quick to advise those with even a little money to consider travelling in the new third class steamers, under the Queensland government's new migration programmes, since 'Passengers in these boats require no papers, and are not subject to any of the perhaps rather inconvenient control and supervision required in emigrant ships'.[2] The 'protection' considered so important for working-class women was thus reduced to the level of an 'inconvenience' for middle-class women. The implications of travelling as a passenger rather than as an emigrant were considerable.

On the other hand, the relative affluence of most middle-class travellers meant that some of their needs were met more directly by shipping companies, without this need for government or philanthropic intervention. For some years the ladies committee of the Anglican Church's British-based Society for Promoting Christian Knowledge (SPCK), which funded the appointment of matrons for small, non-government parties of emigrant women, had also campaigned for the appointment of stewardesses for third-class passengers. The committee noted in 1900:

> There are still ... many ships, carrying women and girls as third-class passengers, where no official protection is thus afforded. It cannot be right or seemly that in cases of sickness there should be even the possibility of young girls being left to the care of male attendants. If such an arrangement would not be countenanced in the first or second class, it seems hardly fitting that poorer people should be treated in a less desirable way.[3]

Far from finding it an inconvenience, a large number of young working-class women and their families consented to and even welcomed the shipboard protection institutionalised through women's organisations. The availability of a system of professional, experienced yet motherly protection was even used as a device to encourage young women to contemplate emigration, since it served to lessen the dread of the passage. Ellen Joyce, who organised matrons for the SPCK, told the Society in 1894:

> The moral and religious influence exercised by the matrons employed by the Society is more and more referred to by travellers of the working class, and the protection of these

parties is sought after by the relations, who recognize the difference in the safety as well as the tone of those who travel
under the matrons' care.[4]

Immigrant women had much at stake in the system of protection provided by colonial governments. The moral and physical dangers they might face, unprotected on board, were real
enough. The perceived absence of adequate protection could
also have serious repercussions. Being named 'disreputable'—
as happened to female emigrants from certain ships—usually
stemmed from the employing public's perception that shipboard
protection was inadequate. The *Aurora Australis* and the *Isles of
the South*, both of which carried parties of immigrant women,
became the subject of a Tasmanian Select Committee inquiry
into immigration in 1861. Though scanty, the evidence presented before the inquiry suggested that the masters of both
vessels had reportedly acted 'improperly' during the passage
out. One of the matrons from the *Isles of the South* had her
gratuity withheld for misconduct after arrival while another, it
was suggested, subsequently kept a brothel.[5] Yet even with
ships' officials found guilty of misconduct, the emigrant women
also emerged as guilty parties. Insinuations along these lines
were sufficient to damn the immigrant women themselves. Not
only was the passage itself considered contaminating but, for
some Hobart citizens, a woman's very submission to the passage
—even a protected passage—implied questionable virtue. Anglican city missionary J. H. Smales asserted that he would not
hire a woman from either vessel.[6] Reverend Benjamin Drake
went on to argue that the very act of choosing to emigrate without natural protectors meant that young women lost any claim
to respectability, noting sourly, 'If single women come to this
Colony in any serious numbers without relatives, they come for
other purposes than earnest and honest servitude, or a well-
directed virtuous purpose of improving their position in life'.[7]
Similar attitudes towards selected single women emigrating to
convict Van Diemen's Land were current in the 1830s, and even
at the end of the century some of those attitudes were still in
circulation.[8]

If the system of protection broke down, the price paid could be high. Colonial governments did not widely publicise allegations about misbehaviour, since they had an interest in seeing new arrivals off government hands and employed, but a reputation earned on board an immigrant vessel or in the depot after arrival could certainly influence the speed with which a woman found work. In 1897 immigrant Hannah Sullivan complained to the authorities in Western Australia that she had not received proper medical care from the doctor nor sufficient attention from the matron, Mary Pittman Monk. All her fellow travellers ridiculed her complaints and the official who questioned her dismissed her criticisms as groundless, describing her as 'an intensely emotional girl of not the most desirable Irish type'. Sullivan was the last emigrant to be engaged from the depot. When a country correspondent wrote seeking a domestic she was mentioned as available, but 'temperamental'.[9]

Over the course of the 1850s and 1860s all colonial governments eventually came to recognise that their financial interests were best served by providing adequate and visible shipboard protection for single female immigrants. Standing in place of the women's natural protectors was one way of demonstrating and maintaining the women's respectability, the most important prerequisite for domestic employment.

Colonial governments did not arrive at this position without some prompting, even unladylike pushing, from British middle-class women. One particular organisation was of critical importance. In 1849 the British Ladies' Female Emigrants Society (BLFES) was established by a group of middle-class women in Britain. Not concerned with the task of promoting female emigration, and not even necessarily condoning it, BLFES aims included 'elevating' and 'purifying' a migration process which was viewed as inevitable. The BLFES concentrated on improving the time single women spent in passage to the colonies and aimed 'to give to the Emigrants those means of employment and instruction, by which they may improve the leisure of a long voyage, and be trained in such habits of industry and self discipline, as will tend to make the Emigrant a better Colonist, whether as servant, wife, or mother'.[10] For the next forty years the chief role of the BLFES was to provide matrons for the long passage out to the Australian colonies. The BLFES was wound up in 1888 on the death of its secretary of thirty years, Miss Caroline Tipple. By that stage the United British Women's Emigration Association (BWEA) and the Society for Promoting Christian Knowledge (SPCK) had jointly taken over the role of providing matrons to accompany women emigrating to the colonies.[11] The efforts of the BLFES ultimately led to professional matrons accompanying all large parties of government-assisted female emigrants to the Australian colonies and, until the turn of the century, matrons remained a standard feature of what the private female migration societies called 'protected emigration'.

Views similar to those of the BLFES had currency within other philanthropic and evangelical organisations. The SPCK had been active in providing moral and spiritual protection for emigrants since 1846 and in 1852 first raised the question of the special needs of female emigrants.[12] Idleness, it was suspected, was the principal cause of the 'vices' affecting young women on board ship and in that year the SPCK established a 'committee of ladies' at Liverpool to provide material for sewing and knitting on the longer passages to the Australian colonies, New Zealand and South Africa.[13]

Similarly the BLFES contracted with the CLEC to supply each emigrant ship carrying parties of women with two boxes or bags of material. One was a hospital bag intended for use in the confinement of married women although it was sometimes used for single women too. The other, a work bag, contained an assortment of sewing, knitting and crochet materials. The single women on board were provided with 65 yards of calico and 89 of cotton print, 5 pounds of patchwork, 200 assorted darning needles, 2 gross of best knitting pins, and half a gross of women's thimbles.[14] In the 1880s and 1890s a similar work bag containing hundreds of yards of print for blouses was provided by some of the colonial governments themselves in order, as the BWEA reported, that the matron could teach the women who needed to learn how to cut out and sew; thus 'the voyage out is made a time of improvement to the girls'.[15]

Members of a colonial ladies committee or the matron of the immigrant depot collected the items made up on board after arrival; they were then sold at reduced rates to the emigrants or given out to reward good behaviour, assessed by the matron and ladies.[16] In fact, for the vigilant colonial women who measured such things, the amount of sewing completed by the women became a measure of the matron herself, a small amount indicating that she had not maintained sufficient discipline or schooled the emigrants adequately. In 1877, Caroline Gawler of the Adelaide Ladies' Committee criticised the matron from the *Robert Lees*:

> Mrs. Borgins only brought a few things made, on the plea that she could not make the women obey her ... The Matrons hitherto have had all the materials made up, which are supplied by the Ladies as the clothes are distributed among those who made them on their arrival at the 'Home'.[17]

Teaching sewing was well enough; but the BLFES wanted its matrons to do more than simply keeping idle single women occupied. It wanted to establish a corps of permanent and professional women trained in the specialist occupation. The BLFES believed that the ideal matron filled a dual role of protector and teacher. Protection, physical and moral, included the idea that the emigration process was an opportunity for the training and socialisation of young women in preparation for their domestic roles in the colony. From the point of view of the nineteenth century reforming bourgeoisie, recreation was to be rational, its ends concrete. The BLFES aim, simply expressed, was to ensure 'that the voyage might be made a season of industry and improvement, and not of idleness and demoralisation'.[18] That goal, BLFES members believed, could be achieved most effectively through the introduction of a class of permanent professional middle-class matrons to accompany parties of single working-class women emigrating to the colonies.

Even before the formation of the BLFES, colonial governments had provided some moral protection for emigrants on the passage to the colonies. All Australian emigrant ships carried a surgeon-superintendent who acted as 'both sanitor and magis-trate' to emigrants on board, male and female.[19] Many vessels carried a shipboard chaplain, often funded by the SPCK. In addition to this, governments had always made some special provision for the physical and moral protection of single women on vessels carrying government-assisted migrants. This com-prised either an accompanying matron, perhaps an older or married woman chosen from amongst the emigrants, or a small number of married couples with families, to stand in place of 'natural protectors'.

The family protection system involved appointing a family or families who were also emigrating to act as informal guardians or stewards of the single women, for a small stipend. However, the system had some drawbacks in practice. Colonial govern-ments were sometimes reluctant to encourage the introduction of families since their labour, or the labour of the male head of the family, was often not needed.[20] Queensland's emigration officials in London were instructed in 1868, on the subject of recruiting single women:

> You may probably experience difficulty in securing any large number of these without being obliged to accept members of families to which they belong; but I am to express the desire of the Government that you will use your utmost endeavors to secure the colony from being burthened with the cost of transport of persons not suited to its requirements.[21]

Like the migration of families generally, family protection also increased shipboard health problems. The amount of space officially allocated to each person or 'soul' on board ship was halved for children, which meant a substantial reduction in the amount of fresh air available between decks for each immigrant. As a result, the level of disease on board a ship was often pro-portionate to the number of children. Further, the greater the number of children per family, the greater the likelihood of the spread of disease. In the 1860s, while acting as selection agent for the Victorian colonial government, Maria Rye ran into more problems with the CLEC over this issue. Because of the govern-ment's refusal to pay for professional matrons, Rye selected families to accompany her women, following the model Caroline Chisholm had used. The CLEC instructed her to favour couples 'without children or [with] as few children as possible' but, of the families she selected for passage on the *Atalanta* in 1867, one had three children aged under seven, another four children under ten.[22] The CLEC rejected these families, despite Rye's argument that the total number of children on the vessel was very low. They argued:

> Experience shows that the health of children on board ship on so long a voyage as that to Australia, depends principally on the amount of care bestowed on their cleanliness, food, clothing, &c.,—which can only be looked for from their Mother. But a woman with a large number of young Children cannot give to each the necessary amount of Care, and illness, once produced, spreads itself, and, eventually, the sanitary condition of the whole ship is deteriorated, and adults, as well as children, suffer. It is not enough, therefore, that the whole number of Children should be limited; it is necessary that a limit should also be applied to each family.[23]

The CLEC was here echoing the findings of a Board of Immigration inquiry, conducted in Maryborough, Queensland, the previous year into the appalling mortality rate on board the Black Ball line vessel *Sultana:*

> Great want of judgement and foresight was displayed by the home authorities in crowding so many children of tender age into one vessel; particularly as it is well known that children require as much pure air as adults, although each adult is held to be equivalent to two children ... Hence ... arises the primary cause of the great mortality amongst the children on board the 'Sultana', there having died 78 children under eight years old.[24]

By the end of the 1860s, all colonial governments had renounced the financial argument and abandoned family protection for matrons. Three different systems operated. Individual women wishing to emigrate but not eligible for free passage, generally because of the upper age limit for assistance, could apply directly to the CLEC for a position as matron, in return for a free passage and a few pounds payment. The BLFES matrons' committee also appointed matrons for the CLEC from its lists of suitable women; and government agents or surgeons-superintendent selected matrons from amongst the older female emigrants at the point of embarkation.[25]

The majority of matrons were selected directly by the surgeons-superintendent who, predictably, favoured this system over the others. Government authorities concurred for some years. In 1852, the immigration agent for Victoria had reported on the 'prejudicial consequences' of the system of appointing matrons recommended by the BLFES. While recognising that not all surgeons-superintendent were of a type to be trusted with the selection of a matron (a prime concern of the BLFES), the immigration agent argued for the ultimate authority of the surgeon-superintendent. He must be in a position to control and, if necessary, replace a matron for 'The assertion of an independent position in the vessel and jurisdiction over the female portion of the emigrants on the part of any Matron cannot fail to give rise to misunderstanding and to be subversive of a steady and systematic discipline on board'.[26]

Similarly in 1859 the CLEC reported that matrons appointed by the surgeons were most successful, though they did admit this judgement was based on the surgeons' own reports. Further, they argued that respectable women selected from amongst the emigrants were better suited to managing their own class than were those of a 'superior' class and education.[27]

The BLFES committee members disagreed. Surgeons, they argued, naturally favoured women 'who were merely their servants', but matrons should be regarded as subordinate government officers, not as emigrants. Though matrons should be subject to the control of the surgeons-superintendent the BLFES advocated their need for some autonomy, that they report directly to the CLEC and that any complaints they made against the surgeon-superintendent be followed up by the appropriate government authorities.[28] The BLFES believed that matrons needed an acknowledged status comparable to the surgeons-superintendent. They should be paid in a similar manner, receiving a fixed gratuity for each voyage with a further amount 'per head' for each emigrant 'landed live', expressions which now seem to smack of animals in holds rather than people. Payment for their return passage was also provided. The occupation of shipboard surgeon was gradually professionalised in the course of the 1850s, with permanent appointments, higher payments for each subsequent journey, and improved conditions of contract and scale of gratuity.[29] Though colonial governments complained to the end of the century about inadequate and inexperienced surgeons being appointed in Britain, neither they nor the CLEC questioned the importance of professionalising the surgeon's role. The BLFES envisioned opening up a parallel professional career structure for its matrons, arguing that only by offering adequate payment could well-qualified women be attracted to the service.

This venture sprang partly from concern with improving employment opportunities for middle-class women. Ellen Layton, for example, secretary of the BLFES in the early 1860s, like Maria Rye was active in the Langham Place feminist group from which emerged the Society for Promoting the Employment of Women (SPEW).[30] Such efforts paralleled the contemporary professionalisation of the nursing service brought about through the work of Florence Nightingale. In demanding a better salary and a permanent employment structure for its matrons, the BLFES also encouraged the employment of 'a better class of woman' who, it believed, would be more suitable for the training of young working-class women than matrons selected from amongst the emigrants. The BLFES argued this would result in a higher standard of protection but it is also a measure of prevailing middle-class belief in the superiority of its own culture and values. From the mid-nineteenth century more educated middle-class women had taken on roles as workhouse guardians, matrons, nurses and inspectors.[31] Introducing a system of shipboard protection based on imposing middle-class notions of femininity on working-class women was yet another aspect of that process.

The women behind this met with significant success in shaping masculine bureaucratic understandings of the value of protection. Certainly the CLEC recognised the value of a tried and tested matron. This was reinforced by their experience with professional surgeons-superintendent:

> We do not doubt that Matrons who have acquired experience in previous voyages should be superior to almost any untried persons, and that even their freedom from Sea sickness and acquaintance with life on board ship would give them considerable influence over female Emigrants.[32]

While the first passage was a trial for all travellers, the training and instruction which the BLFES gave its matrons before embarkation prepared them to some extent for their task.[33] One female emigrant to Melbourne in 1858, Fanny Davis, recorded of a particularly rough trip that their matron, chosen from amongst the emigrants, was as frightened as the rest of them during the first storm.[34] The matron had been seen 'running about crying and, instead of comforting people, making them more frightened':

> [she is] the most cowardly on board, she has been so frightened that this is the first day this week she has been out of bed; she told me today that if they would put her on shore and offer her two hundred pounds to go on board again she should not think of it as she would never wish anybody to go through the frights she has.[35]

But cost was another issue. The BLFES used improved payment and conditions to attract middle-class women to permanent shipboard employment. An average emigrant passage on a sailing vessel, including time spent at the emigration depot before departure and at the reception depot after arrival, could take up to four months, a matron having virtually sole charge of between 50 and 300 single women for that period. Her salary could be as little as £5, although satisfactory performance could earn a bonus. Sometimes no provision was made for a return passage, which virtually precluded the use of a permanent matron.[36] The BLFES wanted this level of remuneration substantially improved but, aware of colonial government reluctance to incur additional expense, the CLEC continued to express its ambivalence about the need for the professional middle-class matron.

Slowly the BLFES view prevailed. In 1859, the New South Wales government became the first to employ permanent matrons. Conditions included a salary of £10, extra payment for subsequent passages and a return trip to England valued at £30 for those matrons who had been responsible for at least 100 young women, who were willing to be re-employed, and whose conduct had satisfied the colonial government.[37] New South Wales authorities found the move fully justified the expense:

> The single women are more under control, and have far better opportunities of benefiting both in a moral and social point of view. For instance many girls have come [on] board so ignorant of the [commonest] household duties, as to be incapable of employment as domestic servants, and have been sufficiently instructed, (chiefly theoretically of course,) during the voyage, as to enable them to take situations in that capacity. Others have been taught needlework, and a larger proportion stimulated to educational exertion with good success.[38]

Nonetheless the Victorian authorities continued to equivocate and, as Maria Rye pointed out, 'a spirit of parsimony' prevailed on this question of permanent employment of matrons at professional salaries.[39] Not until 1869 did the Victorian government agree to offer matrons what the BLFES and the other colonies judged an adequate scale of pay. For that reason matrons were reluctant to work on Victorian government ships except as a last resort. By that stage, New South Wales paid matrons £30 for the first passage, and an extra £5 for each successive voyage to a maximum of £50, with £30 towards the return trip, while South Australia offered £25 for the first trip, with increments of £5 to a maximum payment of £40, and £30 for the return passage.[40]

The BLFES scrutinised employment conditions for its matrons throughout the 1860s and 1870s. It was successful, for example, in arranging that matrons be served better quality food on the passage than were their charges, since the BLFES felt that years of emigrant food would ultimately tax their matrons' strength. So the matrons' food was supplied from the 'cuddy', the captain's table, although for the sake of discipline they ate with the single women.[41] Under the new standardised system, colonial governments additionally provided matrons with free accommodation during their stay in the colonies, at the immigrants' depot or a similar lodging house. The BLFES itself also presented each matron with a gratuity of £3 on her return to England and kept her in free board and lodging for two months afterwards while she awaited appointment to another ship.[42]

The BLFES, however, was less successful in negotiating employment conditions in other spheres. In 1878, it took up the question of a retirement fund for matrons with the South Australian government through the Adelaide Ladies' Committee. The request was rejected. The government conceded the matrons' value to the colony but refused to pay the small annuity requested for the oldest matrons, on the grounds that these women were amply remunerated and should make provision for themselves in their old age.[43] Some were even sacked by the government on the basis of their age.[44] For matrons unable or too old to continue working (as was the case for most working women) the future was bleak.

Emigrant vessels were not pleasant places. As a permanent occupation, the work of emigrant ship matrons was undeniably exhausting and, to some, 'distasteful'. Some women lost their lives in the service. Matron Miss Crockford and submatron Mrs Graham both perished, with all their Irish charges, when the *Kapunda* went down en route to Western Australia in 1887.[45] Others faced life-threatening circumstances. When the *Dacca* foundered on the Daedalus reef in the Red Sea, in May 1890, the matron Mrs Tymons was the last woman over the side. She was in charge of a group of 220 single women, bound for Queensland.[46] In 1896, 50 single women travelling to Western Australia on board the SS *Port Phillip* were evacuated from the vessel at St Helena when the baggage room immediately below their quarters caught fire. Mary Pittman Monk, their highly experienced matron, was, according to the ship's surgeon, 'indefatigable in helping to render assistance and in keeping the girls quiet—she is so well known . . . that it is unnecessary for me to dilate further upon her management—the girls behaved extremely well & caused no trouble whatever, there was an entire absence of panic'.[47]

Other women had their health destroyed by their work. Monk's sister, Susan Monk, a much less experienced matron, served on the *Gulf of Siam* to Western Australia in 1894. Like her sister in the St Helena fire, she was reportedly courageous when fire broke out on that vessel, but her health suffered greatly from the strain and within a year she was completely crippled with rheumatism, quite unable to work. The BWEA attempted to gain Monk an out-pension of £20 per annum from the Royal Hospital for Incurables, and solicited its patrons to vote on her behalf.[48] She had no other financial resources and had made only two trips before the passage of the *Gulf of Siam*.[49]

On the other hand, the professionalisation of the matron service enabled some women to make careers as permanent shipboard matrons. Mary Pittman Monk was one of the system's most successful matrons. She worked as a BWEA matron for twenty years: with the New Zealand government from 1883 to 1888, then taking 21 parties to Western Australia between 1886 and 1901 and a further 14 parties to Canada between 1889 and 1903.[50] Another matron, Jane Chase, made 30 passages to the Australian colonies as matron between 1857 and 1886.[51] For some women, working as an emigrant ship matron was a second career taken on after retirement. Caroline E. Davies, matron on the *Jumna* and the focus of an official inquiry in 1900, took on the post of shipboard matron following her retirement after many years working as a teacher in girls' industrial schools and as a prison matron.[52]

Still others made use of the experience and connections gained working with emigrant women on the passage out to find employment in the colonies. Sophia Morphy served as matron on the *Thomas Arbuthnot*, which sailed to New South Wales in October 1849. She was subsequently appointed matron of the immigration depot in Brisbane, a position she still held in 1874.[53] Taking a different employment option, as we've already seen, one of the submatrons from the infamous *Isles of the South* went on to run a Tasmanian brothel in the 1860s.[54]

Only a few glimpses remain to us of the many women who took on this shipboard life, most of whom remain almost as anonymous as their charges. The impression gained is that these middle-class women, single, married and widowed, were in financially precarious situations, unprovided for by parents or husbands. Their social profiles, in fact, are probably very similar to those few hundred single women who emigrated to the colonies over this period as governesses, although they were probably older and were more likely to have had some form of 'training' than a refined education. Theirs is another hidden story of genteel poverty challenged.

Even after professional matrons became an accepted feature of protected emigration, the BLFES continued to lobby on behalf of its matrons. Matrons were frequently a target of hostility and antagonism, not least because they represented female 'intrusion' into control of the emigration process. They were the most visible symbols of protected emigration and, after the single women themselves, the most vulnerable. In the process of protecting the protectors, the BLFES was often supported by colonial women, organised as 'ladies' committees'. Their primary interest was less the matrons than their charges, but their interest in the structures designed to protect single women in transit made them strong allies.

The BLFES had always argued that a matron's middle-class origins gave her particular advantages in her work. In theory, they earned her the obedience of working-class women, simply by virtue of the class structure, and made her less likely to be manipulated by the surgeon-superintendent or ship's officers who shared her class origins. As a permanent employee too, the matron was judged less likely than an emigrant engaged for a single journey to succumb to coercion or bribery in overlooking 'immorality' on board.[55] Like the women for whom she was responsible, however, the matron's conduct and behaviour were more open to criticism than the behaviour of men of the same class. The matron was under the direct control of the surgeon-superintendent and her future employment and part of her payment were subject to his favourable report. Her role of protecting and policing emigrant women had the potential to earn their enmity and, despite her official status, the matron could not enforce discipline on board ship without the support of superior officers. Her duties could also force her directly onto a path of confrontation with her superiors.

Once ashore, matrons could look to other sources for support and help. Colonial ladies' committees, often comprising the wives or relatives of colonial officials—women such as Lady Young, wife of the Governor of Tasmania, Mrs Millicent, wife of the Bishop of Adelaide, Lady Jervois, wife of the South Australian Governor, with their two daughters, and Ellen Barlee, sister of Western Australia's Colonial Secretary Frederick Barlee —were all influential at different times in shaping protected migration. Particularly in South Australia in the 1860s and 1870s, such women often interceded on behalf of professional matrons when their behaviour was under scrutiny as a result of shipboard tensions. Frequently these cases implicated the matron's male shipboard colleagues but sometimes they were simply an endorsement of a professional matron's right to exercise her own judgement and authority. In an episode in 1876, for example, Matron Jane Chicken from the *Hesperides* had been reported by the surgeon-superintendent for being obstructive and disobeying his directions, including having the floors washed down with water instead of holystoning, or scrubbing with soft dry sandstone, as he had ordered.[56] However, Caroline Gawler of the Adelaide Ladies' Committee suggested that, although there were 'defects of manner and discipline' on Chicken's part during the passage, these were 'trifling'; and that, should Chicken come out again 'with an efficient, patient Doctor', she would do much better.[57] Jane Chicken later became a regular New South Wales matron, working for that colony until the very last days of assistance and completing her nineteenth and probably final passage in charge of female immigrants in 1887.[58] However, she had remained intractable. In 1885 New South Wales immigration agent Wise reprimanded her for failing to keep a journal of the voyage for the third time in two years and informed her once again that she must comply with regulations. Her journal, it seemed, had fallen overboard yet again.[59]

Similarly in 1877, the Adelaide group was quick to offer support to matron Mrs Rogers, reported for insubordination after declining to sail on the *Hydrabad* in 1875, because of her reluctance to obey instructions which conflicted with her own. Rogers was seasoned and professional, well known to the Adelaide committee, with sixteen years' shipboard experience with the South Australian and Victorian governments and five previous passages to South Australia behind her. On a trip to the colony on the *British Enterprise* in 1877 (after the abortive *Hydrabad* trip but before the *Hydrabad* inquiry that year) her surgeon-superintendent Dr Mackintosh spoke of her as an excellent matron, praising the 'strict surveillance' she kept over the female emigrants.[60] On another trip, when the surgeon Dr Blood had died thirty days out to sea after a severe illness, she was commended for the excellent job she had done when the entire superintendence of the immigrants fell upon her and the captain.[61] Her references were beyond reproach and the inquiry vindicated her behaviour, with the Adelaide ladies' committee triumphant. On their behalf Gawler was quick to point out to the South Australian authorities that 'There is no reason why our well tried and experienced matrons should be interfered with as they have been lately, it will create discontent and lose us our best matrons'.[62]

Colonial governments were usually prepared to allow middle-class colonial women some say in protection aspects of female migration, but occasionally this caused antagonism. Until its activities terminated in the late 1880s, the BLFES retained its role of recommending shipboard matrons to colonial Agents-General in London. These men then appointed the matrons but colonial ladies' committees—in this case the committee of the Adelaide Servants' home—reported back to the BLFES about each matron's performance. In late 1875, conflict arose over Mrs (or Miss) Whiting, matron on the *Trevelyan*, who for some reason had been assessed poorly by the Adelaide ladies' committee. The Agent-General in London had appointed Whiting against the advice of the BLFES and resented the Adelaide Ladies' Committee communicating with the BLFES on the subject.[63] In future, he insisted, the ladies' committee must ask government approval before negotiating with the BLFES. The Adelaide ladies refused. It was a battle for power. Vigilant in the government-accredited role of guardian of the moral character and well-being of single female immigrants, Mrs Gawler tied the committee's right to be involved in the appointment of matrons directly to the work it did receiving immigrant women. Like the BWEA in the 1880s, the Adelaide Ladies' Committee explicitly recognised a relationship between the three aspects of the migration process: selection, protection on the passage out and the reception of immigrant women after arrival. Careful orchestration of all these three aspects, the committee believed, enabled the introduction of the sort of women colonial employers wanted. Thus Gawler replied to the Commissioner for Crown Lands and Immigration:

> If our Committee could not rely on the accredited ability of the permanent matrons recommended by the Ladies in London, they would not continue their responsible work here in taking charge of women who arrive here under the evil influence of a person like Miss Whiting, or of any but a matron who knows her work & can maintain proper discipline—hence as the London Committee depend on the report sent from the Adelaide Committee of the conduct of the matrons and must

communicate with the Agent General the result of that report
we fail to see how the wishes of the Agent General . . . can be
complied with.[64]

Such committees, with their influential membership, had the
force of social position behind their trenchant refusal to be over-
ruled. The Commissioner agreed with Gawler, and the Ladies'
Committee carried on.

Following Caroline Chisholm's earlier lead, the BLFES was
intent on feminising and controlling some aspects of single
female emigration. Its particular focus was the emigrant ship
itself. Despite some dispute over territory, the interests of these
middle-class women and of colonial governments coincided, for
a time at least. From the government point of view, shipboard
protection became an appropriate complement to the process
of screening and exclusion undertaken by colonial selection
agents. It was also the price to be paid for securing the services
of middle-class colonial women in the process of receiving
immigrant women.

5

'Gliding over the great waves'

The good ship Cornwall put to sea
One sunny eve in May
And gallantly across the seas
She ploughed her lonely way . . .

The passengers on board the ship
Are varied in their kind
Some of them live in the saloon
The others are behind

The last are guarded jealously
Both when they sleep in bunk
And on the deck, by one they know
As matron—Miss M. Monk.

To see how well her charge she keeps
Look on these maidens fair
And you will see upon each face
Rude health depicted there.

A rigid line is stretched between
These maids—and all the others
For they as Emigrants have left
Home, country Fathers Mothers[1]

MANY ATTEMPTS WERE made over the years to draw that 'rigid line' between emigrant maids and their fellow travellers. Once drawn, no other line was guarded more jealously. Usually the guardianship was successful, with single women kept in their 'proper' place; but there were infringements. Notable breaches of the 'charter party', the contract drawn up to govern conditions of passage, including separation of the sexes, were invariably the subject of investigation. In 1866 a Rockhampton Board of Immigration inquiry was established to examine the behaviour of both the surgeon-superintendent and the captain on board the emigrant vessel *Bayswater*. Ship's surgeon Dr Hallows had been accused of 'improper relations' with at least two of the single women immigrants, identified by the inquiry only as Park and Emma Apted:

> [It was alleged] that he has supplied Emma Apted with drink. That he has been seen lying behind the wheel-house with her during the day in a very indecent position; and that his visits to the apartment of the single girls after ten o'clock at night, on which occasion he invariably visited the apartment occupied by these two girls, lead only to one inevitable conclusion—that, notwithstanding his old age and his grey hairs, Dr. Hallows carried on an illicit connexion with one of those girls so much spoken of.[2]

From the indirect evidence of the witnesses and the fact that since his arrival in Rockhampton Captain Pack had been living at the Fitzroy Hotel with Emma Apted, who passed as Mrs Pack, the inquiry also concluded that, 'in the words of one of the witnesses, the doctor had one of the girls and the captain the other'.[3]

The evidence against the two men was compelling and both were found guilty. But so too was the ship's matron, the woman responsible for the moral protection of the single women. Her 'crime' was less straightforward. As well as failing to prevent the incidents, she had failed to report them. She was seen as complicit in the whole affair.[4]

The *Bayswater* inquiry highlights the most contentious issue associated with the passage to the colonies of single emigrant women: morality. But as the verdict in this case showed, it also demonstrates the ambiguous position of the matron, responsible for protecting the morality of the single women but subordinate to some of the men who most threatened it. Two features of shipboard life were specifically designed to protect the morality of emigrant women: patterns of authority established between the emigrant women and their protectors, and the shipboard spatial arrangements which reinforced them.

The only account we have of the passage of the *Bayswater* is culled from evidence produced before this board of inquiry and it is, by its nature, salacious, dramatic and highly coloured. The very existence of such an account marks the passage out as exceptional but the colonial understanding of 'the emigrant passage' was largely shaped by reports, published in the colonial press, which tended to highlight the scandalous. Immorality on board was the most frequent subject of government inquiry. Subsequently, passages such as the *Bayswater*'s came to represent all emigrant passages, and public generalisations too frequently proclaimed not the immorality of the surgeons or the captains, but of the single women.

From mid-nineteenth century, colonial governments eager to attract emigrants regarded immorality on board emigrant vessels with increasing disquiet, with the damaging publicity associated with such 'public shipboard disorder'[5] at least as troubling as the actual 'immorality'. To return to the *Bayswater*, 'the scenes exhibited on board this ship were most disgraceful, and calculated to interfere seriously with inclinations and tendencies at home which would induce a flow of immigration of respectable persons into this colony',[6] a Queensland immigration official lamented, pessimistic about the chances of seeing the matter quickly covered up. For those interested in conditions in steerage, however, such material demands exposure, providing a readily accessible, tempting, and frequently the sole direct account of shipboard passages. Such inquiries also tell us far more about experiences in steerage, particularly for single women, than they do about cabin class passengers. They are the product of the 'double control' exercised over single women. Like emigrant men and families, their particulars were better documented than those of 'passengers' or those paying their own fares, because they emigrated under the financial auspices of colonial governments; and they were controlled by gender-specific structures designed to police their morality. As a result they were well scrutinised. The people who kept them under surveillance were also accountable to the government, and it was their behaviour—that of the captain, the surgeon-superintendent and the matron—which most frequently became a focus of official inquiries.

Other records give insight of a particular sort into the experience of the passage for single emigrant women. All permanent matrons were required to keep a journal, as were all surgeon-superintendents, and some few have survived, although again, they survive sometimes because they were evidence of an aberrant passage, or the subject of an official inquiry. One exceptional series of diaries documents emigration to Western Australia in the 1890s; other series, briefer, better preserved but also relatively unused by historians, exist for emigration to Western and South Australia in the early twentieth century. Records kept by figures of shipboard authority naturally adopt a certain stance towards single women, as their 'charges'; inquiries necessarily focus on the unusual; yet all these sources can uncover the rhythms of the day to day life of the female emigrant traveller.

For the emigrant diarist, every aspect of the passage was remarkable, and thus noteworthy. One's fellow travellers, the location of the berths, the arrival of meals, were all matters for astonishment, and were recorded in sometimes surprising detail. Hannah Wright's journal is an account of a fairly typical passage after an untoward beginning. She and her sister Mary embarked from Gravesend on the steamer *Merkara* on Tuesday, 4 May 1886. They were bound for Queensland to join their cousins in Ipswich. Early that morning they had left the emigrant home to board the tender which would take them to the *Merkara* at anchor at Gravesend:

At last we are out of sight of this and each one seems to be in deep thought. It may perhaps be of home and the loved ones they have left there—dear ones they will never see again. Again all is noise for we see in the river the ship Merkara and each one seems as if they want to be first to be on her. However all have to wait their turn. All are on at last and now the first thing we single women have to do is to find our own berths. Mary's and mine are No. 57 and 59, top berths, for which we are glad as we do not like the bottom berths, and next each other. Having made up our beds and seen that we have got all we require they bring us some dinner, which is very acceptable, for all seem hungry. Dinner over we go on deck and have now set sail. Some are already dancing and some are feeling sick. We are all called by the matron to go to bed and we are not sorry for we are feeling tired after our day of adventures . . . We have not slept long when a great noise is heard and we are told that the piston rod is broken and we cannot proceed.[7]

The emigrants from the *Merkara* spent a few anxious days waiting before they set off again in another vessel, the *Duke of Westminster*. By that time, the tension had affected some of the women so badly they declined to sail. Apart from that experience, the Wrights' preparation for departure was fairly typical.

Parties of single emigrant women usually assembled before embarkation in emigrants' homes in London or Plymouth. In the 1890s, the BWEA usually collected their government parties together in their Horseferry Road home in London, or in the Blackwall Emigrants' Home where the Wrights had stayed in 1886. Here the women were organised into mess groups and met their matron. Most spent no more than one or two nights in an emigrants' home but time spent there was nonetheless all part of the final stage of screening as well as the emigrants' first inculcation into shipboard discipline.

At the depot, the emigrants had their medical examination, although to judge by the number of conditions which slipped by the medical examiner, particularly advancing pregnancies, the examination was rudimentary. In 1883, the rate of examination of emigrants bound for New South Wales was about one hundred per hour, so no more needs to be said about its thoroughness.[8] 'Character' was also on trial, with attention to female character rather more searching than the physical examination. The master and matron of the emigrants' depot would note any apparently 'undesirable behaviour' and report this to the surgeon-superintendent and matron. For single women, this could even mean rejection. In 1869, after a number of problems with women from the *Zenobia,* the Victorian immigration authorities suggested that the Plymouth depot be used to screen the female emigrants even more rigorously, with a view to excluding 'undesirables'; but British government despatching agent James Chant pointed out that the process of incarceration at the depot was already verging on the unacceptable for the emigrants, and any tightening of controls or extended stay there would heighten their dissatisfaction. As he pointed out too, slowing down the process to permit a more searching moral examination would increase government costs, which may have tipped the balance.[9]

At the Home, the single women were advised how to prepare their belongings and complete their final packing for the voyage. Clothing requirements varied from colony to colony, but generally included 'six chemises, two warm and strong flannel petticoats, six pairs of stockings, two pairs of strong shoes [or boots], two strong gowns, one of which must be warm'.[10] Once steamers started to go via the Red Sea, a wide, shady 'Zulu' hat was also recommended for the Queensland run as a health precaution; and a heavy coat was always welcome on passages taking the southern route round the Cape and far into the Southern Ocean. A woman had to provide her own towels and, though there is no reference to items such as rags used for menstruation, they too would have been part of the emigrant's essential baggage. She was advised 'there is ample accommodation for washing linen' (although this was not always the case), and this may have been a discrete reference to the availability of some facilities for dealing with menstruation.

Before the emigrants boarded the vessel contracted to carry them, it was prepared and partitioned out according to the number of people embarking and their shipboard social status. Some arrangements were fixed.[11] Single emigrant women (defined at different times as those over 12 or over 14) were always berthed together in their own compartment; this was located, as the verses which introduce this chapter say, 'behind' or aft. This was regardless of the presence on board of any 'natural protectors' —fathers, brothers, uncles. Some vessels carried a mixture of emigrants, comprising families, single men and single women. On other occasions, a vessel might carry only single women. Unaccompanied married women without children were usually also berthed with the single women and, like them, were subject to the matron's discipline.

Between their quarters and the single emigrant men, at the other end of the ship but on the same level, were generally located the married couples and their children too young to be lodged with the 'singles'. Sometimes married men were berthed separately from their wives and children, with the single men.

Bathroom facilities and water closets were located where possible—sometimes conveniently, sometimes not. The *Queen Bee*'s facilities were neither convenient nor adequate. On the vessel's passage to New South Wales in 1860–61, the water supply was so poor that no one but the children could get a bath, the water closets lacked water for most of the passage, and the water closet provided for the single women was located on deck and surrounded by men all day. They refused to use it, and presumably fell back on their own alternatives.[12] On the *Abyssinian*, which arrived in Sydney in May 1862, the women's water closet was located in the hospital, to the inconvenience of the women and the surgeon-superintendent. An inquiry suggested that two small water closets, one on each side of the between decks, was the best arrangement.[13] Nor were bath and laundry facilities quite as promised in government emigrant literature and this was particularly hard on the single women who could not, like the men, bath on deck. Lice and fleas were commonplace. After the *Abyssinian* arrived in Sydney, the matron at the Hyde Park Depot, where the female immigrants stayed, reported:

> I found this Morning upon inspecting the Blankets in the Dormitories that they were much covered with vermin the [shipboard] Matron informs me that for at least six weeks the girls have not been able to wash any of there [sic] clothes consequently have scarcely a clean article to put on.[14]

Douglas Darbyshire, surgeon on the SS *Cornwall*, described the procedure of treating head lice at sea, but we have no record of how the woman or her bunkmates reacted. How were head lice regarded in the 1890s? Indignation, humiliation and shame at the prospect of delousing might well have been mixed with a measure of gratitude:

> To-day the matron reported to me that she feared the presence of pediculi in the hair of an Emigrant Mary Daly. I examined her head and found an abundance of 'nits' but no pediculi; the girl's hair was very thick, and as the tresses were covered with nits and almost matted, I cut a good deal of it off. I then had her head thoroughly washed, and rubbed with a solution of perchloride of mercury. I also had her removed from the bunk she was occupying and put her in an outside bunk with an empty bunk between her and her next neighbour. The other girls rubbed their hair with paraffin as a precautionary measure.[15]

Between decks, a locked partition with door to allow entry to the women's quarters for the matron or the doctor (who, regulations decreed, was always to be accompanied by the matron) separated the single women's and the family compartments. The matron's berth was usually placed centrally within the single women's compartment or else she had her own compartment at the entrance, an optimum vantage point for observing her charges. This also ensured the single women had virtually no private space on board the ship.

Organised into groups of about eight or ten, called 'messes' or watches, the women dined and slept in these quarters. Sometimes messes were arranged to take account of place of origin, and religious grouping—the Roman Catholics generally together —was also practised. Meals were cooked outside this area, in the cook house or bake house, and heads of messes would fetch and carry food and supplies between the bunk area and the cook house, as called for; but this was no excursion into foreign terrain. Hannah Wright wrote in 1886, on board the *Duke of Westminster*, '[Heads of messes] have to fetch all the meals from the other end of the ship—I mean the single women's compartment of course. They do not let us go beyond our own limits'.[16] For single women, the bunk area represented virtually the totality of 'their' ship, as they experienced it. The only other areas to which they had access were the segregated recreational space on deck and the sick room.

Regular religious services and occasional concerts and dances in the women's quarters were moments to see fellow travellers. Hannah Wright passed a fair amount of her spare time rehearsing songs and recitations for a small concert to mark the end of their passage.[17] On some vessels, religious instruction was organised for the Protestants by the travelling chaplain (the religious needs of the Catholics seem to have been less well catered for, as some of them complained), and on other occasions a schoolmaster might take lessons. This was generally an informal arrangement, with any more or less qualified person on board stepping into the role. In 1854, Miss Mackrell, sister of the appointed schoolmaster John Mackrell who was paid £10 to instruct the men and children, instructed the fifty-two single women on board the *Pestonjee Bomanjee* but, as Mackrell reported, 'nothing was provided for their use'.[18] With some variation, this loose arrangement seems to have prevailed throughout the period.

Depending on the inclination of the matron and the social composition of the vessel, 'family' visits to the single women's quarters were sometimes permitted, to enable young women to keep in touch with family members travelling on the same vessel.

> I must tell you Sundays and Wednesdays are visiting days with us from half-past three till five o'clock. So you see we are rather grand and have days on board ship for callers. The fathers and mothers come to see their daughters and the brothers come to see their sisters and the single men that are good at telling a cram say they have sisters and come to see the young women. It is very laughable. Some of them will ask you if you have seen their sisters and then tell you they have none on the ship at all.[19]

A vigilant matron would quickly weed out such surrogate brothers. All other social intercourse with the opposite sex was forbidden. There were also occasions when female passengers were uninvited visitors to the emigrant women's quarters, sometimes with 'good works' in mind but more often with an eye to selecting a domestic servant.

From the women's compartment a separate hatchway gave access to the upper deck. Sometimes the hatch, a source of movement, light and air, was also a source of inconvenience and contention. On board the *Star Queen* in 1875, the hatches were left open for air but, as there were apparently no awnings on that vessel, the emigrants were deluged with heavy tropical rains for a fortnight. As a result the women's quarters were flooded daily, necessitating hours of bailing.[20] Officially, the hatchway was to be awned, grated, secured at night with iron bars and padlock, and nightly hidden from prying eyes by a system of canvas screens.[21] But regulations were insufficient to deter the determined and on board the *Star Queen*, the surgeon-superintendent complained that Mr William Nettlingham, travelling out on appointment as a government schoolmaster, continually spoke to the single women through the grate, even providing some of them with brandy and water.[22] On another occasion, in a symbolic masculine penetration of the women's space, the sailors gained vicarious access to the women's quarters by dressing an effigy as a man and throwing it down to the women, who promptly put it in one of the bunks.[23]

In other instances it proved impossible to keep the single women's sanctuary free of men. On the ship *Zamora*, which sailed to Brisbane in 1877, the only access to the sail room was through the single women's quarters. In the circumstances it was clearly impossible to keep men out; however, a committee of inquiry into the matter was told that 'whenever [the sail-room] was opened—which was frequently—the girls had all to be turned out on deck, regardless of the state of the weather'.[24] Presumably little by way of immorality could have occurred while the sailors were simply passing through to the sail room, particularly with the matron invigilating proceedings. None-theless such rigorous policing of the women and their quarters was considered necessary to protect their sanctity, at a cost of exposing the women, day or night, to the far more tangible threat of the weather.

The surgeon was responsible for the health and welfare of all on board but alongside him, the matron took on particular responsibility for the women. She was charged with transform-ing the women's space on board from something alien into something much more domestic and familiar. In the anomalous setting of the creaking, reeking emigrant vessel, surrounded by the masculine trappings of seafaring life, a dedicated matron's duties also included preparing her charges for their new roles as domestic servants in colonial homes. Teaching single women who were often ignorant of such skills how to prepare food (so far as possible, given the physical constraints of their quarters), and overseeing the sewing up of the materials provided to keep idle female fingers occupied, were both part of her role. In short, she kept single women gainfully employed and out of mischief, through a process of moral guardianship and quiet inculcation into the discipline of the domestic workplace.

Shipboard activities and timetables assisted her in this process. The emigrant day was highly regulated. Annie Grattan, a single woman travelling out in 1858, describes the women's pre-breakfast routine:

> We have to get up early, each one folding up their bedclothes
> & roll up the mattrass sweep out her own Berth. Then we take
> it in turns for cleaning out the Cabin, Wednsdays & Saturdays
> it is scoured & the rest of the week swept & rubbed with a
> stone & with sand, all done before breakfast at 8 o'clock.[25]

Other routine activities included cleaning and washing dishes and preparing food. Women's access to the deck and fresh air was restricted, with the time for returning to their quarters stipulated; so too was bedtime and lights out. The single women were also expected to use their time gainfully during the day in closely monitored activities.

For almost all emigrants, the ship was a foreign and forbidding landscape. For that reason a permanent matron was a positive step towards familiarising the landscape for travellers. But the landscape remained a potentially dangerous one. To lessen the danger, governments regulated the physical aspects of the passage, such as health and sanitary conditions. Food rations, availability of fresh water, sleeping space, volume of fresh air and ventilation were all decreed and minimum measures stipulated. In Queensland ships in the 1870s, for example, a bunk to be shared by two single women was to be 3 feet and 1 inch wide (about 94 centimetres), with a minimum of 30 inches (76 centimetres) of head room above. The implications for the spread of lice and vermin, as well as disease, are obvious. Sometimes a woman's individual space was defined by a wooden bedboard: 'We have only just enough room to turn round in our berths. My sister and I have taken out our wooden partition so our beds are like one large one instead of two small ones, which is more comfortable than being cramped up in small ones'.[26] The same space was provided for a married couple but was also shared with their children under 12, while single men were permitted a width of 21 inches (53 centimetres) each.[27] Little wonder that for health reasons, emigration authorities preferred smaller families.

Although all were broadly similar, different colonies adopted their own versions of regulations. In the 1870s, South Australia adopted a system of individual hanging canvas bunks, which could be rolled up daily.[28] Bunk areas could then be cleaned more readily, an important step in controlling disease. An 1876 inquiry into the fatal spread of enteric fever on board the Queensland government vessel the *Gauntlet* focused on the fact that the bottom boards of the sleeping bunks in the women's quarters were effectively immovable, nailed down and so close to the deck of the ship as to make cleaning virtually impossible. 'Filth, often of the most offensive description, . . . collected beneath them', and undoubtedly contributed to the spread of disease.[29] But the wheel was continually reinvented; the complaint about immovable bedboards was still being made on board the *Echuca* to Western Australia in 1892.

Physical hygiene was not the only issue in regulating bunk space. Rolling up canvas bunks produced a larger open space in the women's quarters and made enforcing the daily activities prescribed for the single women, such as needlework, more convenient—at least for the matron. And an earlier experiment with canvas cots was applauded in 1863 because it prevented 'an evil of which every Surgeon-superintendent is constantly complaining . . . the indolent habit of lounging in the bed-places the greater part of the day'.[30] The simple rolling up of a bunk served to turn private sleeping space (a woman's only private space, and even then, usually shared with another woman) into public space unavailable for her personal use. At other times, Queensland emigration authorities adopted a system of closed bunks for female emigrants with two or four single women sharing a small self-contained bunk apartment.[31] Creation of such a semi-private space, however, was not conducive to public order, as Damousi has pointed out with regard to convict vessels.[32] These closed bunks were used for what the authorities deemed illicit sexual activities on numerous occasions, the *Bayswater* the tip of at least a small iceberg.[33]

Other physical elements of shipboard management were less amenable to regulation, with wind and fortune outside the province of government emigration officers. Fire was a constant threat, in both the earlier sail vessels and the later coal-fuelled steamers widely used on the emigrant run by the 1880s. Policing the use of torches was an essential safety requirement but could cause friction. Isaiah de Zouche, whose stint as surgeon on board the *Star Queen* was a litany of disasters from the day in May 1875 when the vessel left Gravesend for Maryborough, wrote: 'One great cause of ill feeling towards me on the part of the ship's officers arose from the fact that I waged an incessant war against the carrying of naked lights in the sail locker, between decks forward steerage, and in the hold'.[34]

When the SS *Port Phillip* left London on 17 March 1896, it had on board a party of fifty single women, under the care of matron Mary Pittman Monk. On 8 April, the vessel was off St Helena. That evening, shortly after the single women were sent below to sleep, smoke began to billow out from the baggage room immediately below their quarters. The bunk room, where the women were effectively trapped by the arrangements designed to protect them, was unlocked by the matron and within fifteen minutes, all the single women had assembled on deck in their night clothes. The crew played water into the hatch all night but even those of the women's tin trunks which were retrieved had to be thrown, red hot, into the water.[35]

The people of St Helena received the destitute immigrants with great hospitality, the Acting Governor quartering them in the mess house formerly occupied by the garrison while Monk obtained essential clothing. In fact, the emigrants evidently enjoyed their interlude in St Helena as an unlooked for holiday. Less pleasant, however, was to arrive in Fremantle destitute and far from family resources, and to find the colonial government unwilling to fill the breach. As Nellie Barratt's irate father wrote to the colony's agent general in London:

> Now that the poor girls have arrived there . . . [they lack] the very things that they spent every farthing for before leaving England, viz:—Dresses, Shoes, Stockings and under linen &c. &c. in order that their outfit should be as far as they were able (according to their means) perfect, I have received a most heart rending letter from my daughter respecting the deplor-

able condition she finds themselves in for want of their things and that the Australian Government have offered them the miserable sum, in compensation for their loss, of £2 each.[36]

Nellie Barratt estimated her loss at £17, though her mother placed the value rather higher. Most of the women put their loss at well over £5. Elizabeth Louisa Johnson claimed £22 4s for the loss of all her worldly goods, which included the works of Tennyson and Goldsmith, brushes and combs, a silver brooch and a feather boa. The more prosaic Annie Jeames claimed only a jacket, worth £1 10s, and a felt hat.[37] (She may have been one of the few women to have had some of their luggage salvaged; she should not have been permitted to embark with such a rudimentary wardrobe.) After some pressure from people such as Barratt, and dire hints at adverse publicity, the Western Australian government advanced the women a little more than the first pittance of £2, and subsequently insured each immigrant's luggage for £10. Another woman wrote home:

You can imagine how pleased we were, for it costs such a lot here to get them anything like we have had at home, I am afraid I shall never get another stock of good clothes like I had before, but we must not mind so that we ourselves were saved.[38]

She was right, of course; all the women on board the SS *Port Phillip* must have believed themselves lucky to have survived. Although tragedies were rare, those embarking for the first time carried with them an awareness of their own mortality. Indeed the Anglican chaplains despatched on emigrant vessels, often provided by the London-based Society for Promoting Christian Knowledge (SPCK), were instructed to capitalise on 'the spiritual moment' of the passage as an opportunity for good Christian work.[39] As the SPCK wrote in 1894 of the work of their long-voyage chaplains, who undertook the passage to Australasia and South Africa:

It is difficult to over-estimate the opportunities of usefulness which a right-minded clergyman may obtain amongst the members of his floating parish. The breaking of old home ties, the enforced leisure, the softening influences of strange surroundings, the whole atmosphere of life on ship-board, give chances for wise counsel and gentle advice which may be recalled and acted upon long after the voyage is over, and the Chaplain and his temporary flock parted.[40]

In late December 1886, the Trinder and Anderson vessel *Kapunda*, an iron ship of 1095 tons register, went down in the Atlantic, somewhere off the coast of Brazil, following an early morning collision with an unknown vessel, which did not stop to pick up survivors. On board were three small parties of single women selected in Britain for Western Australia, 29 in all, 34 emigrants selected by the WA Land Company, and 154 other people nominated by kin in the colony. There were other passengers, and crew. All but eight male passengers and crew perished.[41] Some of them had been sleeping on deck to escape the equatorial heat and they heard the screams of the women trapped below deck as the ship went down.

The impact on the small Western Australian community of the loss of so many eagerly anticipated friends and family members can scarcely be imagined. So too the tragedy rocked the emigration network in Britain. Ellen Joyce, who had been responsible through the BWEA and the GFS for the despatch of eleven single Irish women (two other parties had been selected by Ellen Barlee and Julia Blake), had inspected the *Kapunda* before the vessel's departure from London on 11 December 1886. From London the vessel had made her way to Plymouth where, seven days later, the assembled party of ill-fated single women embarked. Mrs Joyce, in a bid to reassure other prospective emigrants and comfort the friends of those lost, wrote a long letter on the tragedy for the GFS newsletter:

> Miss Crockford ... had taken several parties across to Australia, and when on her last voyage she reached Adelaide, Mrs. Gawler, who is the head of the Women's Immigration Work there, was so thoroughly satisfied with her religious influence over the young women, that she wrote home and

begged she might be sent out again. So we may be quite sure that in the days which passed on the voyage she had used the time to draw the travellers' thoughts up to the Master she had loved so much and had served so well.

Whilst the emigrants were waiting at Plymouth a farewell service was held at the depot by Rev. F. Barnes, the emigrants' chaplain. He writes that they were very attentive, that he had five baptisms and seventy-four communicants:

I believe that nothing solemnises our thoughts so much as a long sea voyage. Many a girl has written back, 'I never thought so seriously before—we seem so alone in the hands of God;' and another, 'It made us feel nearer to the Saviour, because we were so alone from every one else, and when the ship was gliding over the great waves He seemed nearer than ever.'

Of the single women lost, Joyce had this to report:

Many motives may have influenced the persons who made up the number of the *Kapunda* list. One young woman, whose widowed mother had struggled for many years to bring up her family respectably, had emigrated on purpose, by earning higher wages, to help support the little ones . . . Others went out, the pioneers of large families, whom they purposed sending for as soon as they had been long enough in the country to assist them out.

Probably more reassuring for other prospective emigrants was a comment Mrs Joyce passed on from the Queensland despatching officer: 'He had sent 81,700 emigrants in 203 ships to Queensland, and . . . there had been no loss of life from ship-wreck amongst all that number'.[42] The loss of the *Kapunda* was in fact so exceptional that it became a symbol of loss for all emigrants and their friends. Agnes Stokes' recollections of her passage to Queensland on the *Roma* in 1887–88 refer to the loss of the *Katumpah* [sic] just out of the Bay of Biscay, and how her friends, hearing of the wreck, made up their minds that Agnes had perished.[43] Shipwreck, though so rare, was often blamed by anxious friends and family in Britain when the longed-for letter from the colonies failed to arrive. Ellen Joyce recounted another incident of a woman who came to her 'with an anxious face', fearing her daughter lost at sea. 'I heard from my Sarah when she was a fortnight off Brisbane . . . but I am afraid the vessel never got there, for I have not heard since.' The vessel, the *Dorunda*, was by that time back in dock in England preparing for a subsequent passage.[44]

More common if less expected was the freak accident which befell an individual. Maria Luttman left her sister and father in Britain in 1859 to take her chances in Tasmania. On the morning of 11 December, the *Hooghly* was just a few days' sail from Hobart, with three months at sea behind her. It was a fine Sunday morning, with the wind blowing freshly and the ship running free before it at a fair pace, and Maria and her companions decided to take some air on the poop. She was sitting on the lee side when an untimely wave broke over the vessel, washing salt water and spray over a number of the surprised young women. At the sight of her friends drenched to the skin, Maria 'threw up her arms in glee', the inquest tells us, 'and so lost her balance and fell between the after-davit and the life boat'. By chance, the captain had just stepped onto the poop deck. Witnessing the woman disappearing, he shouted to the helm to alter course, but his cries were drowned by the frantic screams of the other terrified women and 'even had they been heard and the ship put about, at least half an hour must have elapsed before any assistance could have been rendered and . . . to lower a boat in such a sea would have been attended with the greatest danger to the Crew'.[45] We do not know whether Maria screamed, whether fate was merciful and she was knocked unconscious against the side of the vessel, nor how rapidly she sank beneath the weight of her sodden and cumbersome clothing, her regulation warm gown and good strong boots, as the *Hooghly* sailed remorselessly on before the fresh winds of the Southern Ocean. The inquest recorded her death as a sad accident, with the captain's decision not to turn back the normal one in the circumstances.

Despite requiring all emigrants to provide a medical certificate as part of their application for passage assistance, despite the further precaution of a medical examination before embarking, illness was an inevitable companion on emigrant vessels. Diarrhoea, bronchitis and menstrual disorders were the most common complaints amongst the single women. Sometimes conditions which should have been detected before embarkation presented themselves on board. Pregnancy for instance; Maria Hill gave birth to a child on board the *Sobraon*, bound for Sydney in 1870, and she was not unique.[46] As well as menorrhagia or excessive menstrual bleeding, amenorrhoea or the absence of menstruation was quite commonly reported on board amongst the single women, and no doubt would have inclined the surgeon to suspect a possible pregnancy, although in most cases it was more likely that the physical and psychological shock of the passage and the prospect of a new life could have caused a rhythmic upset.

The passage itself could also provoke 'instability' and in these cases, colonial authorities sought to discover whether there had been any pre-existing mental health problem, in which case the emigrant, her referees and selectors had obtained her passage under false pretences. In the case of Eliza (or Elizabeth) Bland, a sixteen-year-old woman bound for Sydney on board the *Roslin Castle* in 1882, we know nothing of her earlier medical and personal history except that she habitually suffered from menorrhagia, for which she sought the surgeon's advice on 18 February. She was treated with astringents. Within days she was back in the sick room, suffering from delusions. The surgeon reported that, while she was always 'more or less eccentric', Bland was now 'somewhat excited, & strange in her manner'; in fact, Bland 'fancies her head is a telegraphic office, & herself a clerk'.[47] As well as chloral hydrate at bedtime and a dose of citrate of iron and quinine three times daily after food, she was ordered extra rations in an effort to improve her general physical well-being: port wine, beef tea, arrowroot, tapioca, mutton broth, milk, chicken broth and sago. All of these, as well as iron and quinine, were commonly prescribed for women suffering from shipboard debility. Bland's condition, however, was deemed sufficiently serious to necessitate even more persistent surveillance than usual, with the matron and sub-matron instructed to keep a constant watch on her and a nurse appointed to sleep with her in the locked hospital berths each night. By 24 February, the doctor reported Eliza's concern that 'her food jumps out of her mouth, and that it is no good taking it', although in fact, she did eat. On 25 February, she attempted to jump overboard—the fishes were calling her. She subsequently tried to strangle herself. But of the physical signs the doctor sought, 'headache, vomiting, squinting, or other forms of paralysis', there were none. By 5 March she was 'back to normal'.[48] We know nothing of her later fate and whether her symptoms, which today might be ascribed to a schizophrenic condition, re-emerged in the colonies.

Many passages to the colonies saw at least one death. These were seldom amongst the single women, although in 1899 all three fatalities reported on the Queensland emigration run that year were single women, who died of heat stroke in the Red Sea. (Of 1552 assisted immigrants to the colony that year, 423 were single women.)[49] The passage through the Red Sea taken by steamers to Queensland from the 1880s was always responsible for extreme discomfort amongst the emigrant travellers. The heat could be 'very hot, almost past bearing', as Hannah Wright wrote, but there were few precautions taken to alleviate the situation. One typical Sunday in the Red Sea, when Wright recorded that 'I am one mass of perspiration from head to foot, it pours out of me', Irish stew and plum pudding were cooked and served for Sunday dinner, as usual.[50] Maggie Kelly wrote in June 1900, one day out of Las Palmas, that the 'heat was simply unbearable, none of us could sleep'. Yet cooking and eating went on: 'My puddings were quite a success so the Captain came and asked me if I'd make him one tomorrow. Of course I had to say 'yes' although I'd have done anything to get out of it, the heat downstairs makes me quite ill'.[51]

Eating on deck and sleeping on deck (although this was seldom permitted for the single women) were the only recourse

from the heat: 'All are feeling the heat too much to dance to-
night, so we again retire to our berths, but not to sleep—only to
fan ourselves all night. It is much too hot to sleep'.[52] Inevitably
the heat took its toll among the weak:

> There is one old lady taken bad. They do not think she will
> ever recover. She is with us single women as she is a widow
> woman. She was coming to her son in Australia. The doctor
> is now cutting all her hair off and putting ice to her, and there
> was one death in amongst the married people this morning . . .
> Two deaths, one this morning and one this evening. The
> poor old lady is laid out on our deck. One died of sunstroke
> and other of convulsions . . . There is no wonder at sickness
> and death when we have it so hot. The temperature is 100
> and 60 degrees in the shade to-day.[53]

Space and Authority

After the passage of the British government's Passenger Acts of
1855, the carriage of British emigrants to the colonies was
remarkably well regulated and, if not pleasant, then at least no
longer such a gamble with survival. For single female emigrants,
the greater risk to morality remained. In the latter half of the
nineteenth century, creating a perception of a well-disciplined
passage was fundamental to government intentions in protecting single emigrant women. The provision of matrons and the
rigid segregation of sleeping quarters already described were
two controls pressed upon colonial governments to improve the
way the passage was perceived, both by prospective emigrants
and their prospective colonial employers. They also served the
very real purpose of protecting an extremely vulnerable group
of young women. Middle-class female philanthropists and
emigrationists alike viewed the ship as a moral jungle. Predators
included the crew, the ships' officers (some of whom were no
gentlemen), and the other male emigrants and passengers. Sometimes other women were included amongst the ranks of 'predators', with a number of cases recorded over the years of older

women 'contaminating' young single women—presumably seeking to recruit them for prostitution. Even the occasional matron was guilty of this practice.[54] But this was the exception. The moral enemy was almost universally male.

How real were the dangers on board the typical emigrant vessel? Undoubtedly some were exaggerated for effect, and we probably have to include Maria Rye's shocking tales of gang rape on board the *Wansfell* in this category.[55] However, stories of immorality and associated publicity would have added to the belief that women were at profound physical and moral risk if inadequately protected on board emigrant vessels.[56] No passage to the colonies was ever uneventful. Yet colonial government funds were involved and if it appeared that orders had been disobeyed, money wasted or discipline lax, someone had to be held to account. Shipboard inquiries tended to give the impression that sexual relations on board emigrant vessels were entered into voluntarily by women of low moral character, women who should not have been selected in the first place. Emma Apted and the more anonymous Park, on the *Bayswater* for example, figured in the inquiry as willing accomplices, and on other passages, even where there was no hint of sexual impropriety, there were cases of single women colluding with the surgeon-superintendent, or sometimes the captain, to defy the matron's authority.[57] True or not, the *Wansfell* episode highlights the possibility of an unwilling or immature young woman being coerced, even forced into a sexual relationship on board ship, especially by a male authority figure. Even in the case of Park and Apted, one can only wonder at their fate after the *Bayswater* left Rockhampton, presumably taking the captain and surgeon-superintendent with her.

Colonial emigrant and passenger vessels were floating worlds which in many ways replicated the societies which despatched them. The manipulation of shipboard spaces was one means used to reproduce the social relations of the land, and spatial relationships and even spatial segregation both served to reinforce gender distinctions, as well as the more commonly discussed class distinctions.[58] Single emigrant women were 'contained' by the physical structure of the vessel. But such shipboard arrangements were not themselves sufficient to enforce gender segregation, so emigrants were also subject to a carefully defined hierarchy of shipboard authority. As with the boundaries between classes, shipboard lines of gender demarcation, both physical and social, were often contested.

The professional matron was the first line of defence against moral attack, and spatial confinement was part of her arsenal. By night and for a good part of the day, single women were confined within their quarters where the matron reigned supreme. However, the rest of the vessel was not designed for surveillance. Two levels above the single women was the poop deck, the highest deck on board ship, and here the emigrant women, with the matron, took their fresh air and recreation. Apart from their quarters and, if necessary, the sick bay, this was the only other place on board where single women were allowed.

Activities were varied and dependent on the weather. They included reading, sewing and knitting, often with the matron's assistance; clothes washing and drying; deck games, races, occasional lessons and some of the organised classes. A few—unfortunately not enough for the historian—passed the time writing letters and journals. Strolling and gossiping were also favoured occupations. Other recreation related to social occasions such as Christmas and 'crossing the line'. Sometimes the surgeon-superintendent might also give informal instruction in first aid or ambulance procedures, although this was more often offered to the men on board. All these sorts of activities were single sex.

By regulation on emigrant vessels, the poop was 'strictly apportioned to the sole use of the single women, for the purpose of entirely separating them and cutting off all communication between them and the other emigrants'.[59] But ultimately it was not the other emigrants, nor even the sailors, who represented the greatest 'threat' to the single women. The ship's wheel and compass, signifiers of shipboard authority, were also located on the poop.[60] The single women's presence on the poop placed them alongside the upper echelons of the ship's hierarchy of officers, and it was here that discipline most frequently broke down.

Though in most cases relations between the male officials and the matron were amicable, personality differences and disagreements over ambits of responsibility were potentially a fertile source of grievance. Most passages, certainly from the 1850s on, were sufficiently well-regulated and well-disciplined to meet official colonial scrutiny. However, the men implicated in official inquiries were almost invariably the ship's officers, the captain, and the surgeon-superintendent himself, the only men who legitimately shared any part of the single women's space. The transformation of the male guardians of female emigrants into the role of predator was an easy one. Such a role shift was sometimes welcomed, sometimes initiated by the single women involved.[61]

An inquiry into the *Star of India* revealed that the surgeon-superintendent on board had been so ineffectual, discipline so lax, that two of the single women ended up 'nominally' (the inquiry noted) engaged to the second and third officers; 'the second officer . . . acknowledged that on several occasions he sat on the poop with his arm around the waist of one of the single women'. The doctor also 'permitted the schoolmaster and others to be habitually among the single women on the poop'.[62] In 1855, the captain of the *Royal Albert* was accused of kicking four young Irish women, Ann Scully, Sarah Salmon, Catherine McDonald and Catherine Morison, to prevent them, he said, from hanging around the sailors, leaning too far over the break of the poop to communicate with them. (An inquiry considered his actions unwise but his intentions good; and a severe reprimand was his only punishment.[63]) On the *James Jardine*, Captain Jenkins and Martha Watkins conducted a very public shipboard relationship. They were seen by the matron 'in deep conversation . . . while the others were dancing', and the matron overheard the captain saying to Watkins 'he wished his wife were dead and that no other woman could make him happy', while 'upbraiding her for looking at one of the men during the day'. Three of the ship's men gave evidence that Jenkins had repeatedly been seen sitting and talking with Watkins, putting his hand up her petticoats, touching her breasts and kissing her. All these transgressions were observed on the poop deck. Here too, Watkins drank the glasses of lime juice brought to her by the cabin boy, and ate the meals the captain also had sent to her from the cabin, to the chagrin of the other single women.[64] The poop deck was clearly the setting where the public acts of such shipboard dramas and romances were played out.

It became even more difficult to enforce a strict separation of the sexes on vessels which carried both *emigrants* and *passengers*. The distinction between emigrant and passenger loosely denoted class of origin, 'emigrant' connoting working-class status and receipt of an assisted or free passage. This gave government authorities the right to compel obedience to shipboard rules and regulations, through the person of the surgeon-superintendent. Most colonies followed a system of keeping emigrants and paying passengers in separate vessels throughout the latter part of the nineteenth century. Queensland, however, had taken no such precautions and had greater trouble than any other colony with shipboard discipline. As Queensland's agent for emigration, Henry Jordan, had reported to the colonial authorities in the 1860s:

> If we are to have the advantage of a Middle-Class Emigration, thus introducing Capital *with* labour, there must necessarily be certain minor disadvantages, resulting from the impossibility of maintaining on board our Ships, the same amount of unquestioning obedience to regulations which will be often secured by the iron rule established in ships where all the passengers are of the lowest class, and are going out under the feeling that they are accepting their passage as a kind of charity.[65]

Again, the poop deck was the site of contention. Surgeon-superintendent Dr J. J. Luce, appearing before an 1865 Select Committee inquiry into the *Commodore Perry*, made this abundantly clear:

> (Luce) I think no single females should be sent out in any ship containing first and second class passengers. The ship

would be in much better order without them ... It requires unceasing vigilance to keep matters right, especially where there are so many young men in the saloon, because they must be more or less intermixed; there are no means of keeping them separate, as they always meet on the poop ...

(Question) Then you have no control over the cabin passengers?

(Luce) Not a sufficient control to prevent intercourse with the single women.[66]

Hassam makes much of the social status of the poop deck and the contrivings of different classes of cabin passengers to gain access to it, but his claim that, because of 'the rarity of its social air', the poop deck was absolutely forbidden to steerage passengers', needs to be qualified.[67] To male steerage passengers—largely emigrants—yes, but not to single female emigrants. Such was the desire to keep them from the lower decks where the single emigrant men took their air that they had access, alongside cabin passengers on vessels which carried them, to this the most privileged site on board ship.

It was not, however, the cabin passengers, nor even the system which permitted them proximity to the single women, which were under investigation in the *Commodore Perry* inquiry, but the chief officers. Only the officials employed by the government or the shipping company (the captain, surgeon, matron, and the ship's officers) were the subjects of immigration board inquiries, as passengers were effectively outside the discipline of the government in these matters. What was at issue in such affairs was whether the 'charter party', the agreement or contract between the colonial government and the company which provided vessel and crew, had been breached. 'Any intercourse whatsoever' between the officers and crew and the single women constituted a breach of the charter party.[68] However, as Luce made clear of the *Commodore Perry*, the presence of passengers seemed to undercut discipline and make segregation more difficult, to the point where the ship's officers—and the single women themselves—were less inclined to recognise the restraints officially imposed on fraternisation between the sexes.

As a shipboard site, the poop represents more than simply a staging ground for sexual fraternisation and resistance of shipboard discipline. Daphne Spain has argued that spatial segregation can reinforce gender stratification. Masculine spaces are seen as socially desirable, with women traditionally confined to socially un-valued locations.[69] But the women's use of the socially prestigious poop deck might seem to challenge this. Similarly Hassam's analysis of the social significance of the poop leaves the question of the privileged access of the emigrant women unresolved. We have seen that, by virtue of their commodity status, their economic value to colonial governments as goods bought and paid for to be delivered intact to their destination, single emigrant women required protection. Hens in their coops were also kept on the poop. In fact the hen coops were considered the best seats in the house by privileged poop users,[70] although it was from such a vantage point on board the *Hooghly* that Maria Luttman fell to her death in 1859.[71] Accidents aside, it is clear that the single women were up there for the same reason as the hens were: to be confined. Yet Spain's analysis remains relevant. Giving single emigrant women special access to the poop served to underline their difference and further the process of social segregation which took place between decks.

Some fellow travellers regarded the single women's treatment as privileged: 'The single Woman are Cabin Passengers with use of the Poop & every Comfort with a Matern & under Matern with 3 Constables Selected from Maried Men to wait upon them for which they get £3'.[72] Many of the single women would have agreed. Privileged access to a space, however, might well include the right to use it, to exclude others from it, and to leave it. The single women did not enjoy such rights.

The matron's role as the single women's guardian extended to the poop, but here she ran most risk of direct conflict with the surgeon-superintendent, the captain or the officers. Her authority within the women's quarters was, in theory, supreme, but in other areas of the ship she had challengers to whom she was subordinate by rank, gender and indeed the authority of the natural order itself.

Some emigrant women were travelling by themselves; others embarked with their families. Eighteen-year-old Grace Martin from Cornwall, in the company of Emma and Thomas Trebilcock, her sister and brother-in-law, all sailed to Sydney in 1871 on the *Hawkesbury*;[73] while the sole single male on board the *Dunbar Castle* that year, draper Evan Jones from Monmouthshire, had been permitted passage only because his sister Margaret was also on board. They were travelling out to be near their sister, Jane Jones, who was working in Victoria.[74] While berthed and messed with the other single women, women who legitimately felt they had 'natural protectors' on board the vessel sometimes resented the totality of their enforced separation, leavened only by the occasional well-supervised 'at home' in the women's quarters. Single women, visible to all the other emigrants on the poop, frequently passed notes down to their relatives on the lower deck. Some stopped with the family; others went further afield into the hands of prospective suitors. There was little could be done. 'Some few messages were passed by the married women & children but led to no harm on board', the surgeon-superintendent recorded on board the *Queen Bee* in 1861.[75] More serious was the occasional refusal of single women to heed the matron when their parents or other family members were close by, with parents in particular sometimes outraged at an authoritarian matron presuming to prevent them speaking to their daughters. Mary Monk, for instance, had trouble on board the *Nairnshire* in 1895, noting in her journal her difficulties in controlling young women who sailed as emigrants, while their mother travelled out passenger class.[76]

In all these conflicts, the poop deck emerges as a highly visible, indeed an elevated, stage for contests over social authority, with the single women (the protected), the emigrant men (the excluded), parents and relatives (the supplanted) and sometimes passengers of a different class (the affronted) all vying with the matron for the role of director. Here indeed was theatre in the making.

Sometimes the anomalies built into the matron's position were officially recognised. In 1885, New South Wales experienced immigration agent, George Wise, vehemently opposed the colony's Agent-General's suggestion that she hand over her official journal weekly to the surgeon-superintendent. The Agent-General argued that, as her superior, the surgeon-superintendent had a need to oversee her work. But as Wise pointed out, the matron was herself charged with the responsibility of policing the surgeon-superintendent, and matrons' journals had frequently been used as evidence of 'irregularities' and even 'gross misconduct'. If its production were to be, in effect, censored, 'it will become a useless document as she would not venture to note therein any serious misbehaviour, or any want of attention to the Female Immigrants on the part of the Surgeon Superintendent'.[77]

As the *Bayswater* inquiry had indicated, an assertive response on the matron's part could work to her advantage in cases of 'gross' abuse of authority. In New South Wales in late 1877, an inquiry investigated the conduct of the surgeon-superintendent from the *Star of India*, at the matron Mrs Eagar's instigation. The single women largely supported her. Although the evidence was often contradictory, the inquiry found that Dr Brady had been guilty of a range of offences: drunkenness, undue familiarity with a few chosen women, habitual swearing and 'unbecoming conduct'.[78] While the surgeon denied the charge of intemperance, his explanation that 'I had concussion of the brain some years back, so I fancy a small quantity of spirits has an effect on me', was taken as tacit admission of guilt. His 'objectionable behaviour' included attending single women in the hospital berths without the matron being present and, on occasion, physically preventing her accompanying him. While at the quarantine station he also encouraged the single women to go rowing in boats with himself, the captain and other crew members. All this clearly transgressed government instructions concerning relations between single women and members of the opposite sex. Brady also admitted that in a fit of temper he broke down the lattice work of the water-closet to force two of the single women to vacate it.[79]

As the man responsible for the entire ship, but particularly his own officers, the captain was held accountable, and judged not to have exercised sufficient control or discretion. But of the initiator of the inquiry, the matron, the board reported:

> As the conduct of the Surgeon-Superintendent towards Mrs. Eagar was such as to materially tend to lower her in the estimation of the single women, and thus deprive her of all authority, the Board do not attach any blame to the Matron on account of the want of discipline and irregularities which occurred on board the ship.[80]

Her past good record and the gratitude of most of the single women also weighed in her favour.

There were comparable difficulties on the *Hydrabad*. Even before the ship had embarked for South Australia in 1875, the surgeon-superintendent Dr Worthington, with Captain Deering's support, had urged matron Mrs Rogers to ignore her instructions and allow the single women to attend dances in the evenings, on deck and on the poop. She had worked as a shipboard matron for sixteen years with both the South Australian and Victorian colonial governments, and assented to this unusual request with reluctance; dancing was usually confined to the women's private realm between decks. However, when the doctor announced that he intended to place a second lock on the single women's compartment, to keep the key to this lock himself 'in case any of the women fainted', and then insisted that the matron hand over her own key to him, Mrs Rogers declined to sail with him. As a result, Captain Deering threatened that he would see she was never employed again in any colonial emigration service.[81] Her whole livelihood was at risk if she refused to comply.

There was an inquiry. Not only the matron's authority but the whole structure of shipboard spatial arrangements had been challenged by the surgeon's actions, and colonial officials moved quickly to shore up the logic of their regulations. As the inquiry maintained, what benefit could there be in permitting the doctor free access to the women in case of illness for, if an emergency arose, the women, being locked in, would not be able to alert him? The matron was much closer by design, with her quarters in this instance separate from but adjacent to the single women; and the regulations specifically provided that the surgeon attend the single women only in her presence.

The South Australian Commissioner for Crown Lands and Immigration intervened personally, reiterating the need for a gendered regulation of space:

> While it is considered that the majority of our Surgeons are young, unmarried men, (and in some cases I might almost say boys) it must be obvious to any person who has had any experience of human nature, that it would be undesirable, in many cases, that the Surgeon should have the power at any time during the night, to enter the single women's apartment, without the matron's knowledge.[82]

Nonetheless the support given to the matron was equivocal and resonates with the suggestion that an assertive matron ought still to recognise her place. As the Commissioner wrote to the colony's emigration agent in London:

> Mrs. Rogers was, to a considerable extent (if not altogether) justified in refusing to act under the circumstances ... Mrs. Rogers has been an excellent matron in the past, and I trust she will be employed by you, for I feel bound to admit to you that the stand she took in the matter of the lock and key has caused me to form a very high opinion of her firmness of Character which (if it does not degenerate into obstinacy) is an excellent quality for a matron to possess.[83]

The line between 'firmness of Character' and 'obstinacy' was certainly a tricky one for matrons to negotiate, drawn as it was by men not entirely sympathetic to women asserting independent authority. Questions of gender and status, of a woman confronting a man and one who outranked her professionally, made the endorsement of the matron's 'firmness of Character' a touch ambivalent.

While such obvious cases of abuse of trust were dealt with by immigration board inquiry, friction between surgeon-superintendent and matron was often papered over by unenthusiastic reports of the one about the other. Such reports —and few remain because they are in effect unexceptional— reveal a shipboard climate of petty hostilities and conflict over lines of authority. The matron was well aware of her position and the consequences of insubordination. In 1869, following Dr Prentice's complaints about matron Miss Barker's attitude towards him, the Queensland Colonial Secretary decided that, as she appeared to be growing too old to discharge her duties, Miss Barker was not to be re-employed. She had no avenue of appeal.[84]

On the other hand, relations between the matron and the surgeon or captain could take a different tack. Many such ship-board relationships were completely harmonious and some developed more than a measure of warmth. In 1878, matron Miss Neill who had accompanied single women on the ship *Newcastle* to Brisbane late the previous year, sent a scandalised *frisson* through Brisbane society by openly living on board the vessel in the saloon, in company with Captain Whereat, after all the other emigrants had left the ship. Though suggestions of immorality were loud, ultimately the charge against her was not proven and she was permitted to continue her work on sub-sequent passages, though, interestingly, Captain Whereat was not.[85] Regardless of 'immorality', Neill's behaviour was uncharacteristic for an experienced emigrant matron and, in full view of prurient colonial society, was certainly unwise. There is clearly more to this incident than remains officially or publicly recorded. However, its significance lies not so much in issues of morality, but in reminding us that matrons too were single women far from home, denied the support and companionship of women of their own social class, and that the shipboard passage could temper prudence amongst matrons and other officials just as it did for their charges. In their official roles as authority figures, matrons as women were effectively desexed or masculinised. At the same time, however, they were middle-class women coming into close every day contact with men—the surgeon and captain —who largely shared their class origins. It would be more surprising if relationships never developed.

Judging from remaining sources such as matrons' journals, evidence of inquiries, the observations and correspondence of spectators, and those few accounts left by single women themselves, it seems most single women largely took the matron's role for granted. Some undoubtedly welcomed the shipboard protection offered by the matrons, finding it a comfort in the unfamiliar masculine world of the emigrant vessel. Many a testimonial was drawn up and signed by the single women when their ship finally docked, to attest publicly to the kindliness and friendship of their shipboard matron. But appreciation of the matron was seldom universal. Where there was discontent amongst the single women, the matron's authority was often a factor. She came on board armed with her 'duty statement', a list of regulations which outlined her responsibilities and sphere of influence. The single women, however, had no such clear charter of the lines of shipboard authority. In any case, they had no reason to accept it nor the proprietorial paternalism of colonial governments which, having largely paid the single women's passage, now considered the women colonial property. In an attempt in 1894 to compel women to submit to the matron, Ellen Joyce, working in conjunction with the Western Australian colonial government, insisted that single women sign an agreement to obey the matron as the price of receiving an assisted passage.[86]

The surgeon-superintendent, as the other immediate authority figure on board, also had a hand in disciplining the single women and supporting the matron. More serious incidents such as theft called for his intervention, in 1884, for example, when a woman travelling to Sydney on the steamship *Abergeldie* was 'convicted of having stolen several articles from another single girl'. Dr Beattie described Margaret Minihan as 'of very low caste and appears to be an inveterate thief and liar'. Her punishment was to be kept below deck, 'apart from the other girls of the mess' and to undertake extra work under the matron's supervision. She was 'not to be curtailed in food' (although by implication it seems such a punishment was an option), and was warned that 'if improvement is not evinced and her conduct exemplary for the remainder of the voyage she is to be brought under official notice on arrival in Sydney'. If her conduct was drawn to the attention of the immigration officer in Sydney it did not apparently interfere with her employment prospects, as she was hired out from the immigration depot at the first hiring day after arrival.[87] More severe punishments such as deprivation of food or putting women in irons, a punishment sometimes used against single women migrating to colonial New Zealand, have left no apparent trace in Australian migration records.[88]

Although they could complain about an unduly authoritarian matron or surgeon-superintendent, minor charges made by immigrant women were not usually taken seriously, unless the dissatisfaction was widespread. Two single women's complaints against the matron of the *Samuel Plimsoll* were dismissed in 1878 by the New South Wales Immigration Board as 'frivolous and unworthy of further consideration' despite the fact that the surgeon-superintendent's independent complaints about matron Mrs Kent's 'want of proper control over her temper' on the same passage were treated seriously.[89] In a more serious incident in 1862, Bridget Cannaughan accused the matron of trying to force her to undress in front of all the single women then, when she refused, of dragging her to the matron's compartment where she was stripped in an attempt to ascertain whether or not she was pregnant. In a written complaint addressed to the New South Wales immigration agent, Cannaughan declared, 'it was an insult to me which I will get satisfaction for when I land in Sydney if God spare me'. Perhaps God gave Biddy Cannaughan more satisfaction than the Immigration Board did. Matron Elizabeth Brock was merely cautioned for indiscretion and received her full gratuity of £30; but she suffered a severe fall on her arrival in Sydney, requiring medical attention.[90] From these and other incidents, it also seems that conflict could have been compounded by the question of national origins. Single women occasionally complained against matrons who referred to them as 'nasty Irish beasts', or 'dirty Irish'. While there is insufficient evidence to confirm this empirically, it does seem that the majority of matrons were English, and a significant proportion of single immigrant women were Irish.[91] In any event, shipboard insubordination probably gave greater satisfaction than waiting to lodge a complaint with largely unsympathetic colonial authorities at journey's end.

Emigrant needs were neither uniform nor static but for most single women, the passage to the colonies was a reasonably safe and pleasant watershed between their old world and their new. While some chafed under the authority of the matron and what they experienced as rigid shipboard discipline, the restrictions placed on their behaviour and their movements were probably little different from those they had tolerated in service in Britain. Colonial authorities too considered the financial cost of shipboard protection a necessary bulwark against the expense of introducing women 'tainted' by immorality and consequently unemployable. For the other parties involved (matrons, colonial employers, and the British emigrationists who had been behind the notion of adequate protection in the first place) the stakes were rather different. Ultimately though, most seemed reasonably content with the process of physical and moral protection which evolved in the decades from the 1850s to the 1890s, when assisted migration slowed down.

'No worse than might have been expected'

MANY FEATURES OF female emigration, such as selection, were common across colonies, but others were not. Colonial differences were most apparent in the way single women were treated in transit and after arrival. By the 1890s only Queensland and Western Australia still offered assistance to single immigrant women. Assisted passages to Queensland had tailed off early that decade with Queensland, like the eastern colonies generally, affected by depression; but they were soon revived. First nomination was reintroduced, then free passages for domestics.[1] Over the intervening years, colonial government attitudes to protected female migration had changed considerably and nowhere were these shifts more apparent than in the 1900 Queensland government inquiry into the passage of the steamer *Jumna*, which charted a map for the future of female migration well into the next century. Clearly inscribed on the Queensland inquiry was a push towards a more *laissez-faire* model of protection. That same decade, the Western Australian government handed virtually total control of their programme of female migration to Ellen Joyce of the British Women's Emigration Association (BWEA). Ironically, while Queensland officials were questioning the very basis of protection, 'protective maternalism' (the byword of the British female emigrationists who had influenced migration practices for the previous several decades) had simultaneously reached its zenith on the other side of the continent, in the realm of both shipboard protection and reception practices after arrival. The waning of protective maternalism evident in the *Jumna* inquiry[2] spelled the beginning of the eclipse of the power of the female emigrationists who had worked for half a century to standardise protection practices across the migration process.

The passage of the British India Company steamer *Jumna* was the vanguard of a newly ascendant model of shipboard protection. She left London on 22 September 1900, carrying 431 immigrants bound for the colony of Queensland. They included 282 single women. With Western Australia's programme of assistance winding down and with assisted passages to all the other colonies long withdrawn, Queensland's reopening of assistance in 1896, following its suspension in 1892, succeeded in attracting large numbers to the colony now convalescent after the depression.

Most of the single women were young and had been drawn to the prospect of emigration by the extensive advertising campaign the colonial government had conducted in Britain. Annie Jane Edwards was amongst them. She had obtained references for her passage from her employer and the Vicar of Charlton, in Staffordshire, and had been examined by the ship's doctor, Dr A. Napier Ledingham, before embarkation in London.[3] Martha Copeland embarked with seven or eight other young women who had all applied for migration through the BWEA. Had the West still been recruiting single women at that stage, they undoubtedly would have taken passage for Fremantle.[4] Sisters Gwendoline and Daisy Melville Jones, from Wales, travelled out together as single women; their brother Hugh Norman Jones was also on board, with the single men. Before travelling to London to board the *Jumna*, the Jones girls had lived at home with their parents. They had no experience of paid employment. Two other young sisters, Louisa and Annie Clarke, were bound for Brisbane but ultimately decided to disembark at Thursday Island, where they both found work within a couple of days.[5]

A number of the single women had obtained passages through London selection agent August Larsen. Mary Sands, a 22-year-old domestic servant from London, had seen the colony's advertising in the papers at Wandsworth, and contacted Larsen for further information. After looking at her references and hearing of her stable employment history—Sands had spent more than two years with one employer—Larsen encouraged her to proceed with her application. The usual preliminaries of having her papers signed by a clergyman and a doctor were soon attended to and Sands obtained her orders for the *Jumna*.[6] However, some of Larsen's selections were less straightforward, with Larsen playing the role too often associated with selection agents who were not directly accountable to government authorities: of profiting from applicants' ignorance. Rose Parry had worked as a certificated nurse in the Hereford Hospital. Under the colony's immigration regulations, hospital nurses were not acceptable as prospective emigrants. Nonetheless, Parry was prepared to work as a general servant in the colony and in her application form Larsen described her as a housemaid.[7] He told her not to take out her nursing certificates but she made good use of her medical training by working as a nurse on board the *Jumna*. Similarly he described D. Williams, a certificated nurse in England who worked alongside Parry in the ship's hospital, as a domestic servant.[8]

Parry was apparently happy enough to acquiesce in Larsen's arrangement, but Elizabeth Rimbault was bitter when she realised she had been misled about her prospects in the colony. She was a certificated maternity nurse, had attended Larsen's office in London in her nursing uniform and had outlined her employment experience and capabilities. In Britain, Rimbault earned from eight to ten guineas a month, but Larsen told her prospects in Queensland were even better and that she would be eligible for a free passage. In fact, as a maternity nurse, she would not have been eligible, so Larsen completed her application as a 'nurse', implying unqualified household or child nurse. This ploy enabled Rimbault to take a free passage and

Larsen to pocket his commission.[9] He had tricked her into leaving a stable and remunerative career in Britain for unemployment or at best underemployment in Brisbane.[10]

Other single women needed no help in bending the rules to obtain a free passage. Three reached the colony in an advanced state of pregnancy and others on board were also known to be pregnant.[11] Another, Alice Hill, was a married woman, deserted, she said, by her husband, and she had travelled out on the *Jumna* as a single woman.[12] Leaving Britain as an emigrant without the consent of one's husband was illegal, and if Hill's marital status had been suspected before departure, she would have met the same fate as one of Hannah Wright's fellow emigrants in 1886, of being forcibly removed from the vessel and returned to her husband's home.[13]

Yet another woman, Kate Clouton, had obtained her passage directly through Queensland's Agent-General in London and had provided a reference from her parish clergyman.[14] Few secrets remained hidden on board though, and it was soon whispered that the woman travelling under Kate Clouton's name was *not* Kate Clouton.[15] Obtaining papers from a friend or relative was not unusual and was virtually impossible to detect in the days before photographic identification. It often came about simply as the result of circumstance, rather than as a deliberate attempt to deceive or avoid detection. A prospective emigrant found herself temporarily or permanently unready to depart and so passed her papers on to a friend or relative. Perhaps she would reapply in her own name for a subsequent passage. By that means some emigrants, according to the shipping lists, travelled out to the one colony twice in close succession. In the case of Kate Clouton, she carried with her introductions to Mr R. F. Woodcraft, the Secretary to the Society for the Prevention of Cruelty, who did not know her or her family personally but who knew 'a gentlemen in town who knew her father'.[16] If, as it was alleged, Clouton were not the 'real' Kate Clouton, the imposter obviously knew her well enough to be able to make use of this connection and undoubtedly travelled with Kate Clouton's blessing.

As well as emigrants selected in Britain for assisted passage, many of the emigrants were nominated by friends and relatives in the colony. Employers outside Brisbane were particularly aware of the benefits of the nomination system since selected single women generally disembarked in Brisbane, leaving the northern ports short of domestic servants. Either as relatives or as nominated domestic help, single women H. Andrews, D. Hawkins, M. Donnelly and F. Elmslie all disembarked at Thursday Island, into the charge of Thursday Island residents, Mr Andrews, Mr Burne, and Mrs MacMahon, and Mr L. Armstrong of the northern town of Normanton.[17] Thursday Island had particular attractions. Hannah Wright recorded that 'there are thirty men to one woman at Thursday Island, so if some of us single women were to land . . . I should think we would soon get a husband'.[18] Most women, though, preferred the more concrete prospects of domestic service in southern towns.

Within days of the *Jumna* leaving the London docks under her master, Captain Sanders, tensions simmered on board, with some of the single women already unhappy about their conditions. The focus of complaint was the ship's matron, Caroline E. Davies. Appointed by the Queensland government to take charge of the party of single female emigrants on board, Davies had nearly twenty-five years of employment as both a teacher and a matron behind her. Her qualifications ranged from teacher with the London School Board, to assistant matron and matron at Millbank, Fulham, Woking and Surrey government prisons. She had also worked in girls' industrial schools. Leaving the Prison Department in May 1891 after twelve years' employment in prison institutions, Davies continued to take short-term employment to supplement her retired allowance. In the mid-1890s she began work as an emigrant ship matron, escorting parties of young women to Canada under Ellen Joyce's auspices, and groups of children from Maria Rye's Children's Home in London to Rye's 'Western Home' at Niagara, on Lake Ontario in Canada.

Although we know little about the personal backgrounds of the women who served as permanent emigrant ship matrons in the nineteenth century, Davies' general career pattern and social circumstances were probably reasonably typical. She had worked in positions of authority over young women of a different class from her own, she was single and she apparently had no independent means nor family wealth. In her appointment to the Queensland government, Davies was expected to take sole charge of nearly three hundred young women for nearly two months, for a sum of £40 plus £10 expenses. She could also expect a free second class return fare to Britain. Davies' referees described her as firm, loving and prudent, constantly watchful in her tasks, and exhibiting a strong Christian character.[19] Unfortunately for shipboard discipline, a significant proportion of the single women on board the *Jumna* did not value these qualities highly—or at all.

On 25 September, the surgeon-superintendent Dr Napier Ledingham's journal recorded the first in a series of charges, reports and counter-charges laid on the passage to Queensland. Before the *Jumna* docked in Brisbane, no fewer than nine formal inquiries, with evidence taken and minutes recorded, had been held. Shortly before her arrival in Brisbane, a petition signed by 82 of the single women was presented to John Douglas, a government official on Thursday Island, requesting that he authorise a formal inquiry into the conduct of the matron before the vessel travelled south on the last leg of its journey.[20] Subsequently, the Queensland Immigration Board conducted its own four-day inquiry into the question of discipline on board the vessel.

By 1900, conditions on board immigrant vessels had changed dramatically from the days when the BLFES had first called for the appointment of matrons to protect single women on the long passage to the colonies. Modes of transportation had changed, with modern steamers replacing the old sailing vessels. So too had the route. In an endeavour to cut back on passage times of three to four months, vessels no longer followed the great circle route heading far south into the treacherous icy waters of the Southern Ocean. The *Jumna's* passage was, in navigational terms at least, an unexceptional one and, with weather favourable throughout the passage, took just 59 days, steaming through the Suez Canal and Indian Ocean and then via the Dutch East Indies before first making contact with colonial Queensland at Thursday Island.[21] Queensland vessels had followed this route through the Red Sea and Torres Strait since the 1880s, although emigrants and passenger vessels bound for other colonies continued to come via the Cape.

More significant, in terms of the immigrants' shipboard experience, were the physical and spatial changes on board the steamers. The *Jumna* had three decks or recreational areas for the use of the emigrants: two segregated decks for the use of male and female passengers, and the third a mutual deck where all could gather. Under earlier schemes single female emigrants were kept strictly separate (wherever possible) from crew and fellow travellers, with physical barricades demarcating the male and female sections of the ship. Now these barriers had been completely removed under the system of emigration revived by the Queensland government in the 1890s. The immigration agent's report on the arrival of the *Duke of Portland* in 1899, the first vessel under the new system, described the changes: 'There were no barricades as of old beyond which the single women could not go. They were at liberty to promenade everywhere on deck during the day time, and mix with the single men'.[22]

The removal of the barricades of course equally increased the liberty of the men on board and it is significant that the immigration agent saw the changes—negatively—as a lessening of the controls exercised over the women. In former days, they had been the ones contained and theirs the area demarcated. In a subsequent report on the 1900 passage of the *Duke of Portland*, the immigration agent reiterated this point:

When the 'Duke of Portland' brought her first shipment of passengers here in August last, I mentioned the absence of a barricade to confine the single women to one portion of the ship and pointed out that it remained to be seen whether it was wise to dispense with such a division.

So far as we know, positively, no serious consequences have resulted; but there is very little doubt than an act of immorality referred to elsewhere as having taken place during the last voyage could not have happened had there been a barricade and a proper watch kept to see that no one passed through it ... Certainly, under the present system, but little can be done towards the right enforcement of discipline.[23]

Lines and ambits of authority had changed too. From 1899, the only government appointee on ships bound for Queensland was the matron, and she alone was answerable to the government for the well-being of the single women. Henceforth the surgeon-superintendent was simply the fourth officer in the ship's hierarchy, an employee of the shipping company having no power over superior officers and certainly little influence with the captain. Previously he had been required to keep a detailed log of the passage which, if necessary, could be used as evidence in the event of an inquiry or report into the passage. Although the surgeon on board the *Jumna* had kept a log of the charges against and by the matron, keeping such a journal was no longer a government requirement, a fact regretted by the immigration agent in Brisbane.[24] Long-established patterns of authority which had served to keep emigrants 'disciplined' and matron, surgeon-superintendent and captain in mutually dependent and accountable relationships were henceforth abandoned.

The other most striking difference between the *Jumna* and earlier emigrant vessels was the existence of an open bar on board. Although some restrictions were placed on the single women, all the emigrants were entitled to use it. The restrictions, in any case, proved very flimsy. Single women were not, for example, permitted to buy spirits unless they had the surgeon's permission.[25] In practice they merely needed to request spirits 'for medicinal reasons' in order to be served and, although this was certainly not officially permitted, other people could and did buy spirits for them as well.[26] The matron herself had passed on some of her own supply of wine and spirits to women who she thought needed it, presumably because of ill health, even though, as Dr Ledingham pointed out before the inquiry, this was a distinct breach of the rules.[27] Single women were entitled to order beer or stout on their own behalf whenever they wished, provided they paid for it.[28]

It was not so much the ready availability of alcohol as the existence of the open bar which became an issue on board the *Jumna*. Drinking beer and stout was an acceptable practice for young women in the late nineteenth century. On the *Echuca*, Matron Monk had her own supply of beer and wine, augmented by the doctor when she needed it. Stigma was attached only to the locality where the drink was purchased. On this subject Lady Louisa Knightley, long time president of the BWEA and active in the Girls' Friendly Society (GFS) and in the conservative Primrose League,[29] had written in 1879 of the young single working woman in London whom the GFS sought to help:

> She can have some supper when she returns at night, but she must buy her bread and cheese and beer, herself, or pay some one to fetch it for her, and that she cannot afford to do. To think of a young respectable girl going into a public house at 9, 10, or 11 o'clock at night for a glass of beer, or stout, seems very dreadful, and yet it is a common daily and nightly occurrence . . . It is a demoralising practice, and . . . it is a habit that leads to much evil or misery.[30]

Clearly, it was the place where beer was dispensed, the public house or the ship bar, which carried the taint of immorality. Similar attitudes were held in the colonies, with public drinking a male prerogative.[31] Quietly and privately consumed, however, beer and stout could be legitimate refreshments for the young working-class woman. Spirits were another matter entirely. Thus William McMillan, the clerk aboard the *Jumna*, was severely chastised by the board of inquiry because he admitted bringing a small flask of spirits into the Brisbane depot where the inquiry was held, even though he asserted that 'the girls did not touch the strong drink'.[32]

For many of the single women the bar, like the mutual deck, was a popular site for social and recreational gatherings. Consequently, for the matron, it required policing. At the open bar the single women were able to fraternise fairly readily with the crew, and a number developed friendships with some of the men later named by the matron in her charges. The chief steward Ovenden, for example, was there regularly. Early in the passage Davies spoke to the captain about attempting to prevent the single women from buying from the bar, or at least going there themselves. As a result, Captain Sanders directed the chief steward to put up a notice requesting that the single women stay away. Instead an insulting notice referring to the matron was posted up.[33] This was removed, but no steps were made to investigate who was responsible, which served to reinforce the matron's view that the ship's officers, including the captain, gave her no support against the women and that she alone stood between the single women and corruption.

Just as the emigrant women could be harmed by the suggestion they had been indulging in alcohol, so too could the matron. Several of the single women accused her of having been drunk on a number of occasions, on board and on shore in Brisbane. There is a certain irony to this charge, as the matron was the only person on board actually accused of intoxication. In collusion with one or more of the cabin boys and possibly the chief steward, some of the women had ordered and paid for spirits in the matron's name, leaving a sizeable record of alcohol purchased and by implication consumed by Davies. The matron's wine and spirits account, apparently amounting to nearly £12, was then offered before the inquiry as evidence of her sly drinking, with the chief steward claiming that she was in the habit of ordering brandy on the quiet, late at night, which she then consumed in secret in her cabin.[34]

The charges were thrown out by the inquiry. Walter Ovenden was undoubtedly a hostile witness. Davies had already named him in a charge of 'frivolous and unseemly conduct' brought against the two hospital nurses, Williams and Parry,[35] and both Ovenden and the second officer, Harry Howard Goodwin, had been the subject of rumours suggesting they had slept with some of the single women.[36] More specifically, Davies had charged Ovenden with having spent an hour alone in his cabin with Beatrice Hall, a single woman 'who was freely spoken of aboard as a prostitute', according to passenger Arthur Palmer.[37] That charge had been dismissed and the allegations against Hall never corroborated. However, Ovenden's antagonism towards the matron was both well documented and, it would seem, well grounded.

In more concrete terms, it appeared that the evidence of the wine bill was contrived. Davies claimed that she had embarked with only ten shillings in her possession and, as the captain confirmed, had been compelled to ask him for an advance of two pounds to spend on curios at Port Said.[38] For a single woman in Davies' circumstances, earning her living and hoarding against her future, it might have been surprising if she had embarked with more.

The mud slinging went on. Another single emigrant Annie Brown made a further charge against Davies, that she had seen the matron drunk in town four days after arrival in Brisbane.[39] Fortunately for Davies, she had been visiting a Queen Street dentist, Dr John W. Ward, 'a professional gentleman well known in Brisbane', at just the time that Brown had allegedly seen her drunk, and he made a sworn statement before a justice of the peace attesting that she had been 'perfectly free from the influence of alcohol'.[40] That same afternoon, Davies also paid a fortuitous visit to Dr Thomson, who happened to be a member both of the Immigration Board and the inquiry panel; he too stated that neither he nor his servant had observed or smelt traces of alcohol on the matron.[41] For the many witnesses who were able to claim they had seen Davies drunk, she was able to produce a range of others, including the less than compliant captain and doctor who saw her more frequently than they wanted to, to refute the allegation. Nonetheless, the repeated charges of intoxication and the fabricated liquor bill both stand testimony to the very real contempt, even hatred with which many of the single women regarded Davies. The matron's efforts to control the behaviour of single women was the single most contentious issue on the passage out. The board of inquiry, in fact, asserted that 'with 282 single women, mostly young, it was only natural that trouble to the matron was always more or less imminent', thereby giving the status of inevitability to the *Jumna*'s problems. Yet the matron on board an earlier immigrant vessel under the same system, the *Duke of Portland*, had experienced no difficulty whatsoever. The immigration agent described her work:

> There was a matron (Miss Buchanan), or perhaps I should call her stewardess, for her position was really not defined, and I have no advice as to whether she was appointed by the Queensland Government, or was merely a servant of the ship. She seems to have had no trouble whatever in the management of the women placed under her charge. I am inclined to think that is to be accounted for by the fact that she never interfered with them in any way. This I merely assume from personal observation on board. This lady was at her post alongside the women's quarters, but took no active part in their control. Indeed, I failed to see how she could have done so. There were no constables, or any holding equivalent positions on the ship; and, so far as I could learn, the people had never once during the voyage been mustered by roll-call.[42]

Davies had taken a stricter view of her role. Appointed by the Queensland government, she had been formally instructed that her duties lay 'in the care and supervision of the single women emigrants; in keeping them free from intrusion and unnecessary association with other passengers; and in seeing that they regularly observe the rules laid down . . . for the good order of their part of the ship'.[43]

While Davies was zealous in carrying out those orders, unfortunately for peace and harmony on board she overlooked the other tenet of her instructions:

You will remember that the oversight of the young unmarried females is an important trust, and while you endeavour by firmness to maintain good order and obedience, you will strive to win their esteem by a wise and kind construction of the rules prescribed for their good behaviour.

It was clear from the complaints the single women lodged against her that Davies failed on this count. Within days of leaving London, Davies had earned the reputation of being a strict and unfeeling disciplinarian. Single woman after single woman, questioned concerning their experience of the passage, affirmed that the matron was too strict, and that a kind word occasionally would have done a great deal to gain co-operation. Although many of the immigrants, both single and married, reinforced the general impression that some of the single women had been 'unruly and undisciplined', and that the matron had been 'greatly provoked', they also blamed the matron's high-handed treatment of the young women.

Shipboard conflict was related to a small range of issues: communication between the single women and some of the men (most frequently the crew) on board; behaviour which the matron considered disrespectful; behaviour on the matron's part which the single women resented as heavy-handed, particularly in the matter of her language towards them; and the use of racist language by some of the single women, towards each other and towards other passengers. The first recorded incident, three days out of port, was a typical example. One of the single women, Maud Runt, had been talking with a fellow passenger, a man. However, 'talking' became what the matron judged to be 'unbecoming conduct'. Carrying out what she saw as her duty, Davies took Runt by the collar, presumably to lead her away. According to Davies her hand slipped and came into contact with the woman's face. Runt claimed the matron struck her. Ledingham, the ship's surgeon, cautioned Runt to obey regulations and advised Davies to avoid physical confrontation.[44] Subsequently the incident was reported to the captain, with Runt repeating her accusation that she had been struck.[45]

Although no further action was taken, lines of confrontation were clearly illustrated in this small episode. The matron's view of 'unbecoming conduct' was at odds with the views of the single women and those of the ship's officers too. Many of the single women resented and refused to recognise that the matron had any authority over them, and certainly no one on board but the matron herself believed she had any right to compel single women to obey her instructions.

After this incident, relations between the matron and the single women deteriorated even further, with several complaints made to the medical officer concerning her 'harsh and unnecessary severity' over the next few days.[46] These he smoothed over but, on an evening early in October, some of the single women demonstrated loudly and vocally against Davies, 'hooting' her on her evening rounds and defying her attempts to get them into bed. Her response, according to the women, was to refer to them as pigs. She also threatened that her reports on their behaviour would prevent them getting good employment positions in Brisbane. She certainly believed this was within her power, with her instructions explicitly stating that the women in her care were to 'understand that their future prospects in their new home will probably much depend upon the commencement they make while on their way to it'.[47]

In fact, none of the incidents on board the *Jumna*, nor the findings of the inquiry, named any of the girls as 'disreputable', and nor were they used directly against the women in the matter of employment. In any case, Queensland employers were too desperate for servants to care.

Although the *Jumna* inquiry was set up to investigate the role and conduct of the matron, the behaviour of the immigrant women was also under scrutiny. Two of the women, Beatrice Hall and Dot Atkins, had allegedly slept with the second and third officers, underlining the difficulty the surgeon-superintendent would have faced, as fourth officer, had he attempted to prevent this. Witnesses had seen both women going in and out of those officers' cabins. A male passenger, when asked whether he had seen any of the officers in the hold with the women, replied, 'yes, when we were at Cairns, but of course I could not see whether any familiarity took place, though it was well understood that it was not about boxes they had gone down'.[48] Other women had been 'associating' with the Lascar seamen on board ship and had been seen drinking with them in a hotel in Brisbane after arrival.[49]

The mutual deck, where the men and women could mingle freely during the day, caused further aggravation, with the matron attempting to check every exchange between the single women and the men. On a number of occasions she had reportedly struck women who disobeyed her. One witness recalled, 'I saw the matron smack a girl on the face, but that girl did not, as was alleged by the matron, throw her leg over a man's head'.[50] Another woman recalled that she had seen 'some of the girls lying about on the mutual deck in improper positions with men, rolled up in blankets'. The excuse often made was that the women were merely speaking to their brothers but, when the immigration agent ingenuously asked one female witness, 'might not the men have been [the] girls' brothers?', she replied with alarming candour, 'No I do not think so; at least I should not lie wrapped up in a blanket with my brother; I would rather some other girl's brother'.[51]

Most telling was the claim that the matron had repeatedly told the single women that no 'respectable girl' would emigrate, that they must have come from bad homes to consider leaving them for the colonies, and that if they had had decent friends, they would not have left Britain.[52] Such comments hint at an attitude towards emigration which was still relatively common in Britain despite the best efforts of the BWEA, though it was becoming less evident in the colonies. Emigration, particularly by means of a free or subsidised passage, was still seen as the last resort of the desperate and not to be contemplated by anyone claiming 'respectability'. If those remarks were made by the matron, they also suggest her ambivalence regarding her role and go some way towards explaining her attitude to her 'charges'.

At one of the many shipboard inquiries she instigated, Davies called the single women present 'London Hooligans' and 'scum of the slums', 'taken from the streets by magistrates and sent to homes'. When the captain, who was conducting the inquiry, told Davies that her language was outrageous and left her open to criminal prosecution, Davies replied, 'it is the truth. I have been slumming, and know what "scum of the slum" means.'[53] Although it's plain that some of the complaints and charges against the matron had been exaggerated, even fabricated, there can be little doubt that Davies had attempted to deal with the single women as if they were inmates of a custodial institution. Her employment background, as an official in women's prisons and in industrial schools, predisposed Davies towards this view.

The changed physical structure and spatial arrangements of the ship which permitted the single women to communicate with the men, crew and male emigrants alike, caused most of the aggravation with the matron. Although some of the charges she brought against individual women related to simple insubordination and disobedience, the majority stemmed from her attempts to police most forms of social exchange between the sexes. Elsie Strachan, for example, and the Welsh sisters Gwen and Daisy Melville Jones, were caught by the matron on the number three deck, the men's domain, after the 10.30 pm curfew. Though they appeared to have been simply indulging in some fairly harmless water play, Davies brought them before the captain and medical officer to have them reminded that their presence on the men's deck was 'strictly against the regulations'.[54] 'Kate Clouton' was accused of 'irregularities with the natives', although it was not the matron who made this charge but other members of the emigrant party. 'Clouton', in fact, was known as 'the matron's spy' and, before this accusation being made, had allegedly been 'taking names for the matron'.[55] On this occasion, 'Clouton' was accused of having been alone in the bakery in the early hours of the morning with the 'native baker'; on another occasion, several emigrants allegedly saw her under the port ladder with a 'native'.[56] The steward Suffolk reported that 'I saw the native standing against the natives' door, and he had his arms on her shoulder, her clothing was not in a fit state; it was drawn up above her knees. I saw nothing wrong with the baker's clothing'.[57]

As well, sub-matron Mrs Russell and the ship's constable Smith, who were both antagonistic to matron Davies, had apparently caught the couple 'in the act'.[58] In the absence of any more concrete evidence of 'immoral conduct', however, the charge against 'Clouton' was dismissed, although she was cautioned not to repeat her indiscreet behaviour of going to the galley before regular hours.

Contact between the single women and the 'natives', the Lascar seamen, was not a particularly contentious issue while the *Jumna* was at sea. Once the vessel docked in Brisbane, however, the passage caught the attention of the press. Seizing upon the most titillating aspects of the passage the press were remorseless in playing up allegations of 'bad behaviour', to that extent that Annie Watson, one of the single women called as a witness before the inquiry, made a public protest. Calling for better treatment by the press, she declared that the way the single women were presented was so unsavoury that people would not employ them. She and her shipmates had even been followed in the streets by local youths and treated to remarks such as, 'Let us black our faces; we will have more show as lascars'. As 'friendless girls, in a strange land', Watson felt the immigrants from the *Jumna* deserved protection against treatment of that kind.[59]

Certainly the presence on board of Lascar seamen was not unusual and, except for the 'Kate Clouton' incident and a few references to the 'girls larking with the darkies', it attracted no other adverse comment.[60] In fact, when questioned in general terms about the employment of 'coloured crew', the captain said it was preferable, since such a crew was more amenable to discipline and susceptible to control. The Lascar seamen 'knew their place' and that seems to have included knowing where they were expected to stand in relation to white women.

There was other evidence of racism on board. One of the passengers, a Mrs Sing, was constantly serenaded by the girls with songs such as 'Chinky Chinky Chinaman', and the Irish girls complained that the Melville Jones sisters, amongst others, had referred to them as the 'dirty Irish'. While the matron agreed that this was offensive and cause for further complaint against the Jones girls and their clique, this was of no account to the inquiry.

In fact the board of immigration intended to keep the whole issue as low key as possible. Davies had clearly experienced some disrespect, but the board ultimately felt that she had brought much of the trouble on herself. Her understanding of her duty was at fault. 'It was impossible, under the conditions she had to contend with on the "Jumna", to fully perform her duties as matron as understood by her', concluded the board; therefore they agreed she was 'unwise' in permitting her view of her own responsibilities to prevail. She ought, they concluded, simply to have let things pass and quietly recorded her impressions of unsatisfactory shipboard conditions for the benefit of the immigration agent in Brisbane.[61]

Ever mindful of public perceptions, the inquiry recorded nothing reprehensible about the behaviour of the single women, nor the other emigrants:

> The conduct of the people while on board the 'Jumna' appears on the whole, with the exceptions indicated, to have been good. There was, however, some immorality and indiscreet conduct in isolated cases; but, under the conditions of an ordinary passenger ship such as the 'Jumna' in effect was, matters were certainly no worse than might have been expected.[62]

No worse than might have been expected? Gone was the notion of the single emigrant woman as one requiring close attention, even policing, for the good of her morality and the colonies. In its place was the recognition that women who undertook such a passage did so as independent agents and as such,

deserved some autonomy on board ship. Any idea of the shipboard passage as a time of self-improvement, contemplation and
quiet reflection, a necessary hiatus between the old life and the
new, was fast vanishing by the 1890s. Still evident in the doctrine
of protection espoused and practised by Ellen Joyce in the immigration programmes conducted for the Western Australian
government that decade, its absence was apparent in the new
Queensland system.

Conditions of passage were fundamental to that shift. As well
as the physical changes already mentioned, such as the existence
of the open bar, the abandonment of physical barriers between
the sexes, the mutual deck, and the easy fraternisation between
male and female travellers, shipboard discipline and routines
too had altered. Certainly emigrants still slept in 'quarters', separated on the basis of sex and marital status into the categories
'single women', 'single and married men', 'married women and
children'. The British India steamers which had monopolised
the carriage of emigrants to Queensland since the early 1880s
were still 'dual purpose' vessels, carrying emigrants on the passage to Queensland and cargo back to Britain. While most vessels
had some permanent cabin-class accommodation for wealthier
travellers, emigrants still travelled in quarters fitted out on a
temporary basis, with screens disposed of in port to make way
for the easy carriage of cargo.[63] However, emigrants were no
longer divided into watches or messes, each with its constable,
each responsible for preparation of its own food, keeping their
own quarters clean, participating in shipboard rituals such as
holystoning the decks or scrubbing the latrines. By the turn of
the century, passenger vessels such as the *Jumna* carried an
army of stewards to undertake such cleaning and catering duties.
Roll call was no longer conducted, and the emigrants were in
effect free agents from dawn till well after dusk. By 1900, the
passage to the colonies had taken on much of the aura of the
modern cruise, with shipboard flirtation and harmless romance
a part of that.

What did concern the inquiry was how Queensland's newly
revived system of emigration would be viewed by both Queens-

land residents and prospective emigrants in Britain. If they had long memories, members of the Board would have been aware that Queensland, of all the colonies, had suffered the most from adverse publicity resulting from poor conditions of passage, scandals in the Agent-General's office in London in the 1870s, rorts associated with abuses of the land grant system in the 1860s and a generally unsavoury reputation. Now the Board sought to eliminate any further public damage which might be caused by the inquiry. The chief danger lay in the threat to the nomination system:

> Probably a large proportion of those residents in the colony who nominate friends from Europe are under the impression that every single female they send for will come out under the strong protection of a legal representative of the Queensland Government on board the ship, while, in fact, no such protection exists under the conditions now regulating the introduction of immigrants to Queensland.[64]

Here are expressed the real concerns of the representatives of the colonial State: fears for the continued working of the nomination system, that cheap and effective source of stable settlers, not fear for the well-being of immigrant women, their morality or the morality of colonial homes. The cost of supporting the 'fruits of immorality' was a consideration, with the Board advising a more rigorous medical examination to screen out pregnant women who '[burden] the institutions of the colony'; but the less tangible 'immorality' of some of the *Jumna*'s women was, by 1900, no longer a source of concern.[65]

Ultimately the Board of Inquiry found that, though the matron had shown a lack of discretion in her treatment of her charges, she had been greatly provoked. It also found that her situation had made it quite impossible for her to fulfil her duties as matron, as she had understood them. The impression gained, however, was that the conduct of some of the young women was ultimately really objectionable only to the matron. While it was clear that the behaviour of two or three of the women had been unacceptable even by the inquiry's standards, the majority of the matron's allegations of misconduct were dismissed as high spirits, with the inquiry concurring with the views of one witness, G. Ryland MLA, that they were 'a good lot of girls ... [although] there were evidently exceptions'.[66]

The matron's understanding of the level of protection expected by the immigration authorities and required for the single women was certainly not shared by the women emigrants themselves, and was increasingly at odds with the government's. The evidence which emerged at the inquiry revealed how very lax was the system of control on board compared with that on earlier vessels, with the Immigration Board finding that 'every respectable person connected with a passenger ship would much prefer the old system'.[67] This was explicitly related to a concern with public perception of government responsibility and the damaging consequences of bad publicity for the government's immigration programme. Anxiety about protecting the single women was secondary.[68] The Board's final recommendation was a return to the old days, with the single women isolated from the rest of the passengers, separate accommodation and deck space marked off by a barrier, and communication between crew and single women forbidden.[69] However, within a year or two, with the decline in the numbers migrating to the State, the Queensland government ceased using matrons altogether.

The *Jumna* inquiry, with its detailed interrogation of shipboard conditions, provides an unrivalled insight into shipboard arrangements at the end of the century; but it also stands as testament to changing attitudes towards protection. Shipboard practices pursued by Queensland in the 1890s indicate a significant reassessment of the needs of single women immigrants. A more liberal understanding of the responsibilities and capacities of single migrant women was in the process of being born. By the end of the century, some government authorities no longer believed in the need for protection, considering that single women could protect themselves quite adequately. In this final round of the symbolic battle over protected emigration, disciplinary arrangements were thrown overboard, and the emigrant ship underwent a spatial revolution. While the Queensland emigration authorities were in the vanguard of change, organisations such as the BWEA continued to lobby for the protection of single emigrant women into the new century. Some twenty years later though, even Ellen Joyce could write that 'the modern girl is far better able to take care of herself than her grandmother was'.[70] The abandonment of the old system of protected emigration on the Queensland run heralded the beginning of widespread acceptance of that view.

A Compromise with Conscience

ARRIVAL IN THE colony was, after all, the whole point of the emigration exercise. It was far more than just the moment. The rites of that passage, indeed the whole transition from 'emigrant' through 'immigrant' to 'colonial', continued for some time. And like the shipboard passage now complete, the process of arriving was mediated by outsiders: employers; middle-class women in their shifting roles of philanthropists and employers; and colonial government agents. Long after arrival, relations with people such as these continued to affect an immigrant's experience.

The experience of arrival changed, of course, with time and circumstance. Convict women could anticipate a rowdy welcoming committee of single men, including dock workers and militia, eager to participate in the spectacle of assessing the prospective sexual talent. Later that century, the arrival and the hiring out of single female immigrants still represented something part way between a spectator sport and a meat market. In the 1880s, the wife of the Governor of New South Wales wanted to watch the proceedings when the newly-arrived immigrant women were hired out from the depot, but the immigration officer prevented her. 'She would be shocked by what she would witness', she was told, a rabble of desperate Sydney employers, mostly middle-class and society women, competing for the limited and valuable services of newly-arrived domestics.[1] In

Western Australia a decade later, police were employed to escort the arriving single women from the vessel to the depot and, though the wharf was crowded, male onlookers restricted any expression of emotion to 'three cheers for Old England in good deep voice'.[2] Yet the *Western Mail* still described the hiring process at the Fremantle female immigrant depot as 'not altogether an elevating one', with its suggestion of 'the squatter picking out the best workers from a herd of two-year old cattle'.[3] The scenes had shifted, some of the cast was new, but many aspects of the drama of arrival and reception remained familiar.

Under colonial immigration schemes, the idea was that immigrant women would enter domestic service as soon as possible, an arrangement which equally suited employers seeking servants and colonial governments footing the bill for immigrant board and lodging. Immigrant women were also generally anxious to resume employment after weeks or months without an income although their interests did not always match up with those of colonial governments and employers. Nor did passing out of the government's hands mean an end to government involvement in their lives.

Reception arrangements differed from colony to colony, and from time to time. In some colonies, such as South Australia, or in Queensland from the late 1880s, assisted men and their families were received into an immigrants' depot or had accommodation provided after they disembarked. Elsewhere, in New South Wales for instance, they could remain on board the vessel during what was called its 'lay days', the time taken for unloading and refitting. This could be anything up to ten days. In most cases, single and married men were responsible for finding their own employment after arrival. For single women, however, the situation was different. Caroline Chisholm's work with single immigrant women in New South Wales decades earlier had heralded the provision of some form of accommodation for single female immigrants in all the Australian colonies.[4] By the 1860s, government reception facilities for women ranged from temporary accommodation in boarding houses to the stability of Sydney's Hyde Park Barracks, the place Chisholm herself had seen established as an immigrant reception home. Women who had no family in the colonies to receive them went directly from these various reception centres to the homes of their first colonial employer. That step was also taken under the eye and sometimes the hand of government immigration authorities.

Reception homes and depots were only intended as a temporary shelter, a transition between the passage out and colonial employment. The process of overseeing the reception of single women and their passage into domestic service was taken on eagerly by colonial women and, under female care, some of these temporary shelters became more welcoming, but they were not designed to encourage new arrivals to linger. One woman wrote of the Sydney depot in 1857, 'We arrived to the Depot about twelve oclock and such a miserable place it is'; another wrote, 'we are not allowed to go out side the doors, and we are like so many prisoners caged in'.[5] In some cases, the women were as physically contained there as they had been on board ship. Although reception strategies gradually mellowed with time, the perception that the depots were prisons and immigrant women inmates confined within their doors remained strong amongst the women concerned throughout much of the period. Surgeon-superintendent Douglas Darbyshire, describing the arrival of the women from the SS *Cornwall* at the Fremantle depot in 1898, reached the same conclusion. The women's arrival was accompanied by a great unlocking of doors and, as he recorded in his journal, 'all this turning of keys was horribly suggestive of gaol,' a fact which cannot have escaped the women.[6]

The Fremantle depot was an old and rather decrepit building frequently targeted by vandals. In the 1890s it was still customary to have a policeman stationed outside night and day, although whether his task was to keep people out or in is not entirely clear. In 1894, the caretaker T. McCarthy reported that 'the Glass was broken by some unknown Mischievous persons throwing stones at the Windows. But the sashes are old and rotten from fare [sic] wear'.[7] The depot's defences in fact offered no real barrier to women who wished to explore their new terrain, and sometimes the attendant police officer was as likely to collude as deter. After the arrival of the *Port Pirie* in July 1894, immigrants Lizzie Curry, Minnie Egan and Esther Hodgkinson all managed to escape one evening by climbing over the balcony and then scaling the wall to the Barrack Field. They were spotted by the assistant ship's matron Edith Dransfield, herself an immigrant, but the constable on duty insisted he had not seen them and did not report the incident until shipboard matron Mary Monk heard of it the following morning.[8] Two days later, the same three women accompanied by Martha Blanks, Selina Barrett and Rebecca Stiff were all absent from the eight o'clock roll call and did not return until after midnight. No action was taken, however, for all six had found employment, which was, after all, the government's major rationale for enforcing a strict depot policy.[9]

Regulations issued for the Perth immigrant depot in the 1870s, when a full programme of immigration was in operation, detail the strict segregation of the single women from all other immigrants and families, under a government-appointed matron. They also stipulate other aspects of depot life. The food supplied was fairly standard institutional fare in its range and quantity: 18 ounces of bread, 12 ounces of meat and a pound of potatoes daily; tea, sugar, treacle and salt, and a weekly half pound of soap. Immigrants were roused at 5.30 each summer's morning, an hour earlier than in winter, to clean the depot and air their bedding. Men and women alike were permitted to leave the depot but had to be available between 7am and 1pm to meet prospective employers, and they had to attend roll call four times a day. Single women had to be back at the depot by 6pm; an extra hour and a half liberty was permitted the others. Swearing, indecent conversation and gambling were strictly prohibited, and conduct was to be 'orderly and submissive'.[10] By the 1890s, regulations were if anything a little stricter, with Maggie Kelly reporting of her time in the Fremantle depot, 'We're not to go out until we've got a situation', although conditions otherwise seemed much the same.[11]

In earlier decades, Queensland provided the worst reception facilities in Australia, although the colony's standards were certainly not unique.[12] Writing home to friends in 1862, Isabella Maugham described the government depot in Brisbane:

> not as good as a barn, no windows in it, neither was it floored, merely the bare ground. It had two large doors, and contained two tables and forms, there were 32 beds for 132 girls, but the worst of it was they drove us in like so many cattle and locked us up.[13]

In the same year, Rosamond Smith described the Brisbane depot as dismal and prison-like, with its sparse furnishings and iron-barred windows. Though food was provided—a pound of beef, half a loaf of bread, and tea and sugar daily—it was as monotonous as shipboard diet and equally lacking in fresh fruit and vegetables. Nor were there cooking utensils or stoves; nor washing facilities, another great hardship after months on board ship. Rosamond Smith, like Isabella Maugham, was an impoverished educated woman who had travelled to Brisbane as a government emigrant to enter domestic service. She too wrote home in disgust:

> I believe in prisons the inmates are trusted with things necessary for feeding and keeping themselves clean, and we ought not to be used worse than thieves; but I suppose the Government considers that in giving us a free passage it buys and pays for us and has a right to do as it pleases with us.[14]

Many colonists, including government officials, shared a similar view of immigrant women and resented any assertion of their independent rights. In the 1850s, some of the single women shipped out to Adelaide by the CLEC then sent up country to the Willunga depot when Adelaide people could not employ them, took a stronger line than writing letters of complaint. The local police officer wrote:

> This morning Mr. Kell, as usual, in visiting the Female Immigrant Depot, was repulsed by the females from the place; in consequence of which he called upon me for assistance, which was rendered, and, by great coolness and perseverance, order was restored.

> In the event of any of the girls being apprehended should
> the same occur again, I do not know the result, they are such
> a determined lot. The occasion of it, as far as I can ascertain,
> was Mr. Kell's interference with the girls for visiting those
> who had left for service; also, fearing they might fall in with
> improper company.[15]

The reception system was intended to prevent such displays of
unwonted autonomy and was usually much more successful.

In 1865 colonial visitor Maria Rye, who had been instrumental that decade in the emigration of women such as Rosamond
Smith and Isabella Maugham, launched a further attack on
Queensland reception facilities. By this stage her interests had
shifted more directly to the emigration of working-class women.
Fresh from New Zealand where she had highlighted the inade-
quacies of reception facilities in Dunedin and Christchurch, she
was equally outraged to find that in the Brisbane immigrant
barracks 'the girls, women and children sleep on the floor without any blankets, and if they find that too hard, they can have
iron bedsteads without any pillows or mattrasses [sic]!!'[16] While
the Queensland authorities defended their arrangements, pointing out that immigrants were provided with bedding for the
passage which should be used at the depot on arrival, few
women had time to take their ship bedding with them to the
immigrant barracks, even if it were worth the carriage. Lousy
and worse after three months at sea, most of it was consigned to
the waters at the dock.[17]

Rye brought with her to Queensland a reputation for being
hard to please, and there is no doubt that some of the complaints she made about immigrant facilities were exaggerated.
But in this case other testimony supported her. As late as 1884,
the Queensland government's own emigration lecturer, George
Randall, commented on the continuing unsatisfactory state of
the Brisbane depot, describing the mattresses—now on the
floor—as 'beggarly in the extreme'.[18] Not until the late 1880s
was an adequate depot established in Brisbane.[19] By this stage
the privately managed Lady Musgrave Lodge served as alternative accommodation for governesses and women with any

means coming out to relatives. But this establishment received no government subsidy. Government immigrants and working-class women could not stay there free of charge so were effectively excluded.[20]

Where other colonial governments provided a different style of facility, as in South Australia or Tasmania, this usually resulted from the efforts of local women. Although colonial governments sometimes found their seemingly benevolent maternal concern a nuisance, leading as it frequently did to criticism of spartan government facilities, they were usually happy to allow middle-class women to soften the rough bureaucratic edge of government reception. There is no doubt though that for the immigrant women involved, 'benevolent maternalism' also meant increased interference in their activities and lives.

In 1862, a committee of middle-class Adelaide women led by Mrs Caroline Gawler had established a servants' home to receive single women arriving under the new government assistance programme.[21] Until South Australia withdrew the offer of assistance in the 1880s Gawler and her Ladies' Committee, members of Adelaide's gentry, saw their role as exercising physical and moral supervision over the single women who passed through the Adelaide Servants' Home. This was part of the broader responsibility they assumed for influencing the implementation of female migration policy.[22] For the government, of course, leaving the care of single women in private hands relieved them of a significant and heavy responsibility and over this period there were evidently few complaints made about the quality of care provided through the Home, either from the women who stayed there or from employers. In fact in 1877, emigration lecturer Reverend John Thorne pointed out before a South Australian Select Committee on immigration that the private institution could offer single women a friendliness and sympathy which he doubted they would find under official management.[23]

In Tasmania in the 1850s and early 1860s, middle-class women successfully pressed the government for funds to purchase a building as a home and employment agency for immigrant domestics.[24] In the late 1850s, when parties of immigrant women began to arrive regularly in Hobart and Launceston, the government had accepted responsibility for the women's accommodation until they entered service. Both the Hobart and Launceston depots closed down in 1858 when immigrant couples and families stopped arriving, but the Board of Immigration opened temporary depots as parties of immigrant women arrived.[25] Middle-class women, who had traditionally dealt with the 'out of place' or unemployed servant forced onto the streets, recognised that the needs of single immigrant women went well beyond accommodation on first arriving. Domestic service was a live-in occupation; as a consequence, unemployment almost invariably meant homelessness for single women far from friends and relatives. In 1856 a servants' home was established in a rented house in Argyle Street, Hobart, at the instigation of Mrs Crouch of the Society of Friends.[26] Run by a committee of fourteen ladies with an executive committee of gentlemen, it provided 'temporary residence for female domestic servants and other unprotected females of character'. The home also served as a servant registry.[27]

Two years later, the committee launched an appeal for funds to buy a suitable home to meet the needs of domestic servants, now almost synonymous with single immigrant women. In its petition to the governor requesting funds, the Home's committee put a convincing case for supporting domestic workers:

There can be only one opinion as to the importance of having good female domestic Servants, and of their influence on the comfort of our homes, the morals of our children, and the prosperity of the general community. And whereas young Females leaving the mother country and their natural guardians, when they arrive in the Colonies, finding themselves friendless, and their high hopes disappointed; and sometimes proving incompetent for situations so different from their former occupations, too often become the victims of the designing and depraved, and sink into poverty and vice: Your Petitioners, therefore, are deeply impressed with the conviction, that a Lodging House, or Home, for the

accommodation of female domestic Servants, is greatly needed in this city.[28]

The government gave £500, matching the amount raised by
public subscription, and the committee opened a Home in a
central position in Murray Street, Hobart, with room to house
twenty-two women.[29] The job description of the matron Mrs
Tillard, formerly a matron from the female immigrant vessel the
Constance, included acting as 'a friend' to the servants in residence, and members of the ladies' committee offered them
'sympathy and counsel, and, when necessary ... more direct
influence and protection'.[30] The ladies also devised a system of
incentives: certificates of good character for time spent in the
Home; rewards for 'perseverance' for those who remained in
service with a family for twelve months; and a 'useful household article' upon marriage after good service.[31]

The path which middle-class women thought appropriate for
domestics, from steady service to marriage, was clearly mapped
out through the Home. Its rules and its structures, with rooms
for teaching domestic duties, the matron as figure of kindly
authority, the friendly offices of benevolent community figures,
all served to direct servants towards the values thought proper
for them within middle-class colonial society. The Home was
not a charitable institution and women were expected to pay for
their residence. However, servants of 'good character' but no
means could stay there on condition they earned their keep
working as housemaids. The additional cost was further loss of
liberty; such women were not allowed to go out in the evening,
as could those who paid for their board.[32] Application, deference, early rising and the realisation that acceptance of charity
implied a corresponding obligation, were all lessons taught
through the Hobart Servants' Home.

In colonies where they were active, ladies' committees also
enabled governments to shed some of the cost associated with
immigrant 'failure'. Help could often be obtained privately for
destitute or 'reprobate' immigrants. However, although colonial
governments were willing and quick to make use of this back-

up, the attitudes of colonial officers and of ladies' committees towards discipline and punishment were often poles apart. In Tasmania in 1860, for example, one of the single women from the notorious *Isles of the South*, general servant Elizabeth Dryden, had become an inmate of the Penitents' Home. The Servants' Home refused to accommodate women the ladies' committee considered 'not of good character'; and in the Penitents' Home as well, Dryden had been labelled a bad influence on the other 'penitents'.[33] Lady Young, wife of the Governor and mainstay of the ladies' committee, raised the question of Dryden's future with the government. The Colonial Secretary's response was that 'a little wholesome restraint' would be beneficial. His idea was that she should be dismissed from the Penitents' Home then immediately arrested as a vagrant with no visible means of support. After a few months' sojourn in prison, under the watchful eye of the Cascades matron, she could then return to the Penitents' Home while a job was found for her. 'Her experience of prison discipline, and the prospect of its repetition, would no doubt bear some weight in urging her to pursue a more creditable course in future', he argued.[34] The ladies' committee disagreed with the Colonial Secretary's assessment of the value of wholesome prison discipline, and the Immigration Board finally agreed to defray the cost of Dryden's accommodation while the committee obtained a position for her.[35]

As well as making government reception facilities more extensive and probably more physically comfortable, the involvement of middle-class women also reinforced the patterns of isolation, protection and surveillance established on board ship. Like shipboard matrons, matrons at the colonial homes retained responsibility for moral supervision and domestic instruction. Particularly in the Tasmanian and South Australian homes, preparing immigrant women for paid employment was an important by-product of the extended system of protection.

In other colonies, middle-class women were less involved in the process of reception, even in the 1860s and 1870s when government assistance was at its height. By the 1880s though, with the establishment of colonial branches of the GFS and the YWCA, the reception needs of single immigrant women attracted renewed local attention.[36] The YWCA's concern with female immigrants was manifest in its travellers' aid work. In Britain, the Travellers' Aid Society emerged in 1885 as a joint initiative of the YWCA and another group headed by feminist Louisa Hubbard, publisher of *Work and Leisure*. Evolving from an initial concern with young women and girls at London stations, 'travellers' aid' soon encompassed a more general role of warning and protecting young women travelling to foreign and colonial ports.[37] In the Australian colonies, travellers' aid work commenced in most colonies after assisted female immigration had generally ceased.[38] In Queensland, where government immigration schemes were at their most ambitious during the 1880s, travellers' aid work was not established until 1903.[39] So in that colony in the 1880s and 1890s the YWCA concentrated on providing the type of reception facilities for private immigrants —generally middle-class women—which governments made available to assisted immigrants.

The GFS played a much more significant role in working-class migration. From 1883, stimulated by the opening of its own Emigration Department in Britain, the GFS became actively involved in colonial reception arrangements. Ellen Joyce was the GFS's first emigration representative and from that point dates her close engagement with the emigration of single women to Australia. Sometimes at the request of the organisation in Britain and sometimes spontaneously, local GFS branches gradually introduced a system of meeting their members from immigrant vessels.[40]

In the GFS hierarchy, working-class girls or young women were 'members', and each one had an 'associate', a middle-class woman and a member of the Church of England, who took some personal responsibility for her.[41] In tandem with the British organisation, the colonial GFS appointed immigration 'associates' to whom migrating GFS 'members' could be commended by their associates in Britain. 'Commendation' was an important part of the GFS organisation in Britain, with its emphasis on protecting the purity of its members and with its relatively mobile membership consisting largely of domestic servants. It involved passing a member's name and personal details between associates, as the member moved from one employer to another. Single female immigrants were simply seen as domestic servants in transit and therefore needing protection. They readily fitted the pattern of the itinerant GFS member.

From Britain, Joyce envisaged the establishment of a system of empire-wide commendation of GFS emigrants, and in 1884 she broached the subject with each Australian colonial GFS.[42] Implementing her commendation model, however, was not straightforward. In Queensland, where an ambitious government immigration programme was then underway, there were two particular difficulties. Many emigrating GFS members responded very negatively to the activities of the colonial GFS. And some colonial GFS associates themselves resented Joyce's demands, seeing them as beyond their capabilities and responsibilities.

For some young women, finding the GFS in the colony was a great boon, providing a link both with 'home' and with other immigrant women also working in the isolation of domestic employment. Others though were no longer prepared to respond to the patterns and bonds of relationships they'd left behind in Britain. The GFS system in Britain in the late nineteenth century had developed most effectively in country areas where the relations of obligation, duty and deference on which the system was based were stronger and more intact than in the towns.[43] For that reason selection agents were encouraged to recruit domestics from rural settings. In urban Britain, rapid population growth and a geographically mobile population made sustaining philanthropic relations extremely difficult, and the ties of duty were even looser in the towns and cities of the colonies.[44] In the colonies, middle-class women who sought to establish similar duty-based relations with female immigrants also found them a highly unresponsive group. Once removed by half a world or more from the nurturing closeness of the GFS associate/

member relationship and its idealised village setting, many GFS members declined to recognise any need for GFS care. The protection of the society became distinctly unwelcome.

Not all assistance was rejected. One young woman emigrant wrote back to the GFS in Britain, after her passage to Queensland, 'I must thank you very much for getting me to join the G.F.S., it has made so many kind friends for us out here'.[45] Another wrote of the founder of the Queensland GFS, Mrs Glennie:

> I can never forget her kindness ... I do not know what we should have done had we not joined the G.F.S. Little I thought when I was at home that it would have been such a help to us. We cannot but feel ever thankful to you for all your trouble with us.[46]

But comments recorded by GFS workers in the colony often told a different tale, of reluctant GFS emigrant members declining to contact colonial associates.[47] The annual meeting of the Brisbane GFS learnt in 1890 that, despite the efforts of two immigration associates who visited the immigrant depot on the arrival of every vessel and asked GFS members to contact Vice-President Lady O'Connell, many did not bother.[48] The local press also reported a general lack of interest in organisations such as the GFS: 'In many cases they never attend the classes held for their instruction and amusement, nor in any way report themselves to the society during the year'.[49] And in its annual report for 1892–1893, the Brisbane GFS expressed bewilderment that 'girls don't attend the meetings and seem careless whether they remain members of the Society or not ... This apathy amongst the girls is not to be accounted for'.[50]

Whether one called it disloyalty or laziness (the terms associates most often applied to reluctant GFS members), immigrant arrivals were frequently completely indifferent to the colonial organisation and its expectations about their behaviour as prospective employees, the basis of the GFS associate/member relationship.

Although few records remain of the other side of this relationship, it's not difficult to guess at the reasons. One account—the edited reminiscences of immigrant Agnes Stokes—is telling. Stokes herself was not a GFS member but her former mistress at the 'Great House' in England wrote to Mrs Glennie in Brisbane requesting that she keep an eye on young Agnes after her arrival: in effect, 'commending' her to Glennie.[51] Stokes recorded: 'Mrs Glennie was determined to get me into the Girls' Friendly Society but I was just as determined not to go ... Here I'd got away from all my relations and from people giving me advice and I didn't want it starting again'.[52] Immigrant women had taken the greatest step in their lives in coming out to the colonies so it was hardly surprising that they wished to preserve the independence which had impelled them to make that move in the first place. As colonial associates soon realised, 'girls will *not* be dictated to by the Associate on landing but choose their own way & go or not as they please'.[53]

Immigrant 'intransigence' was not the only difficulty. In the late 1870s Queensland had commenced a massive programme of assistance, with more than twenty thousand single women disembarking at ports along the coastline between 1879 and 1888.[54] Keeping track of hundreds of GFS immigrants would have been hard enough but, in combination with a government policy of relative indifference towards most questions of reception, the Queensland GFS found Ellen Joyce's notion of empire-wide commendation impossible. Her efforts to promote emigration were appreciated but 'her views ... [were] rather too formidable for an infant Society such as ours'. Brisbane associates also objected to her making the GFS 'a kind of stepping stone to help friendless girls who are sent out under the protection of the Society, but who are *not* members'.[55] It was not usual practice to extend the GFS umbrella to women who had not become members and Joyce's conflation of her roles in the GFS Emigration Department and the BWEA was resented.

In Victoria, South Australia and Tasmania, government-assisted immigration of single women had ceased by the early

1880s. Consequently the demands made upon the women of the local GFS were less taxing than in Queensland and New South Wales, where numbers coming in were still high. In fact, once assistance ceased and the number of GFS members arriving was very small, the most energetic GFS branches saw the trickle of immigrants as an opportunity to build up their membership. In Adelaide, Australia's oldest GFS had been active in meeting immigrants since its foundation in 1879, establishing an employment registry for GFS servants and appointing an associate to go to the Servants' Home on the arrival of immigrants, to recruit 'such girls as the Matron can give good characters to' to induce them to join the GFS.[56] Middle-class Adelaide women who had traditionally supervised government reception arrangements became the foundation associates of the GFS, and saw immigrants as a fertile source of GFS recruits rather than a burden. On board the *Cicero*, which arrived in Adelaide in early 1883 as assisted immigration was winding down, were four commended GFS members, and a further fifteen put down their names as 'candidates' or prospective members after a GFS recruiting drive.[57] Once assisted immigration ceased, Adelaide's middle-class women continued to support individual immigrants through the GFS. Similarly in Victoria, though the local GFS declined 'to step beyond their province, and to constitute themselves an Emigration Society', they hoped 'to protect and help, amid the dangers and temptations of a new and untried life, those who emigrate to Victoria.'[58] They opened a GFS Lodge in rooms at 38 Russell Street in Melbourne in 1885.[59] However, the Victorian society maintained its exclusiveness; it did not receive non-GFS immigrants, women not sent out through the English emigration correspondent or any who did not travel under a 'suitable' matron.[60]

There was another problem: the sometimes contradictory roles of the colonial GFS in *caring* for immigrant women and in *employing* them. It was to prove fatal to GFS emigration work in New South Wales. Women in Britain understood protection as primarily to benefit single women emigrants themselves; yet for middle-class colonial women, protecting immigrant women also meant protecting their own prospective employees. The work was unavoidably self-serving. After some protracted public debate on the activities of Sydney philanthropists in 1885, the *Daily Telegraph* encapsulated this dilemma:

> That philanthropy alone can account for the time directed to it by certain leisured ladies is … undoubted. But in dealing with domestic servants it is very difficult to believe that many of the [philanthropic women] are not biased by their own and their friends' household troubles. The compromise with conscience in this matter is so easy, seems to be so shadowy, that it may be often almost or altogether unconsciously made.[61]

Colonial rules permitted GFS members commended to the colony to be received by local associates. These middle-class women would then find employment for the new arrivals with 'respectable' families, or else place them in temporary lodgings. The Victorian GFS, for example, followed this practice in the 1880s, when government-assisted immigration and reception facilities had long been withdrawn.[62] In this case, the GFS was effectively acting as an employment bureau for its own members and associates; but this did not involve government immigrants or colonial money. In New South Wales, GFS associates similarly used their relationship with the colonial government to redefine 'respectable' households as 'GFS' households; but this took place when government immigration was in full swing. Consequently their activities brought the GFS into conflict with both the government and other middle-class employers of servants, at a time when demand for domestic servants was intense. Though no whisper of the episode appears in GFS records and archives, it received enormous coverage in the press and must surely be one of the biggest scandals in Australian GFS history. 'Women's work for women' could mask self-interest along class lines, manifest in this case in the efforts of middle-class women as employers to promote their own access to a valuable and limited supply of domestic labour.

New South Wales' GFS Department for Immigration was organised in March 1884, at a time when many assisted single women were arriving, and Mrs Annie Gordon, founder of the

New South Wales GFS, immediately sought an opportunity to formalise the GFS role in introducing immigrant domestics. The offer was gratefully accepted.[63] Following her representations, New South Wales Premier and Colonial Secretary Alexander Stuart wrote in June 1884:

> I am anxious to take advantage of any organization which may present itself with a view of obtaining good and efficient young women of [the domestic servant] class . . . The objects of this Society are I understand, to afford some moral control and advice to girls in service . . . As by their organization they appear to be able to hold out inducements for young women to come to the colony in domestic service, I gladly avail myself of their help.[64]

In the 1870s and 1880s, single women migrated to New South Wales under both selection and nomination schemes. Both involved the payment of £2, either by selected young women themselves, or by their nominating friends or relatives. All assisted single women travelled out together under a government-appointed matron. On disembarking, they were immediately taken to the Hyde Park Depot. Hiring day was held at the depot on the second or third day after a vessel's arrival, but only those single women who wished to find employment were obliged to attend. Nominated women, most of whom ultimately went to their friends, and selected women who had paid their own deposit but also intended spending time with friends or relatives, formed the great majority of the female immigrants. The government's expectation was that these women would eventually enter domestic service, so they were not compelled to hire out immediately on arrival, as was sometimes the case in other colonies. But as a consequence, relatively few single women were available for hire from the depot. Between January 1884 and May 1885, nearly 2000 single female immigrants arrived in the colony but, to the consternation of the employing public, less than one-third were willing to go straight into employment.[65]

Competition for the available domestic servants was fierce. Only prospective employers certified as 'respectable' after applying to the immigration office, and sometimes even paying an attendance fee, could attend hiring day.[66] Further, in accordance with long-established practice, single women were virtually isolated before hiring day. The only contact they had with the outside world was through lady missionary visitors—the Sisters of Charity who visited the Roman Catholics and, after 1878, the members of the Ladies United Evangelical Association and the Church of England who visited the Anglicans and the Primitive Methodists[67]—and they were particularly instructed to be 'most careful not to confer with the Female Immigrants either directly or indirectly as to the engagement which they should make as Domestic Servants on the day fixed for hiring day. Otherwise the Public will have just reason to complain'.[68]

Complaints had already been made. A *Sydney Morning Herald* correspondent 'lured' to the depot one hiring day in October 1877, in fierce pursuit of one of just fifteen immigrants advertised for hire, found that most of the selected women would only hire out with friends or relatives. The disappointed applicant, aware that the nominated women had already gone to their friends, objected to these selected women choosing to work for relatives who had not paid a deposit. The fact that four of the domestics were already earmarked for the Bishop of Bathurst required no further comment, suggested the writer, who strongly objected to being dragged into town on a fruitless errand.[69]

We need this backdrop of intense and unsatisfied demand to understand the public's extraordinary response to the activities of the Sydney GFS. GFS women attempted to take charge of GFS members commended to them from Britain, and their efforts met with almost hysterical resistance from other would-be employers. In April 1885 the matter came to a head in the press. Despite the confusion of the press debate, the crux of the matter was ultimately simple. Although Premier Stuart had advised the GFS in England that women *nominated* by that body could be despatched to the charge of GFS associates, the GFS had not paid the £2 deposit required to nominate emigrants.[70] The young GFS women in question were in fact *selected* women who had paid their own deposits. Nominating the women and paying the £2 deposit would have given the Sydney GFS some moral claim to the women's services, though nomination did not amount to indentured or contracted employment. And further, even selected women were free to join friends or relatives in the colony and any of the young women who wished to do so could have gone to the GFS. However, the New South Wales GFS clearly considered it had a right to monopolise the small stream of GFS women arriving in the colony. Annie Gordon went so far as to write to the women at the depot, ordering them not to attend hiring day but to wait until a GFS associate came to collect them. 'This is what you *ought* to do, in accordance with the wishes of your associate', she wrote, in a straightforward appeal to the qualities of duty and obedience on which the GFS relationship was based.[71] Unfortunately for the GFS her letters were intercepted and ended up in the hands of the press.

The public soon realised that the GFS was 'interfering' even further, by following up non-GFS domestics in their new employers' homes.[72] Female immigrants were notoriously 'unsettled' after arrival, to use the contemporary term, and it was quite usual for them (depending on the colony's master and servant laws and their terms of engagement) to remain only briefly in their first situation. Employers objected strongly to the GFS exploiting this uncertainty by 'enticing' young women to join the GFS and subsequently take positions in GFS households. In fact in Britain, GFS associates were not permitted to encourage young women to join the GFS without first obtaining the permission of their employers.[73] As 'Sydneyite' wrote to the *Sydney Morning Herald* in mid-1885:

> The sole desire of the ladies forming the committee of the G.F.S. is to provide servants for themselves and their friends without the annoyance of attending the scramble at the hiring-room. Not only do these ladies secure the immigrants on arrival in the colony, but invite others they meet else-

where to join . . . This is a fact which should be made known to show that the society is more for the benefit of the ladies than the girls themselves, at least in this colony.[74]

The GFS denied it had exceeded its role of 'friend' to the immigrants but the press thought otherwise. One *Daily Telegraph* editorial denounced 'petticoat government'; another suggested that 'if the GFS is allowed to continue its immigration operations, it may become necessary to form other societies for the protection of the public against the society in question'.[75] Most correspondents agreed that the GFS existed at the expense of the public, and not for its benefit.

Press interest peaked with the arrival of the SS *Bombay* with another eight GFS members on board, all claimed by Annie Gordon. Two sisters, Agnes and Kate Nicholls, were taken by her from the depot, but when they were advised that one was to go as cook to Mrs Barry, the bishop's wife, they declined. They had hoped for positions together. So Mrs Gordon packed them off to lodgings at the YWCA hostel, Loma House, where they paid eighteen shillings each for board and lodging, before they moved themselves into other lodgings: six shillings a week less, they said, but they were better provided for.[76] At the government depot, they could have lived rent-free until they found work. With the crush of employers passing through the depot clamouring for domestic servants, the well-qualified Nicholls sisters would certainly have found a position together. As it was, after a week without guided access to employers they were unemployed and destitute. Miss Fox, the General Secretary of the YWCA, claimed she had tried and failed to find situations for the Nicholls, but neither Mrs Gordon nor Mrs Barry made any further attempt to contact them.[77]

The press seized on the incident, which seemed to encapsulate all the public's mutterings about GFS behaviour. Quite clearly, the GFS put the well-being of its principals, influential members of the Anglican church, before the well-being of its members. The *Daily Telegraph* produced further evidence of GFS immigrants who had complained of the miserable situations provided for them through the Society, and called on the public to judge. One correspondent wrote:

> Independently of the illegality of the whole transaction, and the wrong to the general public and servant-seeking mistresses in particular, is not a great injury being perpetuated upon freshly-arrived immigrants by this G.F. Society, which assigns them, or consigns them, to situations without consulting the tastes or feelings of the girls themselves?[78]

Such widely-publicised evidence that the welfare of GFS immigrants was not the Society's first priority was the last straw. The GFS told the press that the local Society would receive no more immigrants, and Mrs Joyce and the GFS in Britain were advised not to despatch any more GFS members to New South Wales.[79] Annie Gordon returned to England with her husband soon afterwards.

Other colonies had taken note of what was happening in New South Wales. A year later, as the Western Australian government began to investigate possibilities for a new programme of female immigration, the Board of Immigration warned local GFS women off their patch:

> Immigrant girls are brought out at the expence [sic] of the general public and therefore the general public have the right of engaging them as soon as landed: any private arrangement by which the services of certain girls could be bespoken by ladies before their arrival has many objections and would certainly raise much opposition to the Board— It is therefore the desire of the Board that no engagements should be made for the girls until after they are landed.
>
> Any interest which may be taken by ladies in these girls, should not . . . take any active form until after the public have had the opportunity of engaging them.[80]

As the GFS episode shows, public discontent with government immigration focused upon its failure to meet the demand for domestic servants and seldom on the plight of immigrant women themselves. According to the press, immigrant women were in fact the ultimate winners in the domestic servant market place. This scenario—depot as market, immigrant women as scarce goods for purchase, colonists as desperate bidders—readily lent itself to the view that immigrant domestics could ask and receive whatever level of wages they wished. Such a depiction was common in snide cartoons and caricatures in the press.[81] It was a false image. Through the two tied strategies of isolating new arrivals and forcing them to compete for employment at the government-controlled hiring day, the reception process served both to exclude immigrant domestics from knowledge of the prevailing price of domestic labour and prevented them competing effectively in the local employment market.

For the government, protecting the access of colonial employers to a source of cheap labour was fundamental to protective reception practices. Immigrant women remained largely ignorant of colonial wage levels and conditions until they left the depot with their first colonial employer, but their initial wages were almost invariably lower than those generally paid to local domestic servants. This was despite the fact that the major incentive held out to prospective single female emigrants in Britain was the great demand for domestic servants and the consequent high level of wages. Although doubtless disappointed, immigrant women were compelled by the immigration agent and by the women privately involved in government reception to accept the wages offered. The promise of higher wages some time in the future once they could claim 'colonial experience' was their sop. Small wonder, then, at their 'restlessness', their failure to stay long with their first employer.

It is difficult, perhaps impossible now, to disentangle the level of wages paid to newly-arrived domestics from the level of wages paid outside the depot. Earlier writers acknowledge that immigrant women were occasionally paid less than the prevailing rates but, like colonial government agents, did not consider the problem widespread[82] noting, 'Some experienced colonial workers undoubtedly received higher rates than were usually paid to immigrants, but most of them did not'.[83]

Immigration officials were well aware of the discriminatory wages paid to new arrivals but also preferred not to push the point. In his annual reports throughout the 1860s and 1870s, New South Wales immigration agent George Wise revealed that the wages earned by female immigrants hired from the depot were almost invariably lower than the prevailing market rate, a disparity which he attributed to the immigrant women's in-experience in domestic work.[84] Yet in evidence given in 1880 before the New South Wales Select Committee on assisted mig-ration, Wise failed to admit this. Called to account for the level of wages paid to newly arrived domestics, he preferred to foster the myth that immigrant women set their own wage levels:

(Question) If they were experienced the wages they receive would be very much higher?

(Wise) Anything they ask they usually get.

(Question) Notwithstanding their inexperience?

(Wise) Notwithstanding their inexperience.

(Question) The majority have not been in service before?

(Wise) The majority have not been in service before.[85]

Wise would knowingly reinforce this myth in future years.[86] The fierce competition among prospective employers at hiring day indicates employers were more than ready to overlook colonial inexperience and to employ new arrivals; but clearly a loose agreement existed concerning the price employers assigned to inexperience.

Immigrant ignorance of the existing level of colonial wages also contributed to the low level of wages received. The recep-tion system, of course, had always encouraged this. In 1860, the newly established Queensland government had only recently commenced assisting immigration to the colony and had not yet perfected its system. Before a Select Committee into immigration that year, health officer Dr Hobbs testified that, while no one could visit an immigrant vessel after its arrival, people could talk to single women at the depot. Consequently, newly arrived domestics could speak to local women, find out about prevailing wage rates and even learn the particular merits of individual mistresses. This, Hobbs agreed, was 'prejudicial to the plan'; employers had no chance![87] Hobbs believed that there was no alternative to this system, since immigrant women could not be shut up as though in prison, although he also believed that, unlike single men, they 'should not be allowed to go about the town alone'.[88] In the next two years, however, as the testimony of immigrants Isabella Maugham and Rosamond Smith has already shown, the government depot in Brisbane did adopt the system used elsewhere, of incarceration. Further, Coghlan refers to a list of wages 'which an immigrant could not refuse without forfeiting the right to shelter', posted in a Queensland immigrant depot in 1870.[89] Serious enough for any new arrival, the consequences of being thrown out of the depot were far more daunting for single women than for men.

Similarly in South Australia, the reception system also prevented newly arrived domestic servants from competing for the wages they could command on the open market. In 1877, Caroline Stapley, matron of the Servants' Home, and Caroline Gawler of the Home committee both gave evidence before a Select Committee into immigration that the domestic immigrants in the Home often spoke amongst themselves in 'a light sort of way' of having been misled about the level of wages. It was often difficult, Gawler added, to persuade them to take 'a reasonable offer' of wages. Stapley then explained that, once female immigrants refused 'a reasonable offer', 'we send up to the Commissioner for some one to come and clear them out of the home; and from that time they are watched by one of the Committee ladies and myself, to see that they do not refuse reasonable wages'.[90]

Exaggeration of colonial prospects was a transparent ploy adopted by most British selection agents, widely acknowledged and a surprise to no one but the immigrants. One correspondent wrote to the *West Australian* in 1891: 'When people come 16 000 miles, believing they are to get £4 a month, and then find out that £2 is an outside wage, it is enough to make them indignant'.[91] Equally transparent was the power of the women who ran colonial reception homes to manage the fate of immigrant women. Protecting single women in the depot also enabled those who managed reception to control their movements and their wage levels. While the fine detail remains a matter of speculation, there is no doubt that the wages paid to immigrant domestics were determined by employers in conjunction with immigration officials, and not by immigrant women.

What of the impact of cheap immigrant wages on the existing domestic labour market? Particularly in New South Wales where the anti-immigration campaign was most virulent, working-class opponents of male immigration occasionally honed in on the lower wages received by immigrant women (they were not deceived by press lampoons) in supporting their cause: 'agricultural labourers and domestic servants ... brought in were willing to accept lower rates of wages than those ordinarily demanded'.[92] There is no doubt though, that the reception and controlled hiring arrangements to which immigrant women were subjected, rather than any 'willingness', was responsible for their lower rates of wages. Once aware of how they had been gulled, women were quick to seek better positions. To cite just one instance, in the late 1850s private registry offices in Melbourne were constantly full of servants, relatively new arrivals in the colony seeking new jobs at higher wages, having been compelled to accept lower rates from the government depot.[93] Hence the constant complaint of 'immigrant restlessness'.

In fact, working-class opposition to female immigration was generally muted. The under-representation of working women in anti-immigration organisations and the total lack of organisations for working women in domestic service contributed to this. Once working women were better organised they were able to recognise and protest against the impact of an immigrant group on their wage levels. In 1912, when the Victorian government attempted to introduce over one thousand female factory workers to the state, local women were quick and effective in organising protest meetings. That degree of political organisation was always denied women in the private sphere of domestic service. There was another reason, though. Throughout this period, the colonial demand for domestic servants remained unsatisfied and while that remained the case, the introduction of immigrant domestics did not lead to a fall in the wages paid to domestics outside the depot.

Even after they'd passed through the depot, immigrant women continued to find their other conditions of employment circumscribed after they arrived in the colonies. The notion of a 'free' passage was certainly illusory. Michael Quinlan has pointed to the heavy-handed nature of State intervention into employer/employee relationships in colonial Australia and the experiences of some female immigrants certainly bears this out.[94]

Each colony approached the issue with its own emphasis. In the late 1850s women emigrating to Tasmania at government expense were required to enter into a number of stringent agreements with the colonial government. They were expected to stay in the colony for four years or, failing that, to repay one quarter of their passage money for each year short.[95] They were also distributed between Hobart and Launceston at the immigration agent's direction. Few were happy to take yet another journey after the long passage out but the decision was not theirs.[96]

A similar policy was introduced in Victoria in the late 1860s. Rural distribution of newly arrived domestics was always a problem, with few single women willingly setting out for a situation in the bush. So in an attempt to give more satisfaction to would-be rural employers, the immigration authorities required single women to sign an agreement before embarking, that they would go anywhere in Victoria they were sent. No other assisted immigrants to Victoria had to submit to the policy, in any case recognised as having somewhat suspect legal value; but it would 'have a certain moral effect and may therefore answer the purpose' of providing rural colonists with domestic workers, or so immigration government officials hoped.[97] In fact, even without first placing their signatures on pieces of dubious paper, single immigrant women had been redistributed throughout Victoria ever since the 1850s, despatched west to the coastal towns of Geelong, Portland, Belfast (Port Fairy) and Warrnambool, and sometimes inland to Castlemaine, Sandhurst (Bendigo), and Ballarat. Signing an agreement simply gave a spurious legitimacy to an established practice.

On the other hand, in Western Australia in the 1890s rural employers were specifically left out of the government plans for distribution of immigrants, to the employers' chagrin. Well informed about the new supply of domestic servants, country residents were particularly vocal in requesting immigrant servants. Such general requests, however, could not be met, with servants going only to personal applicants. In 1893, for example, Mrs J. E. Leary of Talbot House, York, offered thirty shillings a month for a general servant, preferably one with country experience, but none of the four women remaining at the depot after the first rush of employers for the *Port Phillip* arrivals would take up the offer. Confident the women would soon be off their hands, the immigration authorities did not insist.[98] In 1895 the SS *Warrigal* disembarked its party of immigrants at Albany in Western Australia and Under-Secretary Octavius Burt was inundated with requests from Albany residents wanting to take advantage of this exceptional opportunity to acquire domestic servants. Despite Burt's intimations that he'd be accommodating, the immigrants were despatched by rail to Beverley under police guard where they connected with a special train to Perth.[99]

In South Australia in the 1850s, with the colony 'burdened' with an apparently excessive number of single female immigrants, the young women were sent to receiving depots in the colony's hinterland to ease the pressure on Adelaide's reception facilities. Others were offered—unsuccessfully—to the Tasmanians, who turned them down on the grounds that women not good enough for South Australia were not good enough for Tasmania either.[1] There is no evidence whether the women were asked about a possible relocation but, given what we know about governments consulting immigrant women, it seems fairly safe to assume they were not.

Even marriage was sometimes no escape from the immigrant's obligations to those who had paid her passage. In Tasmania in 1855, the colony's Attorney-General advised the Catholic Bishop of Hobart that a female immigrant who married before her employment contract expired was still bound to fulfil her term of service, even if this meant living apart from her husband.[2] So much for the British notion of sending out wives to tame the colonial men.

Though legislation controlling conditions of service for working women was in place in all colonies, it resulted in the most visible intervention in the lives of immigrant women in Western Australia and Tasmania. In Western Australia, this can be attributed to the delayed repeal of excessively harsh Master and Servants legislation; in Tasmania there seems little doubt that some colonists regarded immigrant women in a similar light to convict women, as requiring close control.

The substantial programme of assisting female migration introduced in Tasmania in the late 1850s entailed particularly close restrictions on single women. After transportation ended in 1853, the Tasmanian government had turned to assisted immigration to improve the colony's labour supply. With the Victorian goldfields drawing off the bulk of the single men introduced under the colony's bounty system, it seemed that the solution to Tasmania's population problems lay in family growth and for the government, this meant the introduction of more female domestics. As one Tasmanian noted in parliament, 'there is perhaps nothing which more materially affects the comfort of families throughout the Colony'[3] and from the mid-1850s to the early 1860s the introduction of selected single women as domestic servants became the main thrust of Tasmanian government migration policy.

As soon as they arrived, these young women felt the heavy hand of the colonial government. As well as being despatched to whatever part of the colony suited the government, they were also required to sign a promissory note agreeing to repay the government £5 towards their fare. When women entered employment, the government extracted the £5 from the woman's first employer—a charge, in effect, for providing them with a servant. The employer then reclaimed that money from the servant, deducting it in increments from her wages. Although the debt would remain with the immigrant wherever she was employed, this gave an employer a very strong interest in retaining the woman's services. If her wages were insufficient to repay this debt during a first term of engagement, an immigrant found she had effectively lost the right to move freely to another situation.

Wages improved once an immigrant could claim 'colonial experience' so seeking out a new place after fulfilling the terms of her first employment contract was the normal step. There were no legal barriers; yet it is clear that the authority of sex and class became a potent means of encouraging women to stay in their place, a weapon provided by the government and wielded vigorously against immigrant 'restlessness'.

In 1861 two immigrants affected by the Tasmanian regulations, Catherine McLuren and Margaret Lawson, decided to leave their jobs with R. Allwright of Brighton once their employment agreement expired, so they wrote to Hobart's government immigration agent Smith concerning their legal obligations. Only one month's notice was required if, as in this case, the contract of employment had expired.[4] Yet Smith suggested very strongly that the women stay on with Allwright until they had repaid the money he had paid to the government when he first hired them. And although the women had been in Allwright's service almost a year, Smith also implied that the very thought of leaving cast them as flighty. Servants who were 'in the habit' of leaving jobs, he pointed out to them, generally wasted both time and money seeking better ones.[5]

Following what was apparently normal practice in communications with domestic immigrants, Smith's reply to the women was enclosed in a note to their employer, who was informed that Smith had: 'given them such advice as may I trust, induce them to give up the idea of leaving their places until they have repaid you the amount advanced by you on their acct to the Government'.[6] Smith gave the two women no advice concerning the availability of temporary accommodation at Hobart's new permanent Servants' Home, built for the specific purpose of housing servants between jobs; the possibility of continuing to repay Allwright from new positions; or paying up the amount due from their savings. Security of employment—for the employer—clearly ranked higher than a servant's legal rights.

Another immigrant whose interests and rights were marginalised was Sarah Clinch. A cook, Clinch arrived in Hobart in 1860 on the *Isles of the South*. Two days after her arrival, she signed a service agreement with Mr Webster, agent for John Meredith of Cambria, Swansea. She was placed in lodgings and there she remained for a month, waiting for a passage to the rather inaccessible east coast town. The following year some dispute arose between Clinch and Meredith relating to payment due to her, Meredith dating his liability from the date of Clinch's arrival at Cambria. When Sarah Clinch wrote to Hobart's immigration agent Smith for advice concerning her position, he replied not to her but to her employer. Pointing out to Meredith the date of the agreement with Clinch and appealing to his sense of justice, Smith noted: 'I cannot see how the original date can be set aside … [for] it would seem rather hard that she should lose nearly a month's wages, because she happened to take service in a remote locality, immediate access to which was denied her'.[7]

Yet Smith agreed with Meredith that, should it come before the local bench, 'the usual practice + custom alluded to by [him] as prevailing on the East Coast, will bear due weight'.[8] Meredith would have been well aware of this, having served as Swansea magistrate since 1855.[9] Doubtless his first-hand experience with refractory female immigrants prepared him well when he served on the Select Committee to examine immigration to Tasmania appointed five weeks later.

To Clinch, Smith simply wrote that he 'cannot interfere in this matter in any way but would strongly recommend her to arrange it without having recourse to the Police office'.[10] No suggestion here that she was morally and legally in the right! Clearly (and probably correctly) he believed Meredith would override her in the local courts.

Though the interpretation of legislation was weighted in the employers' favour, even in Tasmania there were moments where women were able to thumb their noses at litigious masters, if only metaphorically. On 22 October 1861, Ellen Butler, a general servant who had sailed to Hobart on the *Antipodes,* was engaged by agents Tabart and Webster, on behalf of Mr Buxton of Little Swan Port. She was twenty-one years old, a Roman Catholic from County Cork, and could read but not write. Butler had come out to Tasmania to a prearranged position with William Giles of Bathurst Street, Hobart, to work as a nurse, but this arrangement had fallen through.[11] Six days after signing the agreement with Tabart and Webster (six days of idling in the depot), Butler complained to immigration agent Smith that she had not yet been sent for. His suggestion that there had probably been no vessel to that part of the east coast did little to help, aware as she was of other employers seeking domestic servants in town, and of friends and former ship mates already settled into paying jobs. Declining to wait any longer, she took up an offer of employment from Mr Marshall of Sorell on the 29th, and left the Servants' Home with him. When Tabart and Webster complained, Smith agreed that it was a breach of the Master and Servants Act but successfully advised them against prosecution. Under the Act her punishment would simply be loss of wages due to her to the day of conviction, 'thus making the law, in her case, a dead letter'.[12]

From 1840, the possibility of imprisonment of women under the Master and Servants Act had been gradually written out of the Acts of all the colonies except Western Australia[13] and since that date, only a handful of women had been committed to gaol for breaches of the Act. One was immigrant Mary Watkins. Shortly after her arrival in Adelaide in 1846, Watkins was charged under the South Australian Act with deserting the service of her master, T. C. Bray, and was committed to a week's gaol as punishment. The result was a public outcry against the

Act, which the local press described as a 'disgrace to any civilized country'. Watkins' fine was paid by her father, and he also paid the equivalent of two weeks' wages to the aggrieved Bray, who promptly returned the money as he said he had not anticipated the consequences of charging his employee. That colony's Act was amended the following year and, with the Watkins case a recent memory, women were specifically excluded.[14]

The Western Australian Act was not rewritten until the 1890s, and that too followed an incident involving a single female immigrant. This was at the height of the colony's largest programme of assisting single women. Though there are clear parallels between the South Australian and Western Australian episodes, the Carrie Hall case, and the subsequent amendment of the Western Australian Act, has a significance which illuminates the whole process of female migration to Western Australia and is worth examining in some detail.

On 21 April 1891 a domestic servant named Carrie Hall appeared before two Perth magistrates charged under the Western Australian Master and Servants Act with deserting her master's service. Her employer was Richard Septimus Haynes, lawyer, Perth City Councillor, political radical and co-founder of Western Australia's Eight Hours Association.[15] Haynes had taken both Hall and a fellow servant, Kate Brown, before the Perth Police Court. Brown was discharged with a caution but Hall received a fine or one month in Fremantle Gaol in default. The wages which Haynes had offered Hall were £2 a month; the fine was £4. Hall had been in the colony for a matter of days, having just arrived, like Brown, as an assisted immigrant on board the *Gulf of Martaban*. Her circumstances as a newly arrived single female immigrant made it clear she was quite unable to meet the fine and the magistrates' ruling effectively amounted to a term of imprisonment.[16]

The case led to a flutter of correspondence in the pages of the *West Australian*, with local residents eager to have their say and with Haynes, the Act itself, and the people who implemented it thoroughly savaged. Just nine months later, the Western Australian Master and Servants Act was rewritten to bring it into line with the less coercive acts of the other colonies. The new Act, designed 'to place the master and the servant on a footing of absolute equality', at last transformed the breach of contract between employer and employee into a civil disagreement, although it still permitted the imprisonment of male employees, and workers of course were far less likely to be able to pay their fines than were their masters.[17] Nonetheless the Act represented a significant advance on earlier regulations.

Most of the amendments introduced in the new Act of 1892 had been foreshadowed in a Bill presented in 1884 but subsequently thrown out. One item not foreshadowed in 1884 was a clause abolishing the imprisonment of women under the Act. In moving this amendment before the Assembly in 1892, Mr M. F. A. Canning of East Perth argued that imprisoning women and girls was unduly severe and would result quite simply in the Act becoming inoperative for women workers, since magistrates would refuse to inflict the penalty.[18] The aftermath of the Carrie Hall case had made that a certainty.

Carrie Hall came out as a government-assisted immigrant under the scheme set up in 1888 to introduce a regular supply of domestic servants to the colony from Britain. Her case came as the culmination of two years of Ellen Joyce's work to improve reception and employment arrangements for single women arriving in the colony. It exemplifies both Joyce's extraordinary influence on conditions of colonial domestic employment and the value which the colonial legislature placed on introducing a supply of carefully selected domestic labour.

Protecting the source of labour had always been a government imperative in a colony where labour shortages had sometimes been critical. In 1879, for example, the colony's Governor Ord had instructed resident magistrates to exercise clemency towards Chinese labourers brought before them under the Master and Servants Act, to avoid jeopardising an important supply of cheap labour.[19] Some of the colonists, outraged at the treatment Carrie Hall received, were aware of the more lenient treatment supposedly dealt out to the Chinese. One wrote to the local press:

To impose so harsh and rigorous a sentence upon a pennyless, sick, young English girl for an offence for which more than one healthy Chinamen has got off scot free, merely upon promising to go back to his employment, is not calculated to convey a very high opinion of the colony, its law, or the latter's agents.[20]

Once Joyce became aware of the Hall case, it was inevitable that she would create havoc. It was perhaps equally inevitable that the government, which had acted so often to placate her, would respond. Like the supply of Chinese labour, the supply of domestics had to be protected.

Within weeks of the case, Joyce in Britain knew all about it and wrote a letter of bitter protest to the Crown Agent in London, E. E. Blake:

There appears to have been no one to whom this young woman had a right to appeal or who was prepared to protect her. This is not what I understood by the promises of care being taken of these young women ... All I can say is that if respectable servants cannot withdraw themselves from a situation without rendering themselves liable to go to prison and undergo a months imprisonment I shall not feel inclined to recommend them to select Western Australia as their future home, unless the Masters and Servants' Acts [sic] is modified.[21]

Joyce was particularly incensed at the idea of imprisoning women she herself had vetted as respectable. As she pointed out to the colonial authorities, 'the amount of the fine is nothing compared with the degradation to a respectable servant of being sent to prison'.[22]

In Britain other agents also warned of the ripples spreading from the case. A Perth report of the court proceedings had described how the young woman was removed to the cells 'crying'; by the time the news reached Britain, a press account there had Hall 'weeping piteously' as she was led away.[23] As Crown Agent Blake admonished the Board of Immigration, 'Unless some very satisfactory explanations can be given of the circumstances of C. Hall's case, . . . all the best Women's Emigration Societies in this Country will decline to assist . . . Emigration to the Colony'.[24] Hard-pressed by Joyce and by people such as Blake who recognised her influence in migration circles in Britain, colonial immigration authorities themselves pushed for an inquiry into the Hall affair. In a lengthy 'explanation of the heavy sentence passed on Caroline Hall', presiding justice J. C. H. James argued that the minimum possible punishment was imposed, to operate as 'a punishment and a deterrent', and that the two justices had no choice under the Act. James also pointed out that Hall was never in the cells, before or after conviction, but that was no thanks to the justice system. In fact there was a large body of interested spectators in the court. A number of local coffee houses and hotels were quickly canvassed for support and the money collected, plus the proceeds of a whip round in the court itself, soon made up the necessary £4.[25]

Under attack, James defended the actions of the Crown, but he found it politic to agree that the Master and Servants Act was harsh and one-sided—giving servants no recourse in the event of wrongful dismissal, and inappropriate in dealing with the civil offence of breach of contract under a criminal statute.[26]

If the presiding justices had no choice, Hall's former master Richard Haynes had chosen to exact the utmost from the law. Correspondents in the press had already found Haynes guilty of hypocrisy and political expediency. In response to the many letters in the press attacking the decision of the Bench, Haynes tried to defend his own position: 'Had I sent the girl away without lawful excuse, I would have had to forfeit a sum of £4 at least, and why, may I ask, if the defendant chose to break the agreement should she be treated in any milder manner than myself?'[27]

The defence was a poor one which drew further condemnation of Haynes:

I cannot believe that the writer of the letter signed 'R. S. Haynes' in today's paper, justifying the harsh sentence passed on a penniless, sick young English girl, belonging to the working classes, is Mr R.S. Haynes, the friend of the working man, and who laboured hard for the working man's vote before he failed to get in for West Perth.[28]

Haynes' villainy did not stop there. The day following the trial, this one-time opponent of the Master and Servants Act wrote to the Colonial Secretary pointing out that under section five of the Act, the Immigration Board was liable to prosecution for 'harbouring' Carrie Hall, that is, allowing her to remain at the Immigration Depot after she had left Haynes' service.[29] It was the only home she had in the colony yet, after this letter was received, Hall was told to leave the depot and advised to return to Haynes' service.[30] Once again the Sydney Coffee Palace, where much of Hall's fine had been raised, intervened. On 23 April proprietor John Musson signed a paper agreeing 'to take all risks and responcibility [sic] in reference to engaging Carrie Hall'.[31] Musson left himself open to prosecution by Haynes; but at least Carrie Hall had a place to sleep short of the streets.

Following the Immigration Board's inquiry the Master and Servants Act was amended, with the imprisonment of women and girls expressly prohibited. Western Australia was back in step at last with the other colonies. Ellen Joyce continued selecting domestic servants for Western Australia until the end of the decade. Haynes became mayor of North Perth in 1896. Carrie Hall's subsequent history is less easy to trace but the repercussions of the affair which brought her brief fame spread far beyond the colony. Joyce had the last official word on the matter. In a letter to the Western Australian authorities in February 1892, she pointed out (no doubt with some satisfaction): 'I think it is instructive to note that I could not get a single emigrant from Devonshire or Cornwall as [the] Carrie Hall case was much circulated amongst those parts'.[32]

Like shipboard protection, the process of receiving female immigrants was designed to protect single women from the dangers of the outside world. From that point of view it was largely successful. Adequate reception facilities offered newly-arrived women the immediate material advantages of food, shelter, and a place to recover from the passage. But reception practices were part of the broader two-edged process of protection and control of immigrant women. Shipboard protection policies were largely introduced at the behest of middle-class women in Britain, whose interests combined the nineteenth-century domestic ideology of femininity with a simple concern that women emigrants be treated with the respect they deserved. Similar attitudes underpinned much of the work of middle-class colonial women who became involved in the reception process, but these concerns could be obscured by their class interests as employers.[33] Thus their motives remain ambiguous. As the immediate beneficiaries of the introduction of immigrant domestic servants, middle-class women were even more aware than governments of the advantages for employers of a programme of tightly-controlled reception.

Colonial governments also kept the interest of employers at heart: through both the depot system, which served to keep the level of wages paid to immigrant women at a lower level than locally experienced domestics received; and through legislation which ensured immigrant women remained subject to the control of their employers. Ultimately, the interests of immigrant women themselves were submerged in a process designed to deliver workers to their employers' hands at minimum cost to government, and to see they stayed there.

'Free agents these domestic damsels'

WRITING IN 1890, a British reporter remarked of a party of single women embarking for Queensland, 'they are free agents these domestic damsels—few of us indeed are quite so free'.[1] Those comments speak of the perceived romance of the sea voyage and the prospect of a new life across distant waters, but they were clearly penned by someone who had never experienced government migration—nor life as a domestic servant —first hand. Ten years before the *Jumna* sailed there were few real freedoms on board emigrant vessels. Even after women had passed through colonial depots and hiring rooms into employment, governments continued to intervene in their lives. Some immigrant women were affected more than others. The Wright sisters arrived in Brisbane in 1886 to be reunited with their Ipswich cousins and, although further rites of passage lay before them, their links with the overarching structures of authority which had shaped their experiences over the previous weeks were more or less severed. The links were far more attenuated for women coming out without their 'natural protectors' or with no family to welcome them. The quasi-parental protection which had embraced them (or which they had endured) on board ship remained in place at least until government officials saw the women into the hands of colonial employers; and sometimes, as we have seen, it impinged on their lives even longer.

As they sloughed off the label of 'migrant' and acquired the coveted veneer of 'colonial experience', however, these women's status rose and with it their wages. In other ways too their position changed. As the government relinquished its paternalistic hold, most became less visible to the historian. Occasionally we find women identified as 'immigrants' or 'recent arrivals' in the pages of the press, but such gleanings are meagre and likely to highlight the exceptional. Kate Teehan, twenty-two years old and a Catholic from Ireland, arrived in Fremantle on the SS *Wooloomooloo* early in 1898. She was not well. Her behaviour was later described as 'somewhat eccentric' and in fact she spent two days resting in the Perth Hospital before joining her shipmates at the Women's Depot (the immigration barracks) in Goderich Street, Perth. Early on the morning of 7 February, she apparently dressed herself, saturated her clothing with kerosene, retreated to an outhouse and lit a match. She died in the Perth Hospital of shocking injuries just two hours later.[2]

Records are more articulate about Agnes Howard, another one of Joyce's selection, who was just nineteen when she and her sister Eliza arrived in Western Australia on the SS *Port Philip*, in September 1893. On 2 February 1895, Agnes threw herself down a 53-foot well on the property of her employers, the Stirling family of Claremont. She had only been with the family for three weeks, but Mrs Stirling had already decided she would not suit, and had asked her to look elsewhere. In her brief time with the family, she had left the house only once, to walk on the beach with one of the Stirling children. According to her sister Eliza, Agnes had quarrelled with her 'young man' sometime before leaving England. They separated, he to Canada, she to Western Australia, and she had been morose and unsettled ever since. Their first year in the colony the sisters had been together, working with Mrs Frank Craig of York. Agnes had been moody and uncommunicative, and had already threatened suicide more than once. 'Drowned while temporarily insane' was the verdict of the coroner's jury; the press preferred 'death from melancholia'.[3]

The deaths of these two women were probably due to incidents which had their roots in their lives before coming to the colonies. The more normal fate of immigrant women, like their colonial counterparts, was to marry and raise families. The Domney sisters, both domestic servants, sailed for Queensland on the *Merkara* in September 1891, as free immigrants. The *Merkara* reached Brisbane seven weeks later but Fanny and Emily had already disembarked at Thursday Island (by design or on impulse, we no longer know) and from there they made their way by boat down the Gulf of Carpentaria to Normanton, then on to Croydon. Fanny was married on New Year's Eve that year, only a matter of weeks after their arrival, to Michael Ryan Cody, a miner aged forty-five, at Croydon's Primitive Methodist Church. Soon after her marriage she and her husband, who was said to be a brother of Buffalo Bill Cody, travelled overland in a coach and four from Charters Towers to Wandi, in the Northern Territory.

Fanny had no children but made up for it by acquiring three husbands. Cody worked as a storekeeper until he died in 1897; then Fanny married again in August 1898, to another miner, Thomas George Crush, who later became a member of parliament for the Northern Territory. He and Fanny between them built and managed the Federation Hotel at Brock's Creek. In 1916, three years after Crush's death, Fanny remarried once again, to the grazier Henry (Harry) Haynes. In Brock's Creek she remained until she and her husband were compulsorily evacuated from the north to Adelaide, following the bombing of Darwin.

Reunited with her sister Emily in Sydney, she was an object of fascination for her great nieces and nephews:

> I can recall the time when Aunt Fanny arrived at our home during the war. She was a very short but very broad lady with long silver grey hair and a florid complexion. With her dresses of floor-length brocaded silk she was like someone out of another era.[4]

'Cockney Fan', as she was known at Brock's Creek, was never to return to her beloved north, but died close to her sister's family in Sydney.[5]

Emily Domney's life followed a quieter but scarcely smoother path. When Fanny left for Wandi with her first husband in 1891, Emily remained in Croydon working as a general domestic and waitress. Two years later she married Henry Watson Mathewson, an immigrant from Scotland. They had three children, but the family eventually broke up, Emily taking the children to Townsville where her resourcefulness and thrift enabled her to support them and build up a small nest egg in real estate. She remarried in 1925, and died in 1959, aged eighty-seven.[6]

Julia Neagle left County Tipperary for Western Australia in 1860, at the age of sixteen. She sailed on the *Dolphin*, one of twenty-eight emigrants on board, with the intention of joining her older sister. Margaret Neagle had arrived in the colony on the *Travancore* eight years earlier and just as the British government authorities had hoped, she had married a former convict, Richard Newport. Julia joined them in York, where they had a small mixed farm. Soon the younger woman went into service with the Parkers at Balladong Farm, where she too married a former convict, the Frenchman Aimable Duperouzel, who had been convicted of a number of crimes in the Channel Islands. At the time of his marriage to Julia, Aimable declared himself a widower but family historians believe he left a wife and baby son in Guernsey. Though she was only eighteen at the time of her marriage, Julia also stretched a point, by claiming to be 'above the age of twenty-one'. The Newports had a family of ten children, and the Duperouzels seven. In 1993, Julia Neagle's direct descendants numbered 380.[7]

Such cameos only seldom come the way of the historian and, as in these cases, are sometimes a welcome gift from genealogists. Without them, the reconstructions of the everyday lives led by most of the immigrant women after their arrival in the colonies would be spare indeed. Those who constructed the immigrant passage, established the routes and acted as guardians along the way, have left behind a huge edifice of records of part of the journey but, for the historian interested in following the immigrant away from the docks and the immigrant depot, into the kitchens of colonial employers and beyond, the path is sometimes more difficult to follow. Unfortunately there is nothing comparable to the convict musters used so effectively by writers such as Deborah Oxley, to colour and animate our knowledge of immigrant women.

Of course, the most typical life patterns—marriage and family—are found in abundance in the records of registrars of births, deaths and marriages, but other fates are sometimes harder to track down. Women who did not marry or did not have children leave fewest traces in obvious places; and without descendants, they are seldom the quarry for eager family historians.

Some women used domestic service to their own advantage. Domestic skills guaranteed that a woman could find both home and employment wherever she travelled and so, though domestic service was no vacation, these immigrant women pioneered the 'working holiday', moving on to visit other Australian colonies or even New Zealand or Canada; returning to Britain and sometimes, like modern day migrants, coming back out again. In the days before computer cross-referencing of data, making a second government-assisted passage out to the colonies was sometimes frowned upon by colonial authorities but was practised none the less.

Lucy Spare came out to Launceston on the *Ambrosine* in 1857. In 1859 she went back to England, but in 1862 at the age of thirty-two she returned to Tasmania on the *Aurora Australis*, accompanied by her 20-year-old sister Frances. On this second passage out, she acted as sub-matron, earning £4 19s. After arrival, the Spare sisters were sent north to Launceston by coach, at Lucy's request. Lucy was said to be an excellent servant and was expected to do very well. The question of whether she had complied with the conditions of her first free passage, and repaid a portion of the passage money due on her first trip as she had failed to stay four years, was apparently not raised.[8]

Similarly Emily Dunn, who applied to the BWEA in January 1894 for a free passage to Western Australia, had already spent a year and a half working in Canada. Her passage there had also been arranged through the BWEA. She had returned to England to visit relatives but had no desire to remain there permanently. With passages to the world's farthest corners freely available to a woman of her skills and initiative, it was hardly surprising.[9]

There is no doubt that single women emigrants would have experienced the emotional highs and lows, the euphoria and despair, which are commonly part of the migrant experience regardless of society or gender. Yet there were opportunities too, and women who had had the courage to take that first step and embark on the process of emigration itself, would not have been slow to take up what was available. Mary Corbett was one woman who recognised that she had a choice: accept the constraints imposed on her by colonial society, or speak out. Shortly after she emigrated to Western Australia in the early 1890s, Corbett wrote a passionate letter to the Colonial Secretary's office in which she argued against a view she had encountered since her arrival, that immigrant women owed a debt of gratitude and subservience to the colony:

> Pardon me if I am presumtious but we came out here as Brave English women & as such we . . . [wish] to uphold the right & not be set down as worthless creatures who have been glad to leave their own country & avail ourselves of free passages which we are told should be given to none . . . We do not reckon ourselves with none but came here with the determination to repay by our good services & abiletys [sic] those who were so kind as to place free passages at our disposal.[10]

Corbett was exceptional in choosing to voice her opinions in this manner. But she spoke for most single immigrant women, English, Irish, Scottish, Welsh and Cornish alike. Though the freedoms available were sometimes limited, recognising what they themselves had to offer left immigrant women in a strong position to begin to negotiate and expand the roles they would play in the colonies they had chosen as their new home.

Appendix: Immigration Tables

New South Wales

1 Government-assisted immigrants arriving, by sex, 'country' of origin and family status, 1860–87
2 Government-assisted single female immigrants arriving, by trades and callings, and 'country' of origin, 1859–86
3 Government-assisted single female immigrants hired from the Sydney Immigrants' Depot, and the wages received, with board and lodging, 1860–87
4 Average rate of wages received by women workers, with board and lodging, 1850–70

Victoria

5 Government-assisted immigrants arriving from Britain, by sex and age, 1859–78

South Australia

6 Government-assisted immigrants arriving by sex, family status and nationality, 1860–85
7 Occupations of government-assisted single immigrant women arriving 1860–67

Queensland

8 Passengers embarked for Queensland, 1860–64
9 Government-assisted immigrants arriving from Britain, by sex and family status, 1865–73

10 Government-assisted immigrants despatched from Britain by the Agent-General for Queensland, by sex and family status, 1874–99
11 Government-assisted immigrants despatched from Britain by the Agent-General for Queensland, by 'country' of origin, 1874–99
12 Government-assisted female domestics despatched from Britain by the Agent-General, 1874–95

Western Australia

13 Assisted migration from Britain, conducted at the expense of the British government. Numbers despatched, by sex and family status, 1850–72
14 Government-assisted immigration from Britain. Numbers arriving, by sex, 1873–1900

Tasmania

15 Government-assisted immigration. Numbers arriving, by sex, family status, country of origin and occupation (1883–89), 1859–90

Note on Statistics

The following tables are compiled from the immigration statistics published in the papers of the colonial parliaments, the reports of the colonial immigration agents, the reports of the Agents-General and annual *Statistical Registers* and *Blue Books*. In two cases, for Queensland between 1860 and 1864, and Western Australia between 1850 and 1872, I have used the published statistics of other historians. This is indicated in the tables themselves.

The tables are not entirely complete and consequently I have not provided 'totals'; to do so would misrepresent the authority of the figures. Not all colonies published consistent runs of statistics for every year in which immigration assistance was offered. Some tables record the number of emigrants despatched from Britain; others record the number of immigrants arriving in the colony. The two types of material cannot easily be reconciled. Other problems relate to changes in terminology over the period and the complex structure of colonial assistance policies, which sometimes makes determining which immigrants were 'assisted' and which were not, extremely difficult.

In terms of the number of single female immigrants despatched to the colonies, there are further problems. Not all colonies differentiated between the number of single women and the number of married women arriving under government assistance schemes throughout this period. Nonetheless, I have attempted to estimate the *minimum* number of single women who received government assistance to migrate to the Australian colonies between 1860 and 1900. My estimate is ninety thousand women, who were assisted by the various colonies as follows: 18 000 to New South Wales; 13 000 to Victoria; 9100 to South Australia; 46 000 to Queensland; 1700 to Western Australia; and 1600 to Tasmania. These estimates are conservative. The figures for Victoria and South Australia, for example, were obtained by assuming the difference between the total number of adult males assisted and adult females assisted to be single women, which does not take into account the numbers of single men who also emigrated to the colony under government assistance schemes and who, under this method of estimating the number of single women, mask substantial numbers of single women. It is likely that the number of single women who migrated to the colonies between 1860 and 1900 under government assistance schemes could have been as high as one hundred thousand.

Wage Conversions

All wages are cited in shillings per week or pounds per annum. Wages for female domestic servants included board and lodging.

Shillings per week	Pounds/shillings
5s	£13 0s
6s	£15 12s
7s	£18 4s
8s	£20 16s
9s	£23 8s
10s	£26 0s
11s	£28 12s
12s	£31 4s
13s	£33 16s
14s	£36 8s
15s	£39 0s
16s	£41 12s
17s	£44 4s
18s	£46 16s
19s	£49 8s
20s	£52 0s

Table 1 New South Wales, 1860–1887: government-assisted immigrants arriving, by sex, 'country' of origin, family status

Year	Adults			Children under 12			England	Scotland	Ireland	Other	Total
	Male	Female	Total	Male	Female	Total					
1860	1347	1230	2577	241	255	496	966	311	1780	16	3073
1861	791	604	1395	102	92	194					1589
1862	1175	1046	2221	199	211	410					2631
1863	1967	1871	3838	391	404	795	1028	295	3275	35	4633
1864	1701	1672	3373	289	315	604	732	275	2951	19	3977
1865	1073	1214	2287	213	217	430	495	155	2041	26	2717
1866	501	543	1044	92	68	160	190	64	937	13	1204
1867	385	435	820	66	58	124	123	57	759	5	944
1868	183	215	398	41	31	72	99	41	324	6	470
1869	*the remaining immigrants under the regulations cancelled in 1867										*47
1870	Government-assisted immigration was suspended										
1871	28	299	327	15	15	30	259	10	75	13	357
1872	25	271	296	16	14	30	240	70	7	9	326
1873	13	119	132	3	5	8	104	2	34	–	140
1874	427	411	838	109	133	242	533	108	433	6	1080
1875	395	324	719	135	119	254	494	163	306	10	973
1876	642	429	1071	208	184	392	841	188	407	27	1463
1877	2892	1627	4519	743	756	1499	3689	418	1446	465	6018*
	*includes 761 assisted immigrants who arrived from New York										
1878	2091	1754	3845	699	646	1345	2864	304	1840	182	5190*
	*includes 173 assisted immigrants who arrived from New York										
1879	1906	2141	4047	840	844	1684	2808	700	2125	98	5731
1880	1150	1195	2345	414	375	789	1205	213	1648	68	3134
1881	929	1029	1958	327	292	619	906	211	1389	71	2577
1882	1209	991	2200	509	524	1033	2017	408	764	44	3233
1883	3370	2718	6088	1154	1127	2281	5382	937	1903	147	8369
1884	2785	2606	5391	1095	1082	2177	4626	1314	1503	125	7568
1885	1871	2211	4082	736	736	1472	3249	969	1207	129	5554
1886	1044	1905	2949	572	560	1132	2235	582	1180	84	4081
1887	131	687	818	286	258	544	777	233	289	63	1362

Compiled from the annual reports of the Immigration Agent, and from the statistical registers, NSW *VPLA*.

Table 2a New South Wales, 1859–1869: government-assisted single female immigrants arriving, by trades and callings, and 'country' of origin

Year and 'country' of origin	Housekeepers	Cooks	House servants	Housemaids	Nursemaids	Laundresses	Dairymaids	Farm servants	Other domestics	Total Domestics
					Domestic Servants					
1859										
English & Welsh	32	25	108	57	32	17	8	5	–	284
Scottish	6	4	50	25	4	4	2	5	1	101
Irish	44	13	217	82	62	31	39	246	7	741
Other	–	–	–	–	–	–	–	–	–	–
Total	82	42	375	164	98	52	49	256	8	1126
1860										
English & Welsh	34	12	108	35	14	8	4	2	4	221
Scottish	10	9	39	15	1	2	5	5	–	86
Irish	39	4	252	67	19	21	38	127	3	570
Other	1	–	–	–	–	–	–	–	–	1
Total	84	25	399	117	34	31	47	134	7	878
1861										
English & Welsh	16	11	19	5	–	–	1	–	–	52
Scottish	3	1	8	4	–	–	–	2	–	18
Irish	18	4	178	28	12	10	13	138	1	402
Other	–	–	–	–	1	–	–	–	–	1
Total	37	16	205	37	13	10	14	140	1	473
1862										
English & Welsh	24	2	38	15	4	3	1	1	–	88
Scottish	9	–	16	12	2	–	–	–	–	39
Irish	46	5	373	137	27	6	22	77	–	693
Other	2	–	–	–	–	–	–	–	–	2
Total	81	7	427	160	33	9	23	78	–	822
1863										
English & Welsh	43	3	108	54	2	2	–	1	–	212
Scottish	1	–	37	10	–	1	1	–	–	50
Irish	50	9	641	392	12	6	7	53	6	1176
Other	–	–	10	–	–	–	–	–	–	10
Total	93	12	796	456	14	9	8	54	6	1448

| | Clothing Trades | | | | | Other Callings | | | | | | | |
Dressmaker	Milliner	Tailoress	Needlewoman	Others: clothing	**Total Clothing**	Governess	Shop woman	Matron	Teacher	Food trade	Other Callings	**Total Other**	**Total**
7	–	–	7	1	15	3	–	–	–	–	5	8	307
1	–	–	3	–	4	–	1	–	–	–	1	2	107
10	1	1	15	1	27	5	3	–	–	–	4	12	780
–	–	–	–	–	1	–	–	–	–	–	–	–	1
18	1	1	25	2	47	8	4	–	–	–	10	22	1195
3	3	2	5	3	16	1	–	8	–	–	2	11	248
–	2	–	1	–	3	–	–	–	–	–	–	–	89
8	6	1	11	2	28	1	3	–	–	–	–	4	602
–	–	–	–	–	–	–	–	–	–	–	–	–	1
11	11	3	17	5	47	2	3	8	–	–	2	15	940
4	–	–	6	–	10	–	–	4	1	1	1	7	69
–	–	–	1	–	1	–	–	–	–	–	–	–	19
6	–	–	6	–	12	–	–	–	–	–	–	–	414
–	–	–	–	–	–	–	–	–	–	–	–	–	1
10	–	–	13	–	23	–	–	4	1	1	1	7	503
9	–	1	1	3	14	1	1	2	–	–	1	5	107
1	–	–	1	–	2	1	–	–	–	–	–	1	42
15	2	1	9	–	27	4	2	–	–	1	1	8	728
–	–	1	–	1	2	–	–	–	–	–	–	–	4
25	2	3	11	4	45	6	3	2	–	1	2	14	881
5	1	–	2	1	9	–	–	11	2	–	–	13	234
–	–	–	–	2	2	–	–	–	–	–	–	–	52
24	8	–	16	1	49	–	–	2	2	–	–	4	1229
–	–	–	–	–	–	–	–	–	–	–	–	–	10
29	9	–	18	4	60	–	–	13	4	–	–	17	1525

Table 2a (cont.) New South Wales, 1859–1869: government-assisted single female immigrants arriving, by trades and callings, and 'country' of origin

Year and 'country' of origin	Housekeepers	Cooks	House servants	Housemaids	Nursemaids	Laundresses	Dairymaids	Farm servants	Other domestics	Total Domestics
			Domestic Servants							
1864										
English & Welsh	11	6	110	8	5	–	–	–	3	143
Scottish	–	2	45	5	–	1	–	–	–	53
Irish	1	24	904	76	11	17	11	5	2	1051
Other	–	–	3	–	–	–	–	–	–	3
Total	12	32	1062	89	16	18	11	5	5	1250
1865										
English & Welsh	13	3	55	13	11	1	–	–	–	96
Scottish	2	1	23	1	2	–	1	–	–	30
Irish	29	18	647	67	23	23	26	–	–	833
Other	1	1	1	–	1	–	–	–	–	4
Total	45	23	726	81	37	24	27	–	–	963
1866										
English & Welsh	5	1	25	2	4	–	–	–	–	37
Scottish	3	–	17	–	–	–	–	–	–	20
Irish	20	2	269	28	10	11	24	1	–	365
Other	1	–	3	–	–	–	–	–	–	4
Total	29	3	314	30	14	11	24	1	–	426
1867										
English & Welsh	1	1	21	–	1	–	–	1	1	26
Scottish	6	1	4	1	–	–	–	–	–	12
Irish	14	8	184	16	6	5	7	65	–	305
Other	–	–	1	–	–	–	–	–	–	1
Total	21	10	210	17	7	5	7	66	1	344
1868*										
English & Welsh	9	–	9	–	1	–	–	–	–	19
Scottish	3	1	9	2	1	–	–	–	–	16
Irish	12	–	115	3	4	5	–	11	1	151
Other	1	–	–	–	–	–	–	–	–	1
Total	25	1	133	5	6	5	–	11	1	187

* to 11 April 1869 inclusive

	Clothing Trades					Other Callings							
Dressmaker	Milliner	Tailoress	Needlewoman	Others: clothing	**Total Clothing**	Governess	Shop woman	Matron	Teacher	Food trade	Other Callings	**Total Other**	**Total**
3	1	1	1	–	6	–	–	–	1	–	1	2	151
1	2	–	3	–	6	–	–	–	–	–	–	–	59
18	8	2	14	–	42	–	–	–	4	–	5	9	1102
–	–	–	1	–	1	–	–	–	–	–	–	–	4
22	11	3	19	–	55	–	–	–	5	–	6	11	1316
11	6	4	9	–	30	–	–	–	3	1	2	6	132
1	–	–	–	–	1	–	–	–	–	1	–	1	32
27	11	1	10	3	52	–	–	–	4	1	–	5	890
2	–	–	1	–	3	–	–	–	–	–	–	–	7
41	17	5	20	3	86	–	–	–	7	3	2	12	1061
2	2	–	1	–	5	–	–	3	4	–	–	7	49
2	2	–	–	–	4	–	1	–	–	–	–	1	25
14	3	–	11	–	28	–	6	–	4	–	1	11	404
–	–	–	–	–	–	–	–	–	–	–	–	–	4
18	7	–	12	–	37	–	7	3	8	–	1	19	482
1	–	1	3	–	5	–	1	3	–	–	1	5	36
1	2	–	–	–	3	–	–	–	–	1	–	1	16
12	2	–	5	2	21	–	1	–	6	1	–	8	334
–	–	–	–	–	–	–	–	–	–	–	–	–	1
14	4	1	8	2	29	–	2	3	6	2	1	14	387
4	–	1	7	2	14	–	–	1	–	–	–	1	34
–	–	–	–	–	–	–	–	–	–	–	–	–	16
2	–	–	10	–	12	–	4	–	2	–	–	6	169
–	–	–	–	–	–	–	–	–	–	–	–	–	1
6	–	1	17	2	26	–	4	1	2	–	–	7	220

Table 2b New South Wales, 1871–1886: government-assisted single female immigrants arriving, by trades and callings, and 'country' of origin

Year and 'country' of origin	Domestic Servants	Other callings, including females above 12 years of age coming to or accompanied by relatives	Total
1871			299
1872–1873			354
1877			
English & Welsh	153	167	320
Scottish	17	29	46
Irish	278	65	343
USA	20	11	31
Other	9	6	15
Total	477	278	755
1878			
English & Welsh	211	89	300
Scottish	36	8	44
Irish	581	67	648
USA	8	4	12
Other	8	2	10
Total	844	170	1014
1879	1077	148	1225
1880	866	41	907
1881			
English & Welsh	155	6	161
Scottish	50	1	51
Irish	563	7	570
USA & Canada	2	–	2
Other	18	–	18
Total	788	14	802
1882			
English & Welsh	174	25	199
Scottish	35	3	38
Irish	279	6	285
USA & Canada	1	–	1
Other	3	1	4
Total	492	35	527

Year and 'country' of origin	Domestic Servants	Other callings, including females above 12 years of age coming to or accompanied by relatives	Total
1883			
English & Welsh	594	77	671
Scottish	134	13	147
Irish	762	30	792
Other	29	2	31
Total	1519	122	1641
1884			
English & Welsh	649	39	688
Scottish	188	10	198
Irish	616	15	631
Other	29	5	34
Total	1482	69	1551
1885			
English & Welsh	807	30	
Scottish	231	2	
Irish	526	5	
Other	16	2	
Total	1610	39	1649
1886			
English & Welsh	638	29	667
Scottish	184	20	204
Irish	672	5	677
USA & Canada	4	–	4
Other	35	1	36
Total	1533	55	1588

Compiled from the annual reports of the Immigration Agent, NSW *VPLA*, 1859–90

Table 3 New South Wales, 1860–1887: government-assisted single female immigrants hired from the Sydney Immigrants' Depot, and the wages received, with board and lodging

Year	Occupation	Numbers hired from depot	Wages received per annum
1860	Cooks		£23 13s 0d
	Laundresses		£23 0s 0d
	Housemaids		£20 9s 0d
	Nursemaids		£19 15s 0d
	Generals		£20 12s 0d
	Total	226	
1861	Cooks		£24 10s 0d
	Laundresses		£20 0s 0d
	Housemaids		£16 13s 0d
	Nursemaids		£14 7s 0d
	Generals		£16 12s 0d
	Total	103	
1862	Cooks		£19 0s 0d
	Laundresses		–
	Housemaids		£15 11s 0d
	Nursemaids		£13 14s 0d
	Generals		£17 1s 0d
	Total	183	
1860–62	Cooks	10	
	Laundresses	9	
	Housemaids	42	
	Nursemaids	53	
	Generals	398	
	Total	512	
1863	Cooks	4	£19 10s 0d
	Laundresses	6	£23 10s 0d
	Housemaids	8	£19 12s 6d
	Nursemaids	22	£18 9s 0d
	Generals	312	£17 16s 6d
	Total	352	
1864	Cooks	8	£20 10s 0d
	Laundresses	11	£21 10s 0d
	Housemaids	20	£20 0s 0d
	Nursemaids	35	£15 9s 0d
	Generals	335	£16 12s 0d
	Total	409	

Year	Occupation	Numberss hired from depot	Wages received per annum
1865	Cooks	11	£19 7s 6d
	Laundresses	6	£21 18s 6d
	House servants	15	£18 7s 6d
	Nursemaids	17	£14 17s 0d
	Generals	261	£18 3s 6d
	Total	310	
1866	Cooks	3	£18 3s 0d
	Laundresses	2	£30 0s 0d
	House servants	79	£16 6s 0d
	Nursemaids	14	£14 15s 0d
	Generals	37	£16 10s 0d
	Total	135	
1867	Cooks	2	£26 0s 0d
	Laundresses	2	£26 0s 0d
	Nursemaids	8	£15 15s 0d
	Generals	90	£16 0s 0d
	Total	102	
1871 (including December 1870)		299	£19 17s 6d
1872–73		354	
1874		63	£22 10s 0d
1875			
1876		27	£24 10s 0d
1877		216	£24 18s 0d
1878		407	£23 10s 2d
1879		655	£23 7s 0d
1880			
1881		1617	£24 0s 0d
1882		87	£26 0s 0d
1883		357	£26 0s 0d
1884		505	£27 14s 8d
1885		536	£28 12s 0d
1886		401	£27 6s 0d
1887		114	£25 2s 8d

Compiled from the annual reports of the Immigration Agent, NSW *VPLA*, 1860–90

Table 4 New South Wales, 1850–1870: average rate of wages (£ per annum) received by women workers, with board and lodging

Year	Cooks (plain)	Housemaids	Laundresses	Nursemaids	General house servants	Farm house servants dairy women, etc.
1850	15–19	11–15	13–16	7–12	12–15	11
1851	16–25	14–18	14–18	7–12	14–18	13
1852	18–25	14–18	18–22	15–18	16–18	14
1853	19–28	15–19	18–22	15–18	15–21	15
1854	25–30	18–25	25–30	15–20	25–30	25
1855	25–30	18–25	25–30	15–20	20–26	20–24
1856	24–27	19–22	23–26	16–19	20–24	19–22
1857	25–30	16–18	20–25	15–20	20–25	18–20
1858	26	23	26	19	25	25
1859	25–30	16–18	20–25	15–18	20–25	18–20
1860	25–30	16–25	25–30	15–20	18–25	18–25
1861	25–30	20–25	25–30	15–20	20–25	18–25
1862	26–40	20–26	30–40	15–25	22	25
1863	26–32	20–26	26–32	15–26	18–26	18–26
1864	26–36	20–26	26–30	15–26	20–30	18–26
1865	26–36	25–30	25–30	15–20	20–26	18–26
1866	26	20–26	26	16–20	20–26	20
1867	26–30	20–26	26	16–20	20–26	20–25
1868	26–30	26	30	20	26–30	26
1869						
			Housemaids and other female servants			
1870	30–45		20–30			

Compiled from the annual reports of the Immigration Agent, NSW *VPLA*, 1860–72. Figures for 1870 taken from `Emigration, Report from Sir Clinton Murdoch to Sir Frederick Rogers, Bart, Appendix', NSW *VPLA*, 1870–71, vol. 2, p. 599.

Table 5   Victoria, 1859-1878: government-assisted immigrants arriving from Britain, by sex and age

Year	Adults		Children 1–12 years		Infants under 1 year		Totals		
	Male	Female	Male	Female	Male	Female	Male	Female	Total
1859							552	2599	3151
1860	127	1492	37	45	21	14	185	1551	1736
1861	544	1723	177	191	26	21	747	1935	2682
1862	1249	2533	431	458	30	27	1710	3018	4728
1863	2535	4762	678	647	(Infants henceforth		3213	5409	8622
1864	2120	3451	553	507	included with		2673	3958	6631
1865	1619	2795	336	354	children)		1955	3149	5104
1866	1379	2220	307	288			1686	2508	4194
1867	914	1821	227	240			1141	2061	3202
1868	920	1447	252	252			1172	1699	2871
1869	1473	2023	309	334	45	35	1827	2392	4219
1870	1471	1958	383	417	51	61	1905	2436	4341
1871	1413	1799	(Children and infants henceforth				1413	1799	3212
1872	468	625	included with 'adults')				468	625	1093
1873	456	407					456	407	863
1874	64	85					64	85	149
1875	50	52					50	52	102
1876	34	37					34	37	71
1877	9	8					9	8	17
1878	8	10					8	10	18

Compiled from the statistics of the colony of Victoria (Vic *PP*).

Table 6a South Australia, 1860–1875: government-assisted immigrants arriving by sex, family status and nationality

Year and	Married		Single		Under 12		
'country' of origin	Male	Female	Male	Female	Male	Female	Total
1860							
English	82	81	118	137	87	74	
Irish	4	4	44	30	1	6	
Scottish	26	26	99	86	31	36	
Total	112	111	261	253	119	116	972
1861	Immigration at public expense suspended during 1861						
1862							
English	21	21	97	113	10	31	
Irish	11	10	48	52	7	7	
Scottish	23	22	51	57	13	17	
Total	55	53	196	222	30	55	611
1863							
English	148	153	266	173	131	109	
Irish	19	20	104	98	12	14	
Scottish	39	39	61	58	29	26	
Total	206	212	431	329	172	149	1499
1864							
English	217	229	492	296	191	186	
Irish	53	60	319	268	48	43	
Scottish	31	32	86	48	22	26	
Total	301	321	897	612	261	255	2647
1865							
English	710	715	978	392	440	412	
Irish	92	93	181	91	62	65	
Scottish	26	30	188	119	16	15	
Total	828	838	1347	602	518	492	4625
1866							
English	349	354	582	279	244	220	
Irish	68	72	528	408	84	52	
Scottish	82	84	262	118	49	56	
Total	499	510	1372	805	377	328	3891
1867							
English	28	28	77	65	19	13	
Irish	1	1	12	6	2	1	
Scottish	9	9	49	26	1	2	
Total	38	38	138	97	22	16	349
1868	Immigration suspended						

	Adult Male	Adult Female	Under 12 Male	Female	Total
1869					
English	13	14	10	8	
Irish	3	5	3	1	
Scottish	14	13	–	3	
Total	30	32	13	12	87

Immigration ceased at the end of 1867. Some immigrants arrived in 1869. Assistance resumed July 1873.
Compiled from annual Immigration Returns, SA *PP*.

	Adults Male	Female	Under 12 Male	Female	Total
1873					
English	41	55	18	20	
Irish	34	35	3	5	
Scottish	8	7	–	–	
Foreign	–	–	–	–	
Total	83	97	21	25	226
1874					
English	692	478	227	252	
Irish	136	93	23	34	
Scottish	66	47	24	35	
Foreign	16	10	8	11	
Total	910	628	282	332	2152
1875					
English	572	446	133	142	
Irish	277	208	32	28	
Scottish	67	46	29	20	
Foreign	44	14	2	7	
Total	960	714	196	197	2067

From Statistical Registers for South Australia (SA *PP*).

Table 6b South Australia, 1876–1885: government-assisted immigrants arriving by sex, family status and nationality

Year	Married		Single			English	
	Male	Female	Male	Female	Children under 12	Adult	Children under 12
1876	1121	1123	2486	1019	1839	3883	1263
1877	638	639	1666	902	1102	1912	668
1878	558	558	1376	724	1051	1760	620
1879	416	417	874	686	842	1271	444
1880							
1881	67	68	257	205	186	(M) 110	(M) 56
						(F) 112	(F) 65
1882	81	82	278	447	234	310	131
1883	515	521	841	1085	1170	2023	890
1884						(M) 108	(M) 57
						(F) 199	(F) 87
1885						(M) 14	(M) 10
						(F) 28	(F) 10

From Statistical Registers for South Australia (SA *PP*).

Irish		Scottish		Foreign		
	Children		*Children*		*Children*	*Total*
Adult	*under 12*	*Adult*	*under 12*	*Adult*	*under 12*	*landed*
1151	128	251	84	570	76	7730
1041	139	208	83	693	244	4947
741	106	442	157	273	168	4247
482	65	603	310	40	20	3235
						2513
(M) 176	(M) 20	(M) 24	(M) 9	(M) 15	(M) 9	
(F) 124	(F) 15	(F) 21	(F) 6	(F) 16	(F) 6	783
459	43	67	43	52	17	1122
562	91	226	83	151	106	4132
(M) 131	(M) 24	(M) 16	(M) 15	(M) 56	(M) 20	
(F) 140	(F) 18	(F) 22	(F) 10	(F) 47	(F) 18	968
(M) 90	(M) 3	(M) 4	(M) 1	(M) 4	(M) 4	
(F) 91	(F) 12	(F) 9	(F) –	(F) 5	(F) 8	293

Table 7 South Australia, 1860–1867: occupations of government-assisted single immigrant women arriving 1860–1867

Occupation	1860	1861*	1862	1863	1864	1865	1866	1867
Matron	–		–	–	5	7	10	1
Domestic servant	229		107	302	576	583	770	77
Farm servant	7		–	–	–	–	–	–
Dressmaker	–		–	–	9	6	6	3
Cook	7		–	–	–	–	3	–
Laundress	3		–	–	–	–	–	–
Sempstress	2		4	6	–	1	–	–
Housekeeper	–		–	–	–	4	4	2
Dairymaid	5		2	1	–	–	–	–
Other	–		–	–	6	1	–	6
Not known	–		109†	14	16	–	12	8
TOTAL	253		222	323	612	602	805	97

Compiled from annual Immigration Returns (SA *PP*).

*   Immigration suspended

†   The occupations of 109 single women who arrived on the *Castle Eden* were not recorded.

Table 8 Queensland, 1860–1864: passengers embarked for Queensland

Year	Married		Single		Children to 12 years		Totals		Totals	
	Male	Female	Male	Female	Male	Female	Male	Female	I	II
1860	49	49	88	68	17	29	154	146	300	479
1861	166	169	334	247	129	103	629	519	1235[a]	1201
1862	1143	1169	2601	1364	1045	918	4789	3451	8280[b]	7467
1863	1580	1601	4432	1770	1480	1285	7492	4656	12166[c]	10182
1864	870	894	2804	1240	617	553	4291	2687	7520[d]	6322

Includes [a]87 [b]40 [c]18 [d]542 other passengers.

Compiled from Woolcock, *Rights of Passage*, table 2, p. 348, and Crowley, 'The British Contribution to the Australian Population', appendices 1, 2, pp. 84, 87.

The statistics and total I are derived from Woolcock, *Rights of Passage*. Total II comes from Crowley's two tables, 'Total immigration into Australia from the United Kingdom: 1860–1919', and 'Government immigration into Australia from the United Kingdom: 1860–1919', which, in Crowley's tables, are identical for Queensland for the period 1860–1878

Table 9 Queensland, 1865–1873: government-assisted immigrants arriving from Britain, by sex and family status

Year	Married		Single		Children to 12 years		Totals		Total
	Male	Female	Male	Female	Male	Female	Male	Female	
1865	1593	1628	4026	1641	1081	1010	6700	4279	10979
1866	1282	1312	2832	1266	945	905	5059	3483	8542
1867	115	137	381	202	136	106	632	443	1075
1868	61	68	248	101	41	47	350	216	566
1869	229	241	710	437	152	144	1091	822	1913
1870	308	319	870	511	231	173	1362	1051	2413
1871									1637
(to May)	79	83	230	178	80	55	389	316	705
1872	144	156	317	313	98	78	559	547	1106*
1873	674	705	1533	915	583	533	2790	2153	4943*

* excludes German, and full-paying immigrants conveyed in 'short' ships.

Compiled from Immigration Returns, Qld *VPLA*. The total for 1871 is taken from Crowley, 'The British Contribution to the Australian Population', appendix 2, p. 87.

Table 10 Queensland, 1874–1899: government-assisted immigrants despatched from Britain by the Agent-General for Queensland, by sex and family status

Year	Married Male	Married Female	Single Male	Single Female	Children 1–12 years Male	Children 1–12 years Female	Infants under 1 year Male	Infants under 1 year Female	Total	Notes
1874	1114	1117	2672	1548	831	781	137	134	8334	1874–82: excludes Germans and full-paying emigrants on 'short' ships
1875	609	631	2043	1154	445	453	79	68	5482	
1876	563	596	2038	999	407	388	79	56	5126	
1877	460	493	1759	1066	320	315	56	54	4523	
1878	804	835	2360	1264	520	496	92	111	6482	
1879	142	148	699	638	68	93	18	16	1822	
1880	269	275	983	1184	219	189	39	32	3190	
1881	509	512	1730	1464	383	368	82	67	5115	
1882	1698	1707	4642	3006	1336	1212	254	225	14089	
1883	3899	3925	9096	4466	3105	2965	563	525	28544	1883–86: includes '17th section' or 'bounty' emigrants
1884	1509	1533	4541	2349	1283	1163	209	188	12775	
1885	1132	1151	4733	2462	963	869	184	126	11620	
1886	1098	1120	3839	2412	941	902	180	138	10630	
1887	1154	1174	3703	2975	1206	1097	215	191	11715	
1888	598	598	3215	2340	536	508	106	82	7983	
1889	433	434	2599	2170	403	350	55	71	6515	
1890	131	131	1184	1331	150	140	17	17	3101	
1891	146	146	1188	1142	131	115	23	18	2909	
1892	31	31	205	321	20	36	5	5	654	
1893	–	1	4	8	–	–	–	1	13*	* adult nominees only
1894	4	21	13	40	22	21	1	1	123	
1895	4	5	31	55	4	5	–	2	106	
1896	12	21	89	112	24	15	1	2	276*	* includes 23 full-payers at reduced rate of £12
1897	46	54	227	204	38	62	5	2	638*	* includes 125 full-payers at full rate; and 53 returned Queenslanders from Paraguay
1898	24	36	151	184	24	29	5	1	454*	* includes 1 full-payer at reduced rate
1899	70	80	562	519		152	5	1	1383*	* does not include 518 Scandinavians travelling on free passages

Compiled from the annual reports of the Agent-General, Qld VPLA.

Table 11 Queensland, 1874–1899: government-assisted immigrants despatched from Britain by the Agent-General for Queensland, by 'country' of origin

Year	English	Scottish	Irish	Other	Total	Notes
1874	5910	313	2022	89	8334	
1875	2585	419	2364	114	5482	
1876	2227	533	2260	106	5126	
1877	1835	387	1945	365	4523	
1878	3766	740	1868	108	6482	
1879	900	120	700	102	1822	
1880	1046	173	1752	219	3190	
1881	2095	527	1894	599	5115	
1882	6905	3173	3280	731	14089	
1883	17537	5776	4185	1046	28544	
1884	7039	1334	3473	929	12775	
1885	6322	1572	2980	746	11620	
1886	6414	1481	2176	559	10630	
1887	6657	1598	2726	734	11715	
1888	4787	1077	1869	250	7983	
1889	3818	881	1632	184	6515	
1890	1549	352	1045	155	3101	
1891	1299	263	892	455	2909	
1892	380	26	204	44	654	
1893	2	–	7	4	13	
1894	$43\frac{1}{2}$	8	$24\frac{1}{2}$	$19\frac{1}{2}$	$95\frac{1}{2}$*	$95\frac{1}{2}$ statute adults = 123 individuals
1895	34	6	53	13	106	
1896	111	35	113	17	276	
1897	252	84	215	43	638*	*includes 44 Queensland-born
1898	165	44	201	44	454	
1899	547	303	459	74	1383	

Excludes emigrants despatched from Germany and full-paying emigrants despatched in 'short' ships. Compiled from the annual reports of the Agent-General, Qld *VPLA*.

Table 12 Queensland, 1874–1895: government-assisted female domestics despatched from Britain by the Agent-General

Year	No. of Domestics	Notes
1874	1364	
1875	1026	
1876	920	
1877	1056	
1878	1246	
1879	610	
1880	1074	
1881	1374	
1882	2895	
1883	3949	includes 179 despatched under the '17th section' of the Act
1884	2108	includes 496 despatched under the '17th section' of the Act
1885	2270	includes 217 despatched under the '17th section' of the Act
1886	2192	includes 76 despatched under the '17th section' of the Act
1887	2116	
1888	1880	
1889	1804	
1890	1102	
1891	940	
1892	231	
1893	8	
1894	16	and 5 dressmakers
1895	45	and 2 nurses

Compiled from the annual reports of the Agent-General, Qld *VPLA*.

Table 13 Western Australia, 1850–1872: assisted migration from Britain, conducted at the expense of the British government, by sex and family status

Year	Married		Single		Children*		Infants		Totals		
	Male	Female	Male	Female	Male	Female	Male	Female	Male	Female	Total
1850	35	35	72	59	28	20	2	1	137	115	252
1851	18	18	31	31	10	12	–	1	59	62	121
1852	92	92	43	184	97	100	7	14	239	390	629
1853	135	135	45	300	118	129	12	13	310	577	887
1854	79	79	77	108	41	47	4	8	201	242	443
1855	–	–	2	8	5	4	–	–	7	12	19
1856	18	18	14	31	8	4	2	1	42	54	96
1857	65	65	40	74	27	34	5	4	137	177	314
1858	23	25	6	118	11	12	1	2	41	157	198
1859	58	58	28	219	31	25	7	6	124	308	432
1860	41	43	28	151	17	14	5	4	91	212	303
1861	3	6	19	26	4	8	–	2	26	42	68
1862	86	88	69	207	48	54	12	8	215	357	572
1863	24	26	36	67	13	17	–	3	73	113	186
1864	11	16	37	124	10	10	1	2	59	152	211
1865	9	16	13	82	7	8	1	–	30	106	136
1866	11	11	5	68	9	7	3	–	28	86	114
1867	12	12	4	71	3	1	–	3	19	87	106
1868	13	13	7	96	5	3	1	2	26	114	140
1869	7	7	4	42	2	3	3	1	16	53	69
1870	1	5	1	5	2	1	1	–	5	11	16
1871	–	–	–	–	–	–	–	–	–	–	–
1872	2	3	1	1	2	1	–	–	5	5	10
Total	743	771	582	2072	498	514	67	75	1890	3432	5322

* 'Children' were defined as aged 1–14 years until 1855; thereafter as 1–12 years
Adapted from van den Driesen, 'Convicts and Migrants in Western Australia 1850–1868', table 5, p. 46.

Table 14 Western Australia, 1873–1900: government-assisted immigration from Britain, by sex

Year	Adults		Children under 12		Totals		Total	Notes
	Male	Female	Male	Female	Male	Female		
1873							–	
1874							–	
1875							447	
1876							412	
1877							340	
1878							73*	* no. arrived to April 1878
1879							61	
1880							78	
1881							146	
1882							125*	* no. arrived to 28 July 1882; 131 more expected that year
1883							290	
1884							351	
1885							381	
1886							1556	
1887							1529*	* includes 1024 Western Australian Land Company immigrants
1888							50	
1889							161	
1890							82	
1891							134	
1892					168	149	317	
1893					54	132	186	
1894	11	169	6	13	17	182	199	
1895	23	110	5	6	28	116	144	
1896	9	117	3	7	12	124	136	
1897	25	129	15	11	40	140	180	
1898	29	63	–	5	29	68	97	
1899	17	24	4	4	21	28	49	
1900	25	70	12	17	37	87	124	

Compiled from *Statistical Registers of Western Australia; Blue Books* of Western Australia; annual reports of the Board of Immigration, WA *VP*.

Table 15 Tasmania, 1859–1890: government-assisted immigrants by sex, family status, 'country' of origin, and occupation (1883–89)

Year	Married Male	Female	Single Male	Female	Children Male	Female	Total Male	Female	Total
1859									
English	26	31	20	192	28	45	74	268	342
Irish	5	8	18	82	5	5	28	95	123
Scottish	15	19	95	92	8	21	118	132	250
Total	46	58	133	366	41	71	220	495	715
1860									
English	25	27	14	136	26	36	65	199	264
Irish	8	12	43	109	12	6	63	127	190
Scottish	21	22	51	234	20	13	92	269	361
Other	–	3	–	–	–	–	–	3	3
Total	54	61	108	482	58	55	220	598	818
1861									
English	7	11	6	127	8	5	71	143	164
Irish	9	11	23	76	3	4	35	91	126
Scottish	1	1	4	49	2	2	7	52	59
Other	–	–	–	5	–	–	–	5	5
Total	17	23	33	257	13	11	63	291	354
1862									
English	27	25	30	91	32	20	89	136	225
Irish	5	7	12	52	7	7	24	66	90
Scottish	34	34	93	71	15	21	142	126	268
Total	66	66	135	214	54	48	255	328	583
1863									
English	11	11	9	22	7	8	27	41'	68
Irish	5	5	23	35	3	5	31	45	76
Scottish	1	1	4	18	–	2	5	21	26
Total	17	17	36	75	10	15	63	107	170
1864									
English	5	4	4	6	7	2	16	12	28
Irish	7	7	17	27	9	8	33	42	75
Scottish	2	2	1	4	1	5	4	11	15
Total	14	13	22	37	17	15	53	65	118

Table 15 (continued)

Year	Married Male	Female	Single Male	Female	Children Male	Female	Total Male	Female	Total
1865									
English	3	4	4	5	1	–	8	9	17
Irish	4	3	19	28	5	3	28	34	62
Scottish	2	2	4	2	–	1	6	5	11
Other	–	–	–	–	2	–	2	–	2
Total	9	9	27	35	8	4	44	48	92
1866									
English	–	–	1	2	–	–	1	2	3
Irish	2	2	15	11	4	2	21	15	36
Scottish	1	1	2	4	2	4	5	9	14
Total	3	3	18	17	6	6	27	26	53
1867									
English	2	2	2	1	2	5	6	8	14
Irish	2	2	3	7	5	11	10	20	30
Scottish	1	1	1	–	4	5	6	6	12
Total	5	5	6	8	11	21	22	34	56
1868									
English	1	2	2	1	1	–	4	3	7
Irish	6	4	7	12	9	6	22	22	44
Scottish	–	–	3	2	–	–	3	2	5
Total	7	6	12	15	10	6	29	27	56
1869									
English	1	1	–	1	2	–	3	2	5
Irish	1	1	8	5	3	4	12	10	22
Scottish	–	–	–	1	–	–	–	1	1
Total	2	2	8	7	5	4	15	13	28
1870									
English	2	3	1	4	6	5	9	12	21
Irish	1	1	4	9	1	2	6	12	18
Scottish	–	–	1	1	–	–	1	1	2
German	55	54	38	31	57	66	150	151	301
Total	58	58	44	45	64	73	166	176	342

Year	Married Male	Female	Single Male	Female	Children Male	Female	Total Male	Female	Total
1871									
English	–	–	–	3	–	–	–	3	3
Irish	–	–	2	1	–	–	2	1	3
Scottish	–	–	2	1	–	–	2	1	3
Total	–	–	4	5	–	–	4	5	9
1872									
English	1	1	–	4	2	2	3	7	10
Irish	–	–	3	4	–	–	3	4	7
Scottish	–	–	–	–	–	–	–	–	–
German	32	31	28	13	33	45	93	89	182
Total	33	32	31	21	35	47	99	100	199
1873									
English	–	1	6	1	–	1	6	3	9
Irish	2	2	2	1	8	3	12	6	18
Scottish	–	–	–	–	–	–	–	–	–
Other	–	–	1	–	–	–	1	–	1
Total	2	3	9	2	8	4	19	9	28
1874									
English	1	1	1	2	–	–	2	3	5
Irish	1	1	5	4	2	–	8	5	13
Scottish	–	–	–	–	–	–	–	–	–
Total	2	2	6	6	2	–	10	8	18
1875									
English	–	1	2	1	3	2	5	4	9
Irish	–	–	1	3	–	–	1	3	4
Scottish	–	1	–	–	1	1	1	2	3
Total	–	2	3	4	4	3	7	9	16
1876									
English	7	5	2	2	9	6	18	13	31
Irish	–	–	4	4	–	–	4	4	8
Scottish	2	2	–	–	1	4	3	6	9
Total	9	7	6	6	10	10	25	23	48
1877									
English	1	1	–	1	–	–	1	2	3
Irish	–	–	1	–	–	–	–	1	1
Scottish	–	–	2	1	–	–	2	1	3
Total	1	1	3	2	–	–	3	4	7

Table 15 (continued)

Year	Married Male	Female	Single Male	Female	Children Male	Female	Total Male	Female	Total
1878									
English	2	2	2	8	5	3	9	13	22
Irish	2	2	–	3	4	3	6	8	14
Scottish	1	1	1	–	3	2	5	3	8
Total	5	5	3	11	12	8	20	24	44
1879									
English	8	10	3	6	6	12	17	28	45
Irish	1	1	1	3	–	1	2	5	7
Scottish	–	1	–	–	–	–	–	–	–
Other	1	1	–	1	1	–	2	2	4
Total	10	12	4	10	7	13	21	35	56
1880									
English	4	7	1	6	9	5	14	18	32
Irish	1	1	2	–	4	2	7	3	10
Scottish	2	1	2	2	3	–	7	3	10
Total	7	9	5	8	16	7	28	24	52
1881									
English	3	4	5	5	1	1	9	10	19
Irish	3	3	1	5	3	4	7	12	19
Scottish	3	3	4	3	1	2	8	8	16
Other	1	1	1	–	–	2	2	3	5
Total	10	11	11	13	5	9	26	33	59
1882									
English	13	16	11	14	24	28	48	58	106
Irish	–	2	5	4	6	6	11	12	23
Scottish	1	2	–	4	2	–	3	6	9
Other	–	1	–	–	1	1	1	2	3
Total	14	21	16	22	33	35	63	78	141
1883									
English	71	74	73	42	89	84	233	200	433
Irish	5	4	5	10	6	4	16	18	34
Scottish	17	16	15	17	12	20	44	53	97
Other	6	7	7	2	7	5	20	14	34
Total	99	101	100	71*	114	113	313	285	598

* includes 58 domestic servants

Year	Married Male	Female	Single Male	Female	Children Male	Female	Total Male	Female	Total
1884									
English	114	120	81	72	168	160	363	352	715
Irish	13	11	25	25	19	17	57	53	110
Scottish	15	14	22	18	14	16	51	48	99
Other	5	6	5	4	2	3	12	13	25
Total	147	151	133	119*	203	196	483	466	949

* includes 72 domestics, 7 cooks, 1 dairymaid, 7 house and parlour maids, 2 laundresses, 3 needlewomen, 14 trained and untrained nurses

Year	Married Male	Female	Single Male	Female	Children Male	Female	Total Male	Female	Total
1885									
English	56	62	110	36	56	59	222	157	379
Irish	6	10	12	8	7	7	25	25	50
Scottish	2	2	10	1	4	7	16	10	26
Other	18	17	23	12	25	32	66	16	127
Total	82	91	155	57	90	112	329	253	582
1886									
English	8	31	19	21	26	26	53	78	131
Irish	1	2	4	6	2	1	7	9	16
Scottish	2	4	2	–	3	3	7	7	14
Other	1	1	1	3	–	1	2	5	7
Total	12	38	26	30	31	31	69	99	168
1887									
English	8	24	8	8	14	26	30	58	88
Irish	1	2	4	2	–	1	5	5	10
Scottish	5	6	5	4	10	6	20	16	36
Other	2	6	14	10	8	9	24	25	49
Total	16	38	31	24*	32	42	79	104	183

* includes 20 domestics, 3 dressmakers, 1 schoolmistress

Year	Married Male	Female	Single Male	Female	Children Male	Female	Total Male	Female	Total
1888									
English	1	3	5	4	6	7	12	14	26
Irish	–	–	1	1	–	–	1	1	2
Scottish	–	1	1	–	1	–	2	1	3
Other	–	–	–	1	–	–	–	1	1
Total	1	4	7	6*	7	7	15	17	32

* includes 3 domestics, 1 dressmaker, 1 schoolmistress

Table 15 (continued)

Year	Married Male	Married Female	Single Male	Single Female	Children Male	Children Female	Total Male	Total Female	Total
1889									
English	–	4	1	3	3	6	4	13	17
Irish	–	–	1	1	–	–	1	1	2
Scottish	–	–	–	–	–	–	–	–	–
Other	–	–	–	–	–	–	–	–	–
Total	–	4	2	4*	3	6	5	14	19
	* includes 2 domestics, 2 dressmakers								
1890									3

Compiled from annual statistics, T *HAJ*.

Notes

1 Emigrating Women

1 Joseph Chamberlain, speech delivered before United British Women's Emigration Association, London, 1901.

2 Hannah Wright, diary.

3 Maggie Kelly, diary.

4 These figures are drawn from the statistics included in the Appendix to this book. It is likely that the number of government-assisted single immigrant women arriving in the Australian colonies between 1850 and 1900 could have been closer to one hundred thousand. See 'Note on statistics' in the Appendix for an explanation of difficulties with colonial immigration statistics.

5 Hannah Wright, diary.

6 McConville, 'Peopling the place again', in V. Burgmann and J. Lee (eds), *A Most Valuable Acquisition: A People's History of Australia Since 1788*, Melbourne, 1988, p. 78.

7 O'Farrell, *Letters from Irish Australia 1825–1929*, p. 5. O'Farrell's 1986 work, *The Irish in Australia*, drawing on a different range of sources, gives greater place to the single Irish women who made up such a large proportion of the Irish immigrant population but still not as much as their numerical importance warrants.

8 See, for example, Erickson, *Invisible Immigrants*, p. 20; Erickson, *English Women Immigrants in America in the Nineteenth Century*, p. 1.

9 Hassam, *Sailing to Australia*; Charlwood, *The Long Farewell*.

10 *Friendly Work*, October 1883, p. 229.

11 Dale, Maggie's Journey, pp. 3, 7.

12 *Dunbar Castle*, 4/4993, reel 2486, SRNSW.

13 *Sobraon*, 4/4993, reel 2486, SRNSW.

14 *Hawkesbury*, 4/4996, reel 2486, SRNSW.

[15] See Hammerton, *Emigrant Gentlewomen*; Hammerton, 'Feminism and Female Emigration, 1861–1886'; Monk, *New Horizons*, for accounts of the organisation of middle-class female emigration. Clarke, *The Governesses*, is based on letters sent back to Britain by emigrant British governesses.

[16] Richards, 'Annals of the Australian Immigrant', p. 13, my emphasis.

[17] Caroline Chisholm has been the subject of two book-length biographies. See Kiddle, *Caroline Chisholm*; Hoban, *Fifty-one Pieces of Wedding Cake*.

[18] Damousi, *Depraved and Disorderly*; Oxley, *Convict Maids*; Daniels, *Convict Women*; Snowden, The Irish Female Arsonists; Robinson, *The Hatch and Brood of Time*; Hammerton, *Emigrant Gentlewomen*; McLennan, 'Glimpses of Unassisted English Women'; Kleinig, 'Independent Women'; Curtin, 'Gentility Afloat'; Hamilton, 'Irish Women Immigrants in the Nineteenth Century'; Hamilton, '*No Irish need apply*'; Hamilton, 'Tipperarifying the Moral Atmosphere'.

[19] Macdonald, *A Woman of Good Character*, p. 8.

[20] Cited in Sharpe, 'Female Emigration Schemes', p. 16.

[21] This is to oversimplify forty years of complex policies in six colonies. Victoria and Western Australia are particularly complicated. The intricacies of policy are beyond the scope of this present work but have been analysed in detail in Gothard, Government-assisted Migration.

[22] See Gothard, 'Wives or Workers?'.

[23] *Bulletin*, 12 March 1892, p. 6, quoted in Hicks, '*This Sin and Scandal*', pp. 104–5.

[24] 'Report of the Immigration Agent for 1858', Vic *PP*, 1859–60, vol. 3, no. 6, p. 9.

[25] See, for example, Alford, *Production or Reproduction?*, p. 98.

[26] McBride, *The Domestic Revolution*, p. 47. See also Worthington 'On the Unequal Proportion between the Male and Female Population of Some Manufacturing and Other Towns', 1867, pp. 68–79; Ravenstein, 'The Laws of Migration', 1885, pp. 167–235; and 'The Laws of Migration' (second paper), 1889, pp. 241–305.

[27] See, for example, Stanley (ed.), *The Diaries of Hannah Cullwick*.

[28] McBride, *The Domestic Revolution*, p. 34.

[29] Malcolm Fraser, Agent-General, to Colonial Secretary's Office, 20 March 1896, AG 418/96, minute paper 1258/96, acc. 527, SROWA, notes on file.

[30] Clipping, n.p., n.d., Mrs Ross's Emigration Scrapbook, Fawcett Library, London.

2 *Manchester Cottons and Bermondsey Boots*

[1] 'Reports of the Select Committee of the Legislative Council of South Australia appointed to inquire into the excessive female immigration,

together with minutes of evidence, Select Committee Inquiry into Excessive Female Immigration, First Report', SA *PP*, 1855–56, vol. 2, no. 137, see pp. v–vii, 31–41.

2   Ibid.

3   '24th Report of the CLEC', *BPP*, 1864, XVI, 477, p. 30.

4   Colonial Land and Emigration Commissioners, *Regulations and Conditions*, London, 1861.

5   Newsclippings, various, 1890, Fawcett Library scrapbook.

6   E. T. Wildman, CL&I, to G. S. Walters, Emigration Agent for South Australia, 25 April 1865, Correspondence on emigration, SA *PP*, 1865, vol. 1, no. 34, p. 9.

7   See, for example, 'Immigration regulations', SA *PP*, 1862, vol. 2, no. 13, pp. 2, 3.

8   Application papers, acc. 553, box 1, item 10, SROWA.

9   G. F. Eliot, Immigration Board, to 'Dear Sir', 13 September 1893, box 5, acc. 553; Ellen Heywood to Colonial Secretary's Office, 16 September 1891, notes on file, box 5, acc. 553, SROWA.

10 Application by Henry J. Payton, Form A, notes on form, Colonial Secretary to Under-Secretary, 12 August 1895, box 5, acc. 553, SROWA.

11 Bishop Parry to Colonel Forbes, Secretary, Immigration Board, 24 August 1891, box 5, acc. 553; correspondence from Miss Corless' Nurses Training Institution, May 1894, notes on file, Octavius Burt to Colonial Secretary, 24 July 1894, 1243/94, acc. 527, SROWA.

12 H. Hoost to Inspector of Immigration, 13 September 1894, box 5, acc. 553, SROWA.

13 Ellen Heywood to Colonial Secretary's Office, 16 September 1891, box 5, acc. 553, SROWA.

14 William Henderson to Secretary, Immigration Board, 6 October 1893; Margaret Howard to Octavius Burt, n.d. (received 4 October 1893); box 5, acc. 553, SROWA.

15 Frank to Mother, 23 July 1861, Cole family papers, privately held, Melbourne, Victoria.

16 Evidence of Mrs Mary Anne Pawsey, 'Report from the Select Committee on Immigration', NSW *VPLA*, 1870, vol. 1, p. 790.

17 '33rd Report of the CLEC', *BPP*, 1873, XVIII, 295, p. 1.

18 CSO, Van Diemens Land, to Colonial Secretary, South Australia, 29 October 1855, CSD 1/69/1612, AOT.

19 Chief Secretary, Victoria, to Colonial Secretary, Tasmania, 14 August 1856; Colonial Secretary, Tasmania, to Chief Secretary, Victoria, 29 August 1856, CSD 1/102/2998, AOT.

20 Colonial Secretary to Agent-General, 30 April 1879, 'Suspension of Emigration and Re-organization of the Agent-General's Department', Qld *VPLA*, 1879, vol. 2, p. 171.

21 Board of Immigration to committee members, 14 February 1860, CB 7/5/2, AOT.

22 *Mercury*, 28 December 1860.

23 Orton, *Made of Gold*.

24 Board of Immigration to James Youl, 13 February 1860, CB 7/5/2, AOT.

25 See Gothard, ' "Pity the poor immigrant" ', pp. 104–6, for a discussion of Sidney Herbert's Fund for Promoting Female Emigration, and pp. 102–9, on colonial responses to philanthropic British emigration in the 1850s.

26 'Emigration for Female Prisoners', *Englishwoman's Review*, vol. 10, November 1879, p. 518.

27 Secretary of State to John G. Leyland, 27 November 1855, CO 385/28, PRO Kew.

28 Evidence of W. R. Hunt, 'Report of the Select Committee on Immigration', SA *PP*, 1877, vol. 3, no. 102, p. 49.

29 See Macdonald, *A Woman of Good Character*. Evans, ' "Soiled doves" ', is one of a few secondary sources which picks up the connection between single female immigrants and prostitution.

30 'Immigration Correspondence', SA *PP*, 1858, vol. 1, no. 18, p. 7.

31 S. Walcott, CLEC, to G. S. Walters, 15 February 1865, 'Correspondence on Emigration', SA *PP*, 1865, vol. 1, no. 34, pp. 2–3.

32 'Report of the Select Committee on Immigration', SA *PP*, 1877, vol. 3, no. 102, p. 36.

33 'Immigration (Report from the Agent for 1863)', NSW *VPLA*, 1864, p. 609.

34 'Immigration: Report for the Half-year to June 30, 1863', T *HAJ*, 1864, vol. 2, no. 61, p. 3; 'Report of the Agent-General for the Year 1864', T *HAJ*, 1865, vol. 12, no. 20, p. 3.

35 'Report of the Agent-General for 1897', Qld *VPLA*, 1898, vol. 2, p. 698.

36 S. Walcott to G. S. Walters, 15 February 1865, 'Correspondence on Emigration', SA *PP*, 1865, vol. 1, no. 34, p. 3.

37 'Report of the Agent-General for 1896', Qld *VPLA*, 1897, vol. 2, p. 1055.

38 'Report of the Agent-General for 1898', Qld *VPLA*, 1899, p. 1287.

39 See Gothard, ' "Pity the poor immigrant" ', pp. 97–116.

40 'Immigration: Further Correspondence Relating to', Vic *PP*, vol. 4, no. 62, p. 3.

41 S. Walcott to G. S. Walters, 15 February 1865, 'Correspondence on Emigration', SA *PP*, 1865, vol. 1, no. 34, p. 2.

42 Felgate & Co. to Colonial Secretary, 1 September 1876, 741/46, acc. 36, SROWA.

43 Agent-General to Chief Secretary, 24 March 1871, Z8206, 3991/514, PROV.

44 Agent-General to Chief Secretary, 20 May 1870, X15439, 3991/450, PROV.

45 Anne McManus to Agent-General, n.d., X15439, 3991/450, PROV.
46 Mary Ann Carrow to Agent-General, n.d., X15439, 3991/450, PROV.
47 Mary Ann Roades to Agent-General, 21 April 1870, second letter, X15439, 3991/450, PROV.
48 Agent-General to Chief Secretary, 20 May 1870, X15439, 3991/450, PROV.
49 CL&I to emigration agent, 6 June 1883, GRG 35/41/3, SRSA.
50 Caroline Gawler to CL&I, 20 January 1876, GRG 35/41/2, SRSA.
51 Instructions to agents for the selection of emigrants, 'Correspondence on Emigration', SA *PP*, 1865, vol. 1, no. 34, p. 4.
52 Rye, *'Emigration of Educated Women'*, 1861, p. 6.
53 Evidence of R. J. Day, 'Report of the Select Committee on Immigration', SA *PP*, 1877, vol. 3, no. 102, p. 33.
54 Instructions to agents for the selection of emigrants, 'Correspondence on Emigration', SA *PP*, 1865, vol. 1, no. 34, pp. 3–4.
55 'Report of the Agent-General for 1885', Qld *JLC*, 1886, part 2, p. 2.
56 Emigration office to Herman Merivale, Colonial Office, 10 February 1857, CO 384/98, PRO Kew.
57 Evidence of R. J. Day, 'Report of the Select Committee on Immigration', SA *PP*, 1877, vol. 3, no. 102, p. 33.
58 *The Times*, 21 February 1867.
59 Application for emigration, Elizabeth Jeffreys, box 1, item 10, acc. 553, SROWA.
60 Evidence of R. J. Day, 'Report of the Select Committee on Immigration', SA *PP*, 1877, vol. 3, no. 102, p. 33.
61 Evidence of W. R. Hunt, 'Report of the Select Committee on Immigration', SA *PP*, 1877, vol. 3, no. 102, p. 30.
62 CSO 1203/1892, SROWA, cited in Abbott, '"The aged, infirm and indigent poor"'.
63 John Douglas to Colonial Secretary, 4 November 1870, 'Correspondence between the Government and the Agent-General for Emigration', Qld *VPLA*, 1871, p. 921.
64 Secretary of State to G. A. Hamilton, Treasury, 15 May 1863, CO 385/30, PRO Kew.
65 CLEC to Sir Fredrick Rogers, Bart, 11 May 1869, CO 386/77, PRO Kew.
66 CLEC to Sir Frederick Rogers, 24 September 1869, CO 386/77, PRO Kew.
67 Minutes of the Tasmanian Board of Immigration, 19 May, 16 June, 9 July, 30 July 1885, CB7/7/2, AOT.
68 'Result of Enquiries into Character &c of Female Emigrants Pike, Heather and Baker', S. Walcott to C. F. Verdon, 26 November 1869, V566, 3991/444, PROV.

[69] A. W. Manning, Principal Under-Secretary, to Henry Jordan, 18 January 1865, 'Correspondence between Mr. Jordan, Agent-General for Emigration, and the Government', Qld *VPLA*, 1865, p. 668.

[70] John Douglas to Colonial Secretary, 4 November 1870, 'Correspondence between the Government and the Agent-General for Emigration, Mr. Douglas', Qld *VPLA*, 1871, p. 921.

[71] Instructions to Agents, 'Correspondence on Emigration', SA *PP*, 1865, vol. 1, no. 34, p. 4.

[72] CLEC to Agent-General, 3 January 1870, V2695, 3991/445, PROV.

[73] Denis Brennan to CLEC, 15 December 1869, V2695, 3991/445, PROV.

[74] Agent-General to Chief Secretary, 3 December 1869, V3654, 3991/445 (one of two letters of this description at this location), PROV.

[75] '16th Report of the CLEC', *BPP*, 1856, XXIV, 325, pp. 10–11.

[76] Ibid., p. 19.

[77] S. Walcott, CLEC, to G. S. Walters, 15 February 1865, 'Correspondence on Emigration', SA *PP*, 1865, vol. 1, no. 34, pp. 2–3.

[78] Enclosure, Gov. 105/2189 WA, in, Secretary of State to CLEC, 4 April 1856, CO 385/28, PRO Kew.

[79] Rogers to Merivale, 6 October 1858, CO 386/77, PRO Kew.

[80] '24th Report of the CLEC', *BPP*, 1864, XVI, 477, pp. 17, 32.

[81] Secretary of State to Merivale, 7 July 1855, CO 386/76, PRO Kew. See Haines, *Emigration and the Labouring Poor*.

[82] CLEC to Merivale, 6 October 1858, CO 386/77, PRO Kew.

[83] Ibid.

[84] Secretary of State to CLEC, 13 October 1858, CO 385/29, PRO Kew.

[85] 'Report of the Agent-General for Emigration for 1874', Qld *VPLA*, 1876, vol. 2, pp. 1053–4.

[86] O'Farrell, *The Irish in Australia*, p. 85.

[87] 'Reply to Letter as to Advisability of Increasing Number of Single Female Emigrants', by J. Chatfield Tyler, 19 May 1870, Z1960, 3991/512, PROV; also, Chief Secretary's Office to Agent-General, 21 May 1870, no. 1228, W5057, 1187/17, PROV.

[88] 'Reply to Letter as to Advisability of Increasing Number of Single Female Emigrants', Z1960, 3991/512, PROV.

[89] Fitzpatrick, 'Irish Emigration in the Late Nineteenth Century', p. 136. See also, David Fitzpatrick, A Share of the Honeycomb: Education, Emigration and Women, unpublished paper, for a discussion of nineteenth-century Irish female emigration.

[90] Jackson, 'Women in 19th Century Irish Migration', pp. 1006–7.

[91] 'Report of the Agent-General for 1896', Qld *VPLA*, 1897, vol. 2, p. 1054; 'Report of the Agent-General for 1897', Qld *VPLA*, 1898, vol. 2, pp. 697–8.

[92] See, for example, 'Report of the Assistant Immigration Agent for the Year 1855', Vic *PP*, 1856–57, vol. 4, no. 1, p. v; also, 'Report of

the Assistant Immigration Agent at Geelong', Appendix XVI, Vic *PP*, 1856–57, vol. 4, no. 1, p. 33.

93 Rye, *'Emigration of Educated Women'*, 1861, pp. 1–2.

94 'Report of the Agent-General for 1887', Qld *VPLA*, 1888, vol. 3, p. 147.

95 Evidence of David Sutherland, 'Report of the Select Committee on Immigration', SA *PP*, 1877, vol. 3, no. 102, pp. 63, 66.

96 'Proposed Emigration of Highland Crofters', Qld *VPLA*, 1887, vol. 3, p. 584.

97 Evidence of J. D. Lang, 'Minutes of Evidence before the Select Committee on Immigration', NSW *VPLA*, 1870, vol. 1, p. 769.

98 Evidence of M. A. Pawsey, 'Minutes of Evidence before the Select Committee on Immigration', NSW *VPLA*, 1870, vol. 1, p. 790.

99 J. B. Wilcocks to R. F. Newland, 24 January 1865, 'Correspondence on Emigration', SA *PP*, 1865, vol. 1, no. 34, p. 5.

1 Agent-General to Chief Secretary, 24 March 1871, Z8206, 3991/514, PROV.

2 Eveline Portsmouth to C. F. Verdon, 14 March 1871, Z8206, 3991/514, PROV.

3 See Stedman Jones, *Outcast London*, pp. 127–30, for a discussion of the Victorian perception of the superior morality of the rural dweller.

4 Ravenstein, 'The Laws of Migration', 1885, pp. 196–8, argues, p. 196, that within Britain 'woman is a greater migrant than man.' See also Worthington, 'On the Unequal Proportion between the Male and Female Population', 1867, pp. 68–77, for a discussion of female migration within nineteenth-century Britain. As McBride has pointed out in *The Domestic Revolution*, p. 34, 'The history of domestic service in the nineteenth century is the story of urban migration'.

5 'Scotch Emigration. (First Annual Report. March 1875 to March 1876)', Qld *VPLA*, 1876, vol. 2, p. 1058.

6 Jordan to Colonial Secretary, 26 February 1866, 'Selection of Emigrants. (Correspondence Referring to Article in Brisbane Papers Relative to)', Qld *VPLA*, 1866, p. 1029.

7 G. F. Verdon to Chief Secretary, 25 March 1870, Z1960, 3991/512, PROV.

8 'Reply to Letter as to Advisability of Increasing Number of Single Female Emigrants', by J. Chatfield Tyler, 19 May 1870, Z1960, 3991/512, PROV.

9 R. F. Newland to G. S. Walters, 'Emigration Correspondence', SA *PP*, 1863, vol. 2, no. 68** [sic], p. 6.

10 'Report of the Agent-General for 1887', Qld *VPLA*, 1888, vol. 3, p. 146.

11 Evidence of Caroline Stapley, 'Report of the Select Committee on Immigration', SA *PP*, 1877, vol. 3, no. 102, p. 107.

3 'A reward for good conduct'

[1] Ellen Joyce, 'Letters on Emigration', *Friendly Work*, September 1883, pp. 204–5.

[2] Greg, 'Why are Women Redundant?', 1862.

[3] 'The Emigration of Women', *The Queen, the Lady's Newspaper*, February 1894, Fawcett Library scrapbook.

[4] Hammerton, *Emigrant Gentlewomen*; Clarke, *The Governesses*.

[5] Monk, *New Horizons*, p. 6.

[6] Letter from Florence Hill, *Englishwoman's Review*, October 1873, p. 271.

[7] Pratt, *A Woman's Work for Women*, 1898, p. 30; *Woman's Gazette*, November 1877, p. 218.

[8] *Woman's Gazette*, May 1877, p. 119.

[9] *Woman's Gazette*, June 1877, p. 137.

[10] Monk, *New Horizons*, p. 7.

[11] Pratt, *A Woman's Work for Women*, 1898, p. 66.

[12] *Work and Leisure*, February 1880, p. 57.

[13] Adelaide Ross, *The Times*, 15 November 1883.

[14] 'S.R.', *The Times*, 7 November 1883.

[15] Catherine Helen Spence, *Woman's Gazette*, August 1879, p. 125; September 1879, p. 135.

[16] 'Report of the Agent-General for Emigration for the Year 1882', Qld *VPLA*, 1883, p. 419.

[17] Agent-General to Colonial Secretary, 9 November 1883, 'Immigration Correspondence', Qld *VPLA*, 1883–84, p. 1373.

[18] 'Report of the Agent-General for Emigration for the Year 1882', Qld *VPLA*, 1883, p. 422; 'Correspondence: Female Emigration', *Woman's Gazette*, January 1879, p. 13.

[19] 'Immigration Agent's Report for the Year 1885', Qld *JLC*, 1886, part 2, p. 12.

[20] Agent-General to Gellalty, Hanky, Sewell, and Coy, 30 April 1884, 'Immigration Correspondence', Qld *VPLC*, 1884, part 1, p. 1138.

[21] See, for example, Ross, 'Emigration for Women', 1882, p. 312: 'The chief defect in the history of past emigration has been this—it has been looked at from the wrong point of view, as the last resource of the unlucky and the ne'er-do-weel, not as the legitimate outlet for the energy and strength of our teeming multitudes'.

[22] Despatching officer to Acting Agent-General, 1 February 1884, 'Immigration Correspondence', Qld *JLC*, 1884, part 1, p. 1115.

[23] 'Report of the Agent-General for Emigration for the Year 1883', Qld *JLC*, 1884, part 1, pp. 1174, 1177.

[24] Acting Agent-General to Colonial Secretary, 16 January 1884, 'Immigration Correspondence, Qld *VPLC*, 1884, part 1, p. 1107; see also Ross, 'Emigration for Women', 1882, pp. 313, 315.

[25] See Macdonald, *A Woman of Good Character*, ch. 1.

[26] See, for example, *The Times*, 3 April, 9 April, 23 April, 24 April, 25 April, 28 April, 29 April, 30 April, 1 May, 21 June, 28 July, 16 August, 29 August, 3 September, 5 September, 17 October and 3 November 1862.

[27] *The Times*, 28 July 1862; Jordan to Marsh, 5 August 1862, COL/12, QSA.

[28] Henry Jordan to Colonial Secretary, 25 September 1862, COL/12, QSA.

[29] News clipping, n.p., 10 September [?] 1862, loose in COL/12, QSA.

[30] E. W. Dunlop, 'Marsh, Matthew Henry', *Australian Dictionary of Biography*, Melbourne, 1976, vol. 5, p. 213.

[31] M. H. Marsh to Henry Jordan, 8 August 1862, COL/12, QSA.

[32] Ibid., 3 August 1862.

[33] Henry Jordan to M. H. Marsh, 10 August 1862, COL/12, QSA.

[34] Henry Jordan to Colonial Secretary, 25 August 1862, COL/12, QSA.

[35] Ibid., 27 October 1862.

[36] '24th Report of the CLEC', *BPP*, 1864, XVI, 477, pp. 17, 23.

[37] For some background to Maria Rye's work in the field of female middle-class emigration see Hammerton, *Emigrant Gentlewomen*, chapter 5. Maria Rye's work in New Zealand is discussed in Macdonald, *A Woman of Good Character*, pp. 28–36; and in the chapter, 'Maria Rye in New Zealand, 1863–64', in Macdonald, Single Women as Immigrant Settlers in New Zealand, 1853–1871.

[38] 'Ship "Commodore Perry." Report', pp. 687–8; evidence of Dr J. J. Luce, 'Ship "Commodore Perry." Appendix', p. 699; Qld *VPLA*, 1865.

[39] Maria Rye to S. Walcott, CLEC, 16 September 1865, copy in no. 516, COL/12, QSA.

[40] Ibid.

[41] See, for example, Macdonald, *A Woman of Good Character*, p. 32.

[42] Gothard, Government-assisted Migration, pp. 151–4.

[43] '27th Report of the CLEC', *BPP*, 1867, XIX, 121, p. 10.

[44] Macdonald, Single Women as Immigrant Settlers, p. 78.

[45] *The Times*, 3 July 1866.

[46] S. Walcott to Commissioner, Trade and Customs, 25 May 1866, CO 386/132, PRO Kew.

[47] CLEC to Commissioner, Trade and Customs, 19 December 1866, CO 386/132, PRO Kew.

[48] '27th Report of the CLEC', *BPP*, 1867, XIX, 121, p. 10; S. Walcott to Commissioner, Trade and Customs, 25 May 1866, CO 386/132, PRO Kew.

[49] Pratt, *Pioneer Women in Victoria's Reign*, 1897, pp. 32–3.

[50] See, for example, *The Times*, 3 July, 1 September, 18 September and 25 December 1866, and 21 February 1867.

[51] *The Times*, 25 December 1866.

[52] '27th Report of the CLEC', *BPP*, 1867, XIX, 121, p. 10.
[53] CLEC to Commissioner, Trade and Customs, 19 December 1866, CO 386/132, PRO Kew.
[54] S. Walcott to Commissioner, Trade and Customs, 26 November 1866, CO 386/132, PRO Kew.
[55] Register of assisted immigrants from UK, January 1861–June 1871, VPRS 7310, PROV.
[56] Ship 'Atalanta', Register of assisted immigrants from UK, January 1861–June 1871, VPRS 7310, PROV.
[57] '28th Report of the CLEC', *BPP*, 1867–68, XVII, 787, p. 4; CLEC to Commissioner, Trade and Customs, 24 December 1867, CO 386/132, PRO Kew.
[58] CLEC to Commissioner, Trade and Customs, 27 January 1868, CO 386/133, PRO Kew.
[59] Ibid.
[60] Broome, *The Victorians: Arriving*, p. 96.
[61] *The Times*, 6 May 1869.
[62] Ibid.
[63] Archbishop Tait, 'The Church and Emigration', 20 December 1881, Tait papers, vol. 270, ff. 261, Lambeth Palace Archives, London.
[64] Newsclipping, n.p., n.d. (1883), Benson papers, Lambeth Palace Archives, London.
[65] Benson papers, *passim.*
[66] News clipping, 29 May 1894, n.p., Fawcett Library scrapbook.
[67] See Plant, *S.O.S.B.W.*, pp. 21–2, 32.
[68] This remained a problem throughout the BWEA's history, even into the next century. See, for example, evidence of Lady Knightley of Fawsley and the Hon. Mrs Joyce, 11 October 1912, 'Dominions Royal Commission: Minutes of Evidence', *BPP*, 1912, XVI, 95, p. 45.
[69] *Englishwoman's Review*, February 1882, p. 56.
[70] Board of Immigration meeting, 5 June 1884, acc. 489/5, SROWA.
[71] 'Report of the Board of Immigration for 1888', WA *VPLC*, 1889, second session, p. 179.
[72] 'Report of the Board of Immigration for 1888', pp. 179, 180; Board of Immigration meetings, 14 March and 11 June 1889, acc. 489/5, SROWA.
[73] Board of Immigration meeting, 14 March 1889, acc. 489/5, SROWA.
[74] Board of Immigration meeting, 30 December 1889, acc. 489/5, SROWA.
[75] 'File of Applicants for Immigrants per "Nairnshire"', June and July 1895, box 5, acc. 553, SROWA.
[76] Ellen Joyce to Sir Malcolm Fraser, Agent-General, 1 May 1893; UBWEA preliminary application form no. 5701, 'Alice Hamilton', box 4, acc. 553, SROWA.
[77] Ellen Joyce to Sir Malcolm Fraser, Agent-General, 11 December 1894; cited in Daniels and Murnane, *Uphill All the Way*, pp. 222–3.

78 See for example, Hammerton, '"Without natural protectors"', p. 546.

79 BWEA, *Annual Report for 1894*, p. 10; *Annual Report for 1895*, p. 21.

80 Ellen Joyce to Sir Malcolm Fraser, Agent-General, 11 December 1894; cited in Daniels and Murnane, *Uphill All the Way*, p. 222.

81 Agent-General to Colonial Secretary, 18 May 1894, AG no. 94/94, box 1, acc. 553, SROWA.

82 Maggie Kelly, diary, 24 May 1900.

83 Board of Immigration minutes, 30 December 1889, acc. 489/5, CSO, SROWA.

84 Ellen Joyce to Crown Agents, 23 May 1891, acc. 553, box 5, CSO, SROWA.

85 Board of Immigration minutes, 30 December 1889, acc. 489/5, CSO; Sir William Robinson to Colonial Secretary, 14 March 1891, acc. 553, box 5, CSO; SROWA.

86 Sir William Robinson to Colonial Secretary, 14 March 1891, acc. 553, box 5, CSO, SROWA.

87 Board of Immigration minutes, 13 March 1891, acc. 489/5, CSO, SROWA.

88 Crown Agents to Secretary, Board of Immigration, 20 February 1891; Ellen Joyce to Crown Agents, 23 May 1891; acc. 553, box 5, CSO, SROWA.

89 Mrs Bell to Immigration Office, 9 December 1891, note on file, acc. 553, box 5, CSO, SROWA.

90 CSO to caretaker, Immigration Depot [n.d. 1892?], acc. 553, box 5, CSO, SROWA.

91 William Dale to John McKenna, 28 March 1894, acc. 553, box 4, CSO, SROWA.

92 BWEA, *Annual Report for 1896*, pp. 31–2.

93 See, for example, Ross, 'Emigration for Women', 1882, pp. 312–17; 'Emigration for Educated Englishwomen', *Work and Leisure*, January 1881, p. 5; 'Women's Emigration Society', *Work and Leisure*, February 1881, p. 56.

94 BWEA, *Annual Report for 1895*, pp. 25–6.

95 'The Work of a Women's Emigration Society', part 2, *The Queen, the Lady's Newspaper*, c. April 1890, emigration scrapbook, Fawcett Library, London.

96 *Evening Post*, 27 January 1898, in Fawcett Library scrapbook.

97 *The Queen, the Lady's Newspaper*, 4 December 1886, emigration scrapbook, Fawcett Library, London.

98 'Why Do Single Women Emigrate?', newsclipping, July 1895; Fawcett Library scrapbook.

99 'Openings for Women in the Colonies', newsclipping, 6 March 1897, Fawcett Library scrapbook.

1 'Agent-General's Report for 1899', WA *VPP*, sixth session, third parliament, 1900, vol. 1, p. 669.

4 'A season of industry'

1 Sellars, 'Women's Work for the Welfare of Girls', 1893, p. 40.
2 'Correspondence: Female Emigration', *Woman's Gazette*, January 1879, p. 13.
3 Meeting, 29 June 1900, Society for Promoting Christian Knowledge. Ladies' Emigration Committee minutes (hereafter SPCK Ladies' Committee), 1897–1911, SPCK archives, London.
4 Meeting, 25 October 1894, SPCK Ladies' Committee minutes, 1882–1889, SPCK, London.
5 Evidence of A. H. Boyd, W. Henty, G. Smith, 'Select Committee to Inquire into Immigration for 1861', T *HAJ*, 1861, vol. 7, no. 150, pp. 4, 6, 8.
6 Evidence of J. H. Smales, ibid., pp. 4, 10.
7 Evidence of B. Drake, ibid., p. 13.
8 Hammerton, '"Without natural protectors"', p. 559. The 1861 Tasmanian Select Committee into immigration is discussed more fully in Gothard, '"Radically unsound and mischievous"', pp. 392–4.
9 Needham to Secretary, Education Department, 29 September 1897, 4045/77, acc. 553; Secretary for Education to Under-Treasurer, Perth, 8 October 1897, 4925/77, acc. 553; SROWA.
10 *Report of the British Ladies' Female Emigrants Society for 1852*, n.p.
11 *Imperial Colonist*, vol. 6, December 1908, p. 10.
12 Allen and McClure, *Two Hundred Years*, 1898, p. 402.
13 Ibid., p. 408.
14 Rye, 'Emigrant-ship Matrons', 1860, pp. 32–3.
15 BWEA, *Annual Report for 1891*, p. 39.
16 Ibid., p. 33.
17 Caroline Gawler to CL&I, 24 January 1877, GRG 35/41/2, SRSA.
18 Layton, 'On the Superintendence of Female Emigrants', 1863, p. 616.
19 Rye, 'Emigrant-ship Matrons', 1860, p. 27.
20 See, for example, Board of Immigration to London Selection Committee, 14 February 1860, CB 7/5/2, AOT; CLEC to Merivale, 12 April 1859; CLEC to Frederick Elliot, 13 November 1861; CO 386/77, PRO Kew.
21 'Resumption of Emigration (Correspondence Respecting)', Qld *VPLA*, 1868, first session, p. 361.
22 Walcott to Commissioner, Trade and Customs, Melbourne, 10 April 1867, CO 386/132, PRO Kew.
23 Ibid.
24 'Ship "Sultana". (Report from the Immigration Board, Maryborough, Relative to)', Qld *VPLA*, 1866, p. 1014.
25 CLEC to Merivale, 9 April 1859, Despatches to Governor of Victoria, 1858–1859, typescript duplicate, p. 2844, A2368, ML.

26 Despatch to Sir J. Pakington, 28 December 1859, Despatches from Governor of Victoria, p. 1341a, A2341, ML.
27 CLEC to Merivale, 9 April 1859, Despatches to Governor of Victoria, 1858–1859, p. 2844, A2368, ML.
28 Memorandum on the BLFES forwarded to the CLEC by the Hon. A. Kinnaird, in CLEC to Merivale, 9 April 1859, Despatches to Governor of Victoria, 1858–1859, pp. 2848–9, A2368, ML.
29 See Woolcock, *Rights of Passage*, ch. 5, 'Surgeons', for a discussion of the profession of shipboard surgeon in colonial Queensland.
30 See Hammerton, *Emigrant Gentlewomen*, pp. 125–7, for background to the emigration and employment interests of the Langham Place feminists. See also Rye, 'Emigrant-ship Matrons', 1860; Layton, 'On the Superintendence of Female Emigrants', 1863.
31 Wilson, *Women and the Welfare State*, p. 53.
32 CLEC to Merivale, 9 April 1859, Despatches to Governor of Victoria, 1858–1859, p. 2844, A2368, ML.
33 Unfortunately, I have been unable to find any description of the nature of that training in the few remaining records of the BLFES.
34 Diary of Fanny Davis, 1858, in Charlwood, *The Long Farewell*, p. 281.
35 Ibid., pp. 286, 288.
36 Rye, 'Emigrant-ship Matrons', 1860, p. 28.
37 Memo concerning BLFES, Despatches to Governor of Victoria, 1858–1859, p. 2847, A2368, ML.
38 A. G. Shadforth to Immigration Agent, Melbourne, 27 August 1862, 4/4657, SRNSW.
39 Rye, 'Emigrant-ship Matrons', 1860, p. 34.
40 Caroline Tipple, BLFES, to Agent-General for Victoria, 31 July 1869, V553, 3991/444, PROV.
41 Henry Jordan to Colonial Secretary, 26 November 1863, 'Papers and Correspondence in Reference to Immigration and Conveyance of Immigrants', Qld *VPLA*, 1864, second session, p. 920.
42 Henry Jordan to BLFES, 3 October 1865, COL/12, QSA.
43 Caroline Gawler to Commissioner, CL&I, 10 October 1878; CL&I to Gawler, [?] October 1878; GRG 35/41/2, SRSA.
44 R. Gray to Agent-General for Emigration, 21 December 1869, 'Correspondence between the Government and the Agent-General for Emigration, Mr. Douglas', Qld *VPLA*, 1871, p. 891.
45 *Friendly Leaves*, vol. 12, March 1887, no. 127, p. 75; Board of Immigration minutes, 10 February, 28 April and 2 June 1887, acc. 489/5, SROWA.
46 *Daily News*, 26 May 1890, emigration scrapbook, Fawcett Library, London.
47 Dr Walter Bridgeford to Agent-General, 11 April 1896, box 2, acc. 553, SROWA.

48 BWEA, *Annual Report for 1894*, p. 10; *Report for 1895*, p. 21.
49 *Imperial Colonist*, December 1908, p. 11.
50 Ibid.
51 Evidence of Jane Chase, 'Minutes of Evidence Taken before the Board of Inquiry into Cholera on Board the S.S. "Dorunda" ', Qld *JLC*, 1886, part 2, p. 58.
52 'Report of Immigration Board, Brisbane, on Inquiry into Certain Matters Connected with the Steamer "Jumna"', Qld *VPLA*, 1900, vol. 5, pp. 25–6.
53 'Mrs. Sophia Morphy, Late Matron of the Immigration Depot (Petition)', Qld *VPLA*, 1874, p. 1089.
54 Evidence of A. H. Boyd, 'Select Committee into Immigration', T *HAJ*, 1861, vol. 7, no. 150, p. 6.
55 A. G. Shadforth, Immigration Agent for New South Wales, to Immigration Agent, Trade and Customs, Melbourne, 27 August 1862, 4/4657, SRNSW.
56 Immigration Agent to CL&I, 11 July 1876; CL&I to Emigration Agent, 4 August 1876; GRG 35/41/2, SRSA.
57 C. Gawler to CL&I, 15 July 1876, GRG 35/41/2, SRSA.
58 'Immigration (Reports from Immigration Agent and Others)', NSW *VPLA*, 1887, second session, vol. 2, p. 888.
59 Agent for Immigration to Principal Under-Secretary, 'Immigration (Reports from Immigration Agent and Others)', NSW *VPLA*, 1885–86, vol. 2, p. 838.
60 'Report of the Select Committee on Immigration', SA *PP*, 1877, vol. 3, no. 102, p. 43.
61 Immigration Agent to CL&I, 18 January 1875, GRG 35/45, SRSA.
62 C. Gawler to Commissioner, CL&I, 6 February 1876, GRG 35/41/2, SRSA.
63 Ibid., 20 March 1876.
64 Ibid.

5 *'Gliding over the great waves'*

1 Darbyshire, *In Time for Lunch*, 1898, pp. 77, 80–1.
2 'Ship "Bayswater" ', Qld *VPLA*, 1866, p. 1023.
3 Ibid., pp. 1023–4.
4 Ibid.
5 See Damousi, 'Chaos and Order', pp. 359 *et seq.*
6 'Ship "Bayswater" ', Qld *VPLA*, 1866, p. 1024.
7 Hannah Wright, diary, 4 May 1886.
8 'Mortality on Board Immigrant Ships', NSW *VPLA*, 1883, vol. 2, p. 1080.

[9] Agent-General to Chief Secretary, 3 December 1869, V3654, 3991/445, PROV.

[10] *Friendly Work*, October 1883, p. 229.

[11] See Woolcock, *Rights of Passage*, ch. 4, for a detailed description of physical conditions of passage on Queensland emigrant vessels.

[12] *Queen Bee*, Ships' papers, 9/6280, SRNSW.

[13] *Abyssinian*, Ships' papers, 9/6281, SRNSW.

[14] Hyde Park Daily Reports, 1 June 1862, 9/6181, SRNSW.

[15] Darbyshire, *In Time for Lunch*, 1898, p. 44.

[16] Hannah Wright, diary, 7 June 1886.

[17] Ibid.

[18] Niall and Britain, *Oxford Book of Australian Schooldays*, p. 7.

[19] Hannah Wright, diary, 16 May 1886.

[20] 'Barque "Star Queen"', Qld *VPLA*, 1876, vol. 2, p. 1169.

[21] 'Specification for Fitting Queensland Government Ships', Qld *VPLA*, 1876, vol. 2, p. 1048.

[22] 'Barque "Star Queen"', Qld *VPLA*, 1876, vol. 2, p. 1141.

[23] Maria Steley, diary, 20 January 1864, cited in Hassam, *Sailing to Australia*, p. 117.

[24] Committee of Inquiry to Colonial Secretary, 9 May 1877, 'Immigrant Ship "Zamora"', Qld *VPLA*, 1877, vol. 2, p. 1151.

[25] Annie Grattan, 12 June 1858, cited in Hassam, *Sailing to Australia*, p. 139.

[26] Hannah Wright, diary, 5 May 1886.

[27] 'Specification for Fitting Queensland Government Ships', Qld *VPLA*, 1876, vol. 2, p. 1047.

[28] 'Improved Fittings in Emigrant Ship, no. 255', SA *PP*, 1874, vol. 3.

[29] 'Ship "Gauntlet"', Qld *VPLA*, 1876, vol. 2, p. 1097.

[30] 'Report by the Immigration Agent for 1862', SA *PP*, 1863, no. 22, p. 1.

[31] Correspondence from Henry Jordan, Queensland Emigration Agent, 26 January 1863 (1864?), COL/12, QSA.

[32] Damousi, 'Chaos and Order', p. 352.

[33] 'Ship "Bayswater"', Qld *VPLA*, 1866, pp. 1023 *et seq.*

[34] 'Barque "Star Queen"', Qld *VPLA*, 1876, vol. 2, p. 1142.

[35] Acting-Governor, St Helena, Jersey, to Sir Malcolm Fraser, 22 April 1896; M. P. Monk to Sir Malcolm Fraser, 11 April 1896; box 2, acc. 553, SROWA.

[36] J. W. Barratt, Station Master, to Sir Malcolm Fraser, Agent-General, 14 July 1896, box 2, acc. 553, SROWA.

[37] List of goods lost by each immigrant off the SS *Port Phillip*, box 2, acc. 553, SROWA.

[38] L. H. to Mrs Joyce, BWEA, *Annual Report for 1896*, p. 34.

[39] Allen and McClure, *Two Hundred Years*, 1898, p. 402.

40 Annual Report of SPCK, 21 June 1894, Emigration Committee minutes, 1890–1895, SPCK archives, London.

41 *West Australian*, 2 Februry 1887; WA Board of Immigration meeting, 10 February, 28 April and 2 June 1887, acc. 489/5, SROWA.

42 *Friendly Leaves*. vol. xii, no. 127, March 1887, p. 75.

43 Vellacott (ed.), *A Girl at Government House*, pp. 21–2.

44 *Friendly Work*, October 1883, p. 229.

45 Board of Immigration Letterbook, Outletters, 4 January 1859–29 April 1862: 13 January 1860, CB7/5/1, AOT.

46 *Sobraon*, 4/4993, reel 2486, SRNSW.

47 Surgeon's journals, *Roslin Castle*, 1882, 4/4698.4, reel 2582, SRNSW.

48 Ibid.

49 'Immigration Agent's Report for the Year 1899', Qld *VPLA*, 1900, vol. 5, p. 675.

50 Hannah Wright, diary, 30 May 1886.

51 Maggie Kelly, diary, 7 June 1900.

52 Hannah Wright, diary, 1 June 1886.

53 Ibid.

54 See Gothard. ' "Radically Unsound and Mischievous" ', p. 393.

55 For Rye's reputation for exaggeration see also Macdonald, *A Woman of Good Character*, p. 32.

56 *Manchester Examiner*, 29 June 1866; Rye to Walcott, 16 September 1865, in Emigration Commissioners to T. M. Walcott, 29 November 1865 (copy); Jordan to Walcott, 2 December 1865, no. 516, COL/12, QSA.

57 See L'Esperance, 'Woman's Mission to Woman', for a discussion of working-class women in collusion with middle-class men against middle-class female authority.

58 See Hassam, *Sailing to Australia*, p. 115, on space and class relations on board ship. On space and gender see Spain, *Gendered Spaces*.

59 Report of the Board of Immigration, 15 December 1877, NSW *VPLA*, 1877–78, vol. 2, p. 796.

60 Hassam, *Sailing to Australia*, p. 118.

61 Damousi, 'Chaos and Order', p. 365, similarly suggests that female convict women used their sexuality to negotiate their treatment and for empowerment.

62 Report of the Board of Immigration, 15 December 1877, NSW *VPLA*, 1877–78, vol. 2, p. 796.

63 Entry for 13 December 1855, 'Accounts of Investigations by the Immigration Board into Complaints and Disorders on Immigrant Vessels', 1855–59, GRG 35/302/6, SRSA.

64 Ibid., Entries for 4, 9, 20 July 1859.

65 Henry Jordan, 'Report on Working of Emigrant Arrangements', c. 1866, included with correspondence on Maria Rye, 66/24, LWO/A29, QSA.

66 Evidence of Dr J. J. Luce, 'Ship "Commodore Perry"', Appendix, Qld *VPLA*, 1865, p. 699.

67 Hassam, *Sailing to Australia*, pp. 117, 118.

68 See, for example, Ships' papers, 9/6280, SRNSW.

69 Spain, *Gendered Spaces*, pp. 10–11.

70 Hassam, *Sailing to Australia*, p. 119.

71 Board of Immigration Letterbook, Outletters, 13 January 1860, CB 7/5/1, AOT.

72 Mr M., 23 August 1877, in Hassam, *Sailing to Australia*, p. 140.

73 Ship *Hawkesbury*, 4/4996, reel 2486, SRNSW.

74 Ship *Dunbar Castle*, 4/4993, reel 2486, SRNSW.

75 *Queen Bee*, Ships' papers, 9/6280, SRNSW.

76 Matron's journal, *Nairnshire*, acc. 504, SROWA.

77 Wise to Principal Under-Secretary, 26 June 1885, 4/4662, SRNSW.

78 'Immigration. (Reports of the Board of Immigration, 15 December 1877)', NSW *VPLA*, 1877–78, vol. 2, p. 796; see also 'Immigrant ship "Star of India"', ibid., pp. 813–14.

79 'Immigration', ibid., p. 796.

80 Ibid., p. 797.

81 Rogers to Chief Secretary, 7 December 1877, GRG 35/41/2, SRSA.

82 CL&I to Emigration Agent, 1 February 1878, GRG 35/41/2, SRSA.

83 Ibid.

84 R. Gray to Agent-General for Emigration, 21 December 1869, Qld *VPLA*, 1871, p. 891.

85 'Case of the Ship "Newcastle"', Qld *VPLA*, 1878, vol. 2, pp. 23–4.

86 Ellen Joyce to Sir Malcolm Fraser, 11 December 1894, cited in Daniels and Murnane, *Uphill All the Way*, pp. 222, 224.

87 Minute respecting the immigrant Minihan, Unregistered papers 1880–1886, 9/6186, SRNSW.

88 Macdonald, *A Woman of Good Character*, p. 87.

89 'Samuel Plimsoll', Agent for Immigration to Under-Secretary, 12 August 1878, NSW *VPLA*, 1878–79, vol. 7.

90 *Abyssinian*, Ships' papers, 9/6281, SRNSW.

91 See Appendix: Immigration Tables, pp. 209–40.

6 *'No worse than might have been expected'*

1 'Report of the Agent-General for Queensland for 1898', Qld *VPLA*, 1899, p. 1251.

2 'Report of Immigration Board, Brisbane, on Inquiry into Certain Matters Connected with Voyage of Steamer "Jumna"' Qld *VPLA*, 1900, vol. 5.

3 Ibid., p. 8.

4 Ibid., p. 9.

5   Ibid., exhibit B, p. 24.
6   Ibid., p. 8.
7   Ibid., p. 13.
8   Ibid., p. 3.
9   Ibid., pp. 3, 14.
10   Ibid., p. 14.
11   Ibid., p. 3.
12   Ibid., p. 7.
13   Ibid., p. 6; Hannah Wright, diary, 5 May 1886.
14   Ibid., p. 10.
15   Ibid., exhibit VIII, p. 21.
16   Ibid., p. 7.
17   Ibid., exhibit B, p. 24.
18   Hannah Wright, diary, 26 June 1886.
19   'Report on the Steamer "Jumna"', pp. 25–6.
20   Ibid., exhibit C, p. 24.
21   Ibid., exhibit XIV, p. 23.
22   Ibid., exhibit XII, p. 23.
23   Ibid., exhibit XIII. p. 23.
24   Ibid., exhibit XII, p. 23.
25   Ibid., p. 5.
26   Ibid., p. 7.
27   Ibid., p. 16.
28   Ibid., p. 2.
29   Harrison, 'For Church, Queen and Family', p. 113.
30   Louisa Knightley, 'The Girls' Friendly Society', *Englishwoman's Review*,
      15 May 1879, pp. 202–3.
31   See Lake, 'The Politics of Respectability', p. 8.
32   'Report on the Steamer "Jumna"', p. 12.
33   Ibid., p. 15.
34   Ibid., p. 19.
35   Ibid., p. 4.
36   Ibid., p. 11.
37   Ibid., exhibit VII, pp. 10, 20.
38   Ibid., p. 16.
39   Ibid., p. 9.
40   Ibid., exhibit X.
41   Ibid., p. 9.
42   Ibid., exhibit XII, p. 23.
43   Ibid., exhibit XI, p. 22.
44   Ibid., p. 5.
45   Ibid., p. 4.
46   Ibid., p. 5.
47   Ibid., exhibit XI, p. 22.
48   Ibid., pp. 8, 10, 11.

[49] Ibid., pp. 2, 7, 10, 11.
[50] Ibid., p. 9.
[51] Ibid., p. 8.
[52] See, for example, ibid., exhibit I, p. 17.
[53] Ibid., exhibit V, p. 19.
[54] Ibid., exhibit IV, pp. 18–19.
[55] Ibid., p. 9; exhibit VIII, p. 23.
[56] Ibid., p. 9.
[57] Ibid., exhibit VIII, p. 21.
[58] Ibid., p. 9.
[59] Ibid., p. 10.
[60] Ibid.
[61] Ibid., p. 2
[62] Ibid.
[63] Woolcock, *Rights of Passage*, p. 56.
[64] 'Report on the Steamer "Jumna"', p. 2.
[65] Ibid., p. 3.
[66] Ibid., p. 11.
[67] Ibid., p. 2.
[68] Ibid.
[69] Ibid., p. 3.
[70] Ellen Joyce, Head of Migration Department, to Girls' Friendly Society, 6 November 1920, 2/263, GFS (UK) records.

7 A Compromise with Conscience

[1] 'Immigration (Report of the Agent for Immigration on Complaints as to Manner of Hiring Immigrants per S.S. "Parthia")', NSW *VPLA*, 1885–86, vol. 2, pp. 867–8; *Sydney Morning Herald*, 21 January 1886.
[2] Darbyshire, *In Time for Lunch*, 1898, p. 91.
[3] *Western Mail*, September 1897; press collection, Fawcett Library, London.
[4] For background to Chisholm's colonial reception work see Kiddle, *Caroline Chisholm*, 'The Female Emigrants' Home'.
[5] Letter to Mr Charles King; letter to Mr Edwards; April 1857[?], 9/6213, SRNSW.
[6] Darbyshire, *In Time for Lunch*, 1898, p. 95.
[7] T. McCarthy, Caretaker, to Under-Secretary, 1 October 1894, acc. 1816/187, SROWA.
[8] Police report 185/94, box 1, acc. 553, SROWA.
[9] T. McCarthy to Colonial Under-Secretary, 14 July 1894, box 1, acc. 553, SROWA. For other incidents see also T. McCarthy to Under-Secretary, 20 March 1894; memo, T. McCarthy to Under-Secretary, 21 March 1894; notes on ibid., box 5, acc. 553, SROWA.

10 *Immigration Depot, Perth. Regulations*, Perth, 1877. CSO vol. 866/244, SROWA.

11 Maggie Kelly, diary, 12 July 1900.

12 See Macdonald, *A Woman of Good Character*, pp. 30–2, on the Dunedin immigration barracks, described in 1863 as 'not fit for occupation by human beings' (p. 30).

13 Letter from Isabella Maugham, 10 February; enclosure in Messrs Story and Green to Commissioner of Emigration, 25 April 1862, 62/1576, COL/A30, QSA.

14 R[osamond] S[mith] to Miss Merryweather, 12 January 1862, *English Woman's Journal*, vol. 9, August 1862, pp. 407–8.

15 W. F. Richards, Corporal-in-Charge, Police Station, Willunga, to George Hamilton, Senior Inspector of Mounted Police, 10 October 1855, 'Appendix to Minutes of Evidence on Excessive Female Immigration', SA *PP*, 1855–56, vol. 2, p. xi.

16 See Macdonald, *A Woman of Good Character*, pp. 28–36, for an account of Rye's time in New Zealand; Maria Rye to Stephen Walcott, CLEC, 16 September 1865, no. 516, COL/12, QSA.

17 Henry Jordan to Stephen Walcott, 2 December 1865, no. 516, COL/12, QSA.

18 George Randall to S. W. Griffith, Colonial Secretary, 1 March 1884, COL/A609, QSA.

19 *'Yungaba'. Part of Queensland history*, Division of Migrant Services, Brisbane, n.d., p. 3.

20 *Rules and Twenty-ninth Annual Report of the Lady Musgrave Lodge, for the Year Ended 30 June, 1914*, COL/292, QSA.

21 'Servants' Home Receipts and Disbursements', SA *PP*, 1865, vol. 2, no. 105, p. 1.

22 See, for example, Caroline Gawler to CL&I, 20 January 1876; CL&I to Emigration Agent, 26 February 1876; GRG 35/41/2, SRSA.

23 Evidence of Rev. J. Thorne, 'Report of the Select Committee of the House of Assembly on Immigration; Together with Minutes of Evidence and Appendix', SA *PP*, 1877, vol. 3, no. 102, pp. 7–8.

24 Petition from the executive committee of the Servants' Home to the Governor of Tasmania, Sir Henry Fox Young, 2 [?] September 1858, CSD 1/133/4829, AOT.

25 G. Smith to F. W. Steiglitz, 18 February 1862, CB7/5/1; Mrs Mary Lewis, late matron of the immigration depot, to Board of Immigration, 23 December 1858, CSD 1/106/3248, AOT.

26 *Walch's Almanac for 1864*, Hobart, p. 132; Hobart *Mercury*, 23 April 1862, p. 4.

27 Rules and regulations of Servants' Home, Hobart Town, 12 November 1858, CSD 1/133/4829, AOT.

28 Petition from the executive committee of the Servants' Home, 1858, CSD 1/133/4829, AOT.

29 Hobart *Mercury*, 23 April 1862, p. 4.

30 Ibid., 10 September 1861, p. 2; petition to Governor, 1858, CSD 1/133/4829, AOT. The matron is also referred to as Mrs Tilley: Hobart *Mercury*, 23 April 1862, p. 4.

31 Hobart *Mercury*, 23 April 1862, p. 4.

32 Ibid.

33 Ibid., 14 September 1860, p. 3.

34 Smith to Lady Young, 29 May 1861, CB7/5/1, AOT.

35 Ibid., 6 June 1861.

36 There is no adequate history of the Australian work of either the YWCA or the GFS despite the abundance of archival material, particularly relating to the YWCA.

37 *Travellers' Aid Society Report for 1886*, pp. 1–2, Fawcett Library, London.

38 For background to travellers' aid work in South Australia, see '1880–1980: The Adelaide Y.W.C.A.', typescript, n.d., YWCA archives, Adelaide; see also, *The Blue Triangle*, Adelaide, June 1929, p. 7. For Victoria, see 'The Melbourne Young Women's Christian Association 1882–1876: A Summary of 94 Years' Development Compiled from Annual Reports', typescript, n.d., miscellaneous box, 'Potted Histories', YWCA archives, Melbourne.

39 YWCA Brisbane, 'Annual Report for 1902–03', typescript, YWCA archives, Brisbane.

40 Heath Stubbs, *Friendship's Highway*, pp. 70–2.

41 Harrison, 'For Church, Queen and Family', p. 111.

42 Notes on 'Extract from Letter to Mrs. Joyce', enclosed in letter to all colonial GFS branches from Mrs Glennie, GFS, Brisbane, 21 March 1884, in GFS (Queensland) minute book, 3 November 1882–6 November 1891, GFS archives, Brisbane.

43 Harrison, 'For Church, Queen and Family', p. 118.

44 Godden, 'British Models and Colonial Experience', pp. 43–4.

45 [Girls' Friendly Society for Ireland,] *Seventh Report for the Year Ending 31st December 1883*, Dublin, 1884, p. 7, GFS archives, London.

46 Ibid.

47 See especially GFS (Queensland) minute book, 1882–1891, *passim*. See also GFS commendation registers, vols 4/60, 4/61, GFS archives, London, for similar evidence in the early twentieth century.

48 Annual meeting of 6 November 1890, GFS (Queensland) minute book, 1882–1891, GFS archives, Brisbane.

49 *Courier*, 7[?] November 1890, in GFS (Queensland) minute book, 1882–1891, GFS archives, Brisbane.

50 GFS (Queensland) Annual Report for 1892–1893, p. 8, GFS archives, Brisbane.

51 Vellacott (ed.), *A Girl at Government House*, p. 19.

52 Ibid., p. 37.

53 Notes on 'Extract from Letter to Mrs. Joyce', GFS (Queensland) minute book, 1882–1891, GFS archives, Brisbane.

54 'Report from the Select Committee on Colonisation', Appendix, *BPP*, 1890, XIII, 1, p. 483.

55 Glennie, GFS, Brisbane, to colonial GFS societies, meeting of 21 March 1884, GFS (Queensland) minute book, 1882–1891, GFS archives, Brisbane.

56 Committee meeting, 31 August 1881, committee minute book, GFS archives, Adelaide.

57 Ibid., 25 April 1883.

58 GFS (Victoria) Annual Report for 1885, p. 5, GFS archives, Melbourne.

59 Johnson, *G.F.S. Its Story*, p. 26.

60 'Rules for Emigration', GFS (Victoria) Annual Report for 1885, p. 19.

61 *Daily Telegraph*, April 1885, Immigration Agent's scrapbook, 9/6174 (part), SRNSW.

62 Ibid.

63 Annual Report of the New South Wales GFS, June 1883–December 1884, p. 11, GFS archives, Sydney.

64 Alexander Stuart to Saul Samuel, 30 June 1884, 9/6174 (part), SRNSW.

65 G. F. Wise to Principal Under-Secretary, 26 May 1885, 4/4662, SRNSW.

66 Ibid., 30 January 1886.

67 Colonial Secretary to Agent for Immigration, 4 April and 21 August 1878, 9/6174 (part), SRNSW.

68 Notes by G. F. Wise on letter, William Cowper, Diocesan Registry to Colonial Secretary, 10 August 1878, 9/6174 (part), SRNSW.

69 Letter to the editor, dated 28 October 1877, *Sydney Morning Herald*, c. 29 October 1877; Immigration Agent's scrapbook, 4/4692, SRNSW.

70 Wise to Principal Under-Secretary, 1 June 1885, 4/4661, SRNSW.

71 Letter from Mrs A. Gordon, 9/6174 (part), SRNSW.

72 *Sydney Morning Herald*, 11 April 1885.

73 L. Knightley, 'The Girls' Friendly Society', *Englishwoman's Review*, vol. 10, May 1879, p. 200.

74 *Sydney Morning Herald*, 11 April 1885.

75 *Daily Telegraph*, 13 June 1885; clipping, Immigration Agent's scrapbook, n.p., n.d., 9/6174 (part), SRNSW.

76 Statement of Agnes Beatrice Nicholls and Kate Isabel Nicholls, 9/6174, SRNSW.

77 Letter from S. Fore, General Secretary of the YWCA, 19 June 1885, 9/6174 (part), SRNSW.

78 *Daily Telegraph*, 18 June 1885.

79 *Sydney Morning Herald*, 27 July 1885.

80 Board of Immigration meeting, 19 August 1886, acc. 489/5, SROWA.

81 See Hamilton, *'No Irish need apply'*.

82 See Coghlan, *Labour and Industry in Australia*, vol. 1, p. 206; vol. 2, pp. 1045–6.

83 Ibid., vol. 2, p. 1062.

84 See for example, 'Report of the Immigration Agent for 1865', NSW *VPLA*, 1866, vol. 4, p. 195 for wages received from the depot in 1865; p. 204 for average wages paid to domestics for the year 1865.

85 Evidence of G. F. Wise, 'Minutes of Evidence Taken Before the Select Committee on Assisted Immigration', NSW *VPLA*, 1879–80, vol. 5, p. 732.

86 Memorandum from Mr Wise, Immigration Agent, 3 April 1885, 9/6174, SRNSW.

87 Evidence of Dr Hobbs, 'Report from the Select Committee on Immigration', Qld *VPLA*, 1860, pp. 657–8.

88 Ibid., p. 658.

89 Coghlan, *Labour and Industry in Australia*, vol. 2, p. 1062.

90 'Report of the Select Committee on Immigration; Together with Minutes of Evidence', SA *PP*, 1877, vol. 3, no. 102, p. 106.

91 'Our Immigrants', *West Australian*, 29 April 1891.

92 Coghlan, *Labour and Industry in Australia*, vol. 2, p. 1020.

93 'Report of the Immigration Agent for the Year 1859', Vic *PP*, 1859–60, vol. 3, no. 57, p. 7.

94 Michael Quinlan, ' "Pre-arbitral" Labour Legislation in Australia'.

95 Gothard, ' "Radically unsound and mischievous" ', p. 388.

96 Ibid., p. 390.

97 Agent-General to Chief Secretary, 8 October 1869, T11184, 3991/383 (1869), PROV.

98 Mrs J. E. Leary to [Under-Secretary], 27 September 1893; T. M. McCarthy to Under-Secretary, 30 September 1893; box 5, acc. 553, SROWA.

99 Dalgety & Co., Ltd, to Under-Secretary, 19 November 1895; telegram, Albany, to Under-Secretary, 20 November 1895, box 5, acc. 553, SROWA.

1 CSO, Van Diemens Land, to Colonial Secretary, South Australia, 29 October 1855, CSD 1/69/1612, AOT.

2 Gothard, ' "Radically unsound and mischievous" ', p. 387.

3 T *HAJ*, 1856, vol. 1, no. 4, p. 6.

4 Quinlan, ' "Pre-arbitral" Labour Legislation in Australia', p. 31.

5 Smith to McCluren and Lawson, 5 November 1861, CB7/5/1, AOT.

6 Smith to R. Allwright, 2 April 1861, CB7/5/1, AOT.

7 Smith to John Meredith, 30 July 1861, CB7/5/1, AOT.

8 Ibid.

9 'George Meredith', in *Australian Dictionary of Biography*, vol. 2, p. 225.

10 Smith to Sarah Clinch, 30 July 1861, CB7/5/1, AOT.

11 'Antipodes' (2nd), CB7/12/10, AOT.

[12] Smith to Tabart and Webster, 5 November 1861, CB7/5/1, AOT.

[13] Quinlan, '"Pre-arbitral" Labour Legislation in Australia', p. 46, note 11.

[14] Jones, *In Her Own Name*, p. 49.

[15] R. Erickson (ed.), *Bicentennial Dictionary of Western Australia pre 1829–1888*, vol. II, D–J, Crawley, 1987, p. 1418; C. T. Stannage, *The People of Perth*, Perth, 1979, p. 197.

[16] *West Australian*, 22 April 1891.

[17] Crowley, 'Master and Servant in Western Australia 1851–1901', pp. 20, 25, 26.

[18] WA *PD*, 3 February 1892, p. 449.

[19] Acc. 527, 1264/1800, CSO, SROWA.

[20] *West Australian*, 22 April 1891.

[21] E. Joyce to Crown Agents, 28 May 1891, acc. 553, box 5, SROWA.

[22] Ibid.

[23] *West Australian*, 22 April 1891; British press clipping (n.p., n.d.), Fawcett Library scrapbook, Fawcett Library, London.

[24] E. E. Blake, Crown Agent, to Chairman, Board of Immigration, 4 June 1891, acc. 553, box 5, SROWA.

[25] *West Australian*, 22 April 1891.

[26] 'Remarks in Explanation of the Heavy Sentence Passed on Caroline Hall', prepared by J. C. H. James, 8 July 1891, acc. 553, box 5, SROWA.

[27] *West Australian*, 24 April 1891.

[28] Ibid., 25 April 1891.

[29] R. S. Haynes to Colonial Secretary, 22 April 1891, acc. 553, box 5, SROWA.

[30] Chairman, Board of Immigration, to R. S. Haynes, 24 April 1891, acc. 553, box 5; See Quinlan, '"Pre-arbitral" Labour Legislation', p. 31, for a discussion of the provisions of the Master and Servants Act against 'harbouring and enticement'.

[31] Note written by John Musson, acc. 553, box 5, SROWA.

[32] Ellen Joyce to Shenton, 11 February 1892, acc. 553, box 4, item 2, SROWA.

[33] See Godden on the class interests and ideology of philanthropists in '"The work for them, and the glory for us!"', p. 85.

8 *'Free agents these domestic damsels'*

[1] *Daily News*, 2 May 1890, emigration scrapbook, Fawcett Library, London.

[2] *Daily News*, 8 February 1898.

[3] Police file 327/1895 (AN 5/1 acc. 430), SROWA; *Western Mail*, 9 February 1895.

4 Personal correspondence, Mrs Avis Davis to Jan Gothard, 8 October 1985.

5 Hill, *The Territory*, pp. 406–7.

6 Personal correspondence, Mrs Avis Davis to Jan Gothard, 8 October 1985.

7 Groom, *Four Julias*.

8 Gothard, ' "Radically unsound and mischievous" ', p. 401.

9 Immigration. Letters and other documents Feb. 1891–Jan. 1896, box 5, acc. 553, SROWA.

10 Mary Corbett to Colonial Secretary's Office, 13 June 1892, box 4, acc. 553, SROWA.

Select Bibliography

Primary Sources

Government Records, Unpublished, Britain
Public Record Office, Kew (PRO Kew), London
Colonial Office, papers and correspondence.
Government Emigration Board, correspondence.

Government Records, Unpublished, Australia
Archives Office of Tasmania (AOT), Hobart
Board of Immigration, letterbooks, descriptive lists of immigrants, minutes.
Chief Secretary's Department, correspondence.
Premier's Department, correspondence and index.

Mitchell Library (ML), Sydney
Despatches from Governor of Victoria; Despatches to Governor of Victoria, 1858–59.

Public Record Office Victoria (PROV), Melbourne
Agent-General, correspondence.
Colonial Secretary's Office, correspondence.
Register of assisted immigrants.

Queensland State Archives (QSA), Brisbane
Colonial Secretary's Office, general correspondence.
Correspondence from Henry Jordan.

Home Office, benevolent societies.
Immigration Agents, Bowen and Maryborough, miscellaneous correspondence, circulars and registers of immigrants.

State Records New South Wales (SRNSW), Sydney
Agent for Immigration, journals, correspondence, scrapbooks, miscellaneous papers.
Bounty lists.
Colonial Secretary, special bundles.
Immigration Department, correspondence.
Immigration Office, miscellaneous papers, correspondence and reports.
Immigration reports and lists.
Passenger lists.
Reports of surgeons on immigrant health.
Ships' papers.

State Records Office of Western Australia (SROWA), Perth
Agent-General, correspondence, applications for passage, and other documents.
Board of Immigration, minutes of meetings.
Colonial Secretary's Office, correspondence.

State Records South Australia (SRSA), Adelaide
Crown Land and Immigration Department, letterbooks, papers.
Immigration Agent, correspondence and papers.

Government Records, Published, Britain
British Parliamentary Papers (BPP), 1850–1920.

Government Records, Published, Australia
New South Wales, *Votes and Proceedings of the Legislative Assembly* (NSW *VPLA*), 1858–1900.
Queensland, *Journals of the Legislative Council* (Qld *JLC*), 1883.
—— *Votes and Proceedings of the Legislative Assembly* (Qld *VPLA*), 1860–1900.
—— *Votes and Proceedings of the Legislative Council* (Qld *VPLC*), 1884–86.
South Australia, *Proceedings of Parliament* (SA *PP*), 1856–1900.
Tasmania, *House of Assembly Journals* (T *HAJ*), 1856–83.
—— *Journals and Papers of Parliament* (T *PP*), 1884–1900.

Victoria, *Papers Presented to Parliament* (Vic *PP*), 1856–1900.

—— *Report of the Immigration Agent [for 1853], Colonial Immigration and Emigration*, Melbourne, 1854, printed 27/9/1854, paper no. A8/1854–55.

—— *Report of the Immigration Agent [for 1854], Colonial Immigration and Emigration*, Melbourne, 1855, printed 28/11/55, paper no. A7/1855–56.

Western Australia, *Blue Books*.

—— *Parliamentary Debates*.

—— *Statistical Registers*.

—— *Votes and Proceedings of Parliament* (WA *VPP*), 1890–1900.

—— *Votes and Proceedings of the Legislative Council* (WA *VPLC*), 1870–89.

Non-government Records, Britain

Church of England Children's Society, London

Annual reports of the Waifs and Strays Society, 1886–1921.

Fawcett Library, London Guild University, London

Autograph collection.
Female Middle-class Emigration Society, letterbooks and reports.
Pamphlet collection.
Press collection.
Travellers' Aid Society, reports.
United British Women's Emigration Association (BWEA), annual reports, emigration scrapbooks and minutes.

Girls' Friendly Society (GFS), Townsend House, London

Commendation registers.
Correspondence and papers.

Greater London Record Office and History Library, London

Lucy Osburn correspondence.
Nightingale Training School papers.

Lambeth Palace Library, London

Benson, Tait correspondence and papers.

Modern Records Centre, University of Warwick

Young Women's Christian Association, papers.

Royal Commonwealth Society, London

Sedgwick collection of press cuttings.

Scottish Record Office, West Register House, Edinburgh
Highland and Island Emigration Society, papers.

Society for Promoting Christian Knowledge (SPCK), Holy
Trinity Church, London
Emigration Committee and the Ladies' Emigration Committee,
minute books.

Non-government Records, Australia
Girls' Friendly Society of New South Wales, Sydney
Circulars, annual reports.

Girls' Friendly Society of Queensland, Brisbane
Annual reports, minutes.

Girls' Friendly Society of South Australia, Adelaide
Annual reports, minutes.

Girls' Friendly Society of Victoria, Melbourne
Annual reports.

Young Women's Christian Association of Adelaide, Mortlock
Library, Adelaide
Annual reports and papers.

Young Women's Christian Association of Brisbane, Brisbane
Annual reports and papers.

Young Women's Christian Association of Melbourne, University
of Melbourne Archives, Melbourne
Minutes, papers and reports.

Young Women's Christian Association of Sydney, Mitchell
Library, Sydney
Minute books, scrap books and ephemera.

Diaries, journals, family papers
Cole family papers, private collection, Melbourne.
Dale, Lyn, Maggie's Journey, typescript, Perth, 1998.
Journals Kept by Matrons, Surgeons and Religious Instructors, 1875,
    1892–1898, 1910, State Records Office of Western Australia.

Kelly, Maggie, Diary of a Voyage from London to Fremantle, 1900, typescript, courtesy of Lyn Dale, Perth.

Wright [Kidd], Hannah, Diary of a Voyage from London to Brisbane on the Duke of Westminster, 1886, manuscript, Fryer Library, University of Queensland.

de Zouche, Isaiah, Journal of the Surgeon-Superintendent on Board the Star Queen to Queensland, 1875, Oxley Library, Brisbane.

Contemporary newspapers and journals

Britain

English Woman's Journal, 1859–1864.

Englishwoman's Review, 1873–1910.

Friendly Leaves, the Girls' Friendly Society Reporter.

Friendly Work, the Older Member's Magazine.

Imperial Colonist, 1902–1927.

Our Herald, 1889–1890.

Our Own Gazette (YWCA monthly journal).

Our Waifs and Strays, 1884–1924.

The Times, 1860–1920.

Woman's Gazette, 1876–1879.

Work and Leisure, 1880–1893.

Australia

Observer (Adelaide), 1880–83.

Mercury (Hobart), 1860–62.

West Australian, 1887–91.

Contemporary books, pamphlets and articles

Allen, W. O. B., and Edmund McClure, *Two Hundred Years: The History of the Society for Promoting Christian Knowledge 1698–1898*, London, 1898.

Brice, Arthur Montefiore, 'Emigration for Gentlewomen', *The Nineteenth Century*, April 1901.

British Ladies' Female Emigrants Society, *Third Annual Report of the British Ladies' Female Emigrants Society*, 1852.

Bulley, A. Amy, 'Domestic Service: A Social Study', *Westminster Review*, vol. 135, 1891.

Burdett Coutts, Baroness Angela (ed.), *Woman's Mission: A Series of Congress Papers on the Philanthropic Work of Women by Eminent Writers*, London, 1893.

Chisholm, Caroline and Charles Dickens, 'A Bundle of Emigrants' Letters', *Household Words*, vol. 1, 1850.

Clokey, Robert F., 'Irish Female Emigration from Workhouses', *Statistical and Social Inquiry Society of Ireland, Journal*, 1861–63, July 1863.

[The Committee for Promoting the Emigration of Females to the Australian Colonies], *A Free Passage for Single Women and Widows*, London, 1836.

Darbyshire, Douglas E., *In Time for Lunch: The Personal Diary and the Official Journal of Douglas E. Darbyshire, Surgeon-in-charge of the Young Women Emigrants Sailing in the S.S. Cornwall from England to Australia, 1898*, South Fremantle, 1991.

Evans, Mary Sanger, 'Domestic Servants in Australia: A Rejoinder', *Westminster Review*, vol. 136, 1891.

General Instructions for the Guidance of Emigration Officers, London, 1855.

Girls' Friendly Society (Ireland), *Seventh Report for the Year Ending 31 December 1883*.

Greg, William R., 'Why are Women Redundant?', *National Review*, vol. 28, April 1862.

Herbert, Sidney, *Fund for Promoting Female Emigration: First Report of the Committee*, March 1851.

—— *Fund for Promoting Female Emigration*, January 1853.

Joyce, Ellen, 'Emigration: or, Hopeful Homes for Hard Workers', *Our Own Gazette*, vol. 4, no. 34, March 1887.

—— *Letter to Young Women on Leaving England*, seventh edition, Winchester, 1913.

—— 'Letters on Emigration', *Friendly Work*, September 1883.

Knightley, Louisa, 'The Girls' Friendly Society', *Englishwoman's Review*, 15 May 1879.

Layton, Ellen, 'On the Superintendence of Female Emigrants', *Transactions of the National Association for the Promotion of Social Science*, Edinburgh, 1863.

Lewin, Jane E., 'Female Middle-class Emigration', *Transactions of the National Association for the Promotion of Social Science*, Edinburgh, 1863.

Lockett, Jeannie, 'The Labour Battle in Australia', *Westminster Review*, vol. 135, 1891.

Miss Rye's Emigration Home for Destitute Little Girls, Peckham, c.1880.

'Modern Domestic Service', *Edinburgh Review*, vol. 115, April 1862.

O'Brien, Charlotte G., *The Separation of the Sexes on Emigrant Vessels: A Letter from Charlotte G. O'Brien to the Right Hon. Joseph Chamberlain, President of the Board of Trade*, Dublin, 1881.

Pratt, Edwin, *Pioneer Women in Victoria's Reign, being Short Histories of Great Movements*, London, 1897.

—— *A Woman's Work for Women, being the Aims, Efforts, and Aspirations of 'L.M.H.' (Miss Louisa M. Hubbard)*, London, 1898.

Ravenstein, E. G., 'The Laws of Migration', *Journal of the Royal Statistical Society*, vol. 48, 1885.

—— 'The Laws of Migration' (second paper), *Journal of the Royal Statistical Society*, vol. 52, 1889.

Ross, Adelaide, 'Emigration for Women', *Macmillan's Magazine*, vol. 45, 1882.

Rowe, C. J., 'Housekeeping Troubles in the Australian Colonies', *Westminster Review*, vol. 134, 1890.

Rye, Maria S., *'Emigration of Educated Women', a Paper Read at the Social Science Congress in Dublin, 1861. Reprinted from* The English Woman's Journal, London, March 1862.

—— [M.S.R.], 'Emigrant-ship Matrons', *English Woman's Journal*, vol. 5, August 1860.

Sellars, E., 'Women's Work for the Welfare of Girls', in Burdett Coutts, A., (ed.), *Woman's Mission: A Series of Congress Papers on the Philanthropic Work of Women by Eminent Writers*, London, 1893.

[Society for Promoting Christian Knowledge], *A Few Words for Female Emigrants*, London, n.d.

[——], *Parting Words to Emigrant Parents*, London, 1850.

[——], *The Emigrant's Call*, London, n.d.

Spence, Catherine Helen, *Some Social Aspects of South Australian Life by a Colonist of 1839* (reprinted from the *South Australian Register*), Adelaide, 1878.

—— *Clara Morison*, Adelaide, 1971, first published 1854.

Twining, Louisa, *Workhouses and Pauperism*, London, 1898.

Twopeny, Richard, *Town Life in Australia*, Harmondsworth, 1973, first published 1883.

Willis, W. H., 'Safety for Female Emigrants', *Household Words*, vol. 3, 1851.

Worthington, A. W., 'On the Unequal Proportion between the Male and Female Population of Some Manufacturing and Other Towns', *Journal of the Statistical Society of London*, vol. 30, 1867.

Secondary Sources

Abbott, Kellie, 'The aged, infirm and indigent poor': The Perth Female Poor House, 1890–1900, unpublished paper, 1998.

Ackerman, Jessie, *Australia from a Woman's Point of View*, London, New York and Melbourne, 1913.

Alford, Katrina, *Production or Reproduction? An Economic History of Women in Australia, 1788–1850*, Melbourne, 1984.

Armitage, Susan, & Elizabeth Jameson (eds), *The Women's West*, Norman and London, 1987.

Australian Dictionary of Biography, Melbourne.

Barbalet, Margaret, *Far From a Low Gutter Girl: The Forgotten World of State Wards South Australia 1887–1940*, Melbourne, 1983.

Barber, Marilyn, 'The Women Ontario Welcomed: Immigrant Domestics for Ontario Homes, 1870–1930', *Ontario History*, vol. 72, no. 3, September 1980.

Beer, Jane, Charles Fahey, Patricia Grimshaw, Melanie Raymond, *Colonial Frontiers and Family Fortunes: Two Studies of Rural and Urban Victoria*, Melbourne, 1989.

Broome, Richard, *The Victorians: Arriving*, Melbourne, 1984.

Buckley, Suzanne, 'British Female Emigration and Imperial Development: Experiments in Canada, 1885–1931', *Hecate*, vol. 3, no. 2, July 1977.

Bush, Julia, *Edwardian Ladies and Imperial Power*, Leicester, 2000.

Carrier, N. H., and J. R. Jeffery, *External Migration: A Study of the Available Statistics 1815–1950*, London, 1953.

Carrothers, W. A., *Emigration from the British Isles, with Special Reference to the Development of the Overseas Dominions*, London, 1929.

Charlwood, Don, *The Long Farewell*, Melbourne, 1983.

Clarke, Patricia, *The Governesses: Letters from the Colonies 1862–1882*, London, 1985.

Coghlan, T. A., *Labour and Industry in Australia: From the First Settlement of 1788 to the Establishment of the Commonwealth in 1901*, four volumes, London, 1918.

Crowley, F. K., 'Master and Servant in Western Australia 1851–1901', *Journal and Proceedings of the Western Australian Historical Society*, vol. 4, part 6, 1954.

—— 'The British Contribution to the Australian Population: 1860–1919', *University Studies in History and Economics*, vol. 2, no. 2, July 1954.

—— 'Immigration into Tasmania from the United Kingdom, 1860–1919', *Tasmanian Historical Research Association: Papers and Proceedings*, vol. 3, no. 6, October 1954.

Curthoys, Ann, 'History in a Vacuum: A Review of Katrina Alford, *Production or Reproduction? An Economic History of Women in Australia, 1788–1850*, Oxford University Press, 1984', *Hecate*, vol. 10, no. 1, 1984.

Curtin, Emma, 'Gentility Afloat: Gentlewomen's Diaries and the Voyage to Australia, 1830–1880', *Australian Historical Studies*, vol. 26, no. 105, October 1995.

Damousi, Joy, 'Chaos and Order: Gender, Space and Sexuality on Female Convict Ships', *Australian Historical Studies*, vol. 26, no. 104, April 1995.

—— *Depraved and Disorderly: Female Convicts, Sexuality and Gender in Australia*, Cambridge, 1997.

Daniels, Kay, *Convict Women*, St Leonards NSW, 1998.

Daniels, Kay (ed.), *So Much Hard Work: Women and Prostitution in Australian History*, Sydney, 1984.

Daniels, Kay, and Mary Murnane, *Uphill All the Way: A Documentary History of Women in Australia*, St Lucia, 1980.

Davidoff, Leonore, 'Mastered for Life: Servant and Wife in Victorian and Edwardian England', *Journal of Social History*, vol. 7, no. 4, 1974.

Diner, Hasia R., *Erin's Daughters in America: Irish Immigrant Women in the Nineteenth Century*, Baltimore and London, 1983.

Dixson, Miriam, *The Real Matilda: Women and Identity in Australia 1788 to 1975*, Melbourne, 1976.

Duncan, Ross, 'Case Studies in Emigration: Cornwall, Gloucestershire and New South Wales, 1877–1886', *Economic History Review*, second series, vol. 16, no. 1, 1963.

—— 'Late Nineteenth-century Immigration into New South Wales from the United Kingdom', *Australian Economic History Review*, vol. 14, no. 1, March 1974.

Duning, Becky, 'Being Poor and Female in Colonial Western Australia: New Perspectives on Women's History', *Hecate*, vol. 3, no. 2, July 1977.

Erickson, Charlotte, *Invisible Immigrants: The Adaption of English and Scottish Immigrants in Nineteenth-Century America*, London, 1972.

—— *English Women Immigrants in America in the Nineteenth Century: Expectations and Reality*, Fawcett Library Papers no. 7, London, 1983.

Erickson, Charlotte (ed.), *Emigration from Europe 1815–1914: Select Documents*, London, 1976.

Erickson, Rica, *Old Toodyay and Newcastle*, Toodyay, 1974.

—— *The Bride Ships*, Perth, 1992.

Evans, Raymond, 'The Hidden Colonist: Deviance and Social Control in Colonial Queensland', in J. Roe (ed.), *Social Policy in Australia: Some Perspectives on 1901–1975*, Melbourne, 1976.

—— '"Soiled doves": Prostitution in Colonial Queensland', in Daniels, Kay (ed.), *So Much Hard Work: Women and Prostitution in Australian History*, Sydney, 1984.

Fisher, S. H., 'An Accumulation of Misery?', *Labour History*, no. 40, May 1981.

Fisher, Shirley, 'Sydney Women and the Workforce 1870–90', in Max Kelly (ed.), *Nineteenth-Century Sydney: Essays in Urban History*, Sydney, 1978.

—— 'The Pastoral Interest and Sydney's Public Health', *Historical Studies*, vol. 20, no. 78, April 1982.

—— 'The Family and the Sydney Economy in the Late Nineteenth Century', in P. Grimshaw, C. McConville and E. McEwen, *Families in Colonial Australia*, Sydney, London, Boston, 1985.

Fitzpatrick, David, 'Irish Emigration in the Late Nineteenth Century', *Irish Historical Studies*, vol. 22, no. 86, September 1986.

—— '"Oceans of consolation": Letters and Irish Immigration to Australasia', in E. Richards, R. Reid and D. Fitzpatrick, *Visible Immigrants: Neglected Sources for the History of Australian Immigration*, Canberra, 1989.

—— *Oceans of Consolation: Personal Accounts of Irish Migration to Australia*, Melbourne, 1995.

—— A Share of the Honeycomb: Education, Emigration and Women, unpublished paper, n.d.

Fox, Charlie, *Working Australia*, North Sydney, 1991.

Godden, Judith, '"The work for them, and the glory for us!": Sydney Women's Philanthropy, 1870–1900', in R. Kennedy (ed.), *Australian Welfare History*, Melbourne, 1982.

—— 'British Models and Colonial Experience: Women's Philanthropy in Late Nineteenth Century Sydney', *Journal of Australian Studies*, no. 19, November 1986.

Gothard, Jan, 'Assisted Female Migration 1860–1920', in James Jupp (ed.), *The Australian People: An Encyclopedia of the Nation, Its People and their Origins*, Sydney, 1988.

—— '"Radically unsound and mischievous": Female Migration to Tasmania, 1856–1863', *Australian Historical Studies*, vol. 23, no. 93, October 1989.

—— '"The healthy, wholesome British domestic girl": Single Female Emigration and the Empire Settlement Act, 1922–1930', in S. Constantine (ed.), *Emigrants and Empire: British Settlement in the Dominions between the Wars*, Manchester, 1990.

—— 'Protecting Labour: Carrie Hall and the Master and Servants Act', *Papers in Labour History*, no. 6, November 1990.

—— '"Pity the poor immigrant": Assisted Single Female Migration to Colonial Australia', in Eric Richards (ed.), *Poor Australian Immigrants in the Nineteenth Century. Visible Immigrants: Two*, Canberra, 1991.

—— Government-assisted Migration of Single Women from Britain to Australia, 1860–1900, PhD thesis, Murdoch University, 1991.

—— '"A compromise with conscience". The Reception of Female Immigrant Domestic Servants in Eastern Australia, 1860–1885', *Labour History*, no. 62, May 1992.

—— 'Space, Authority and the Female Emigrant Afloat', *Australian Historical Studies*, vol. 30, no. 112, April 1999.

—— 'Wives or Workers? Single British Female Migration to Colonial Australia', in Pam Sharpe (ed.), *Women, Gender and Labour Migration: Historical and Global Perspectives*, London, 2001.

Grimshaw, Patricia, Chris McConville, Ellen McEwen, *Families in Colonial Australia*, Sydney, London and Boston, 1985.

Groom, Susan Ovens, *Four Julias: One Hundred Years in York*, Perth, 1993.

Haines, Robin F., *Emigration and the Labouring Poor: Australian Recruitment in Britain and Ireland, 1831–60*, Houndsmill, 1997.

Hall, Catherine, 'The Early Formation of Victorian Domestic Ideology', in Sandra Burman (ed.), *Fit Work for Women*, London, 1979.

Hamilton, Paula, 'No Irish need apply': Prejudice as a Factor in the Development of Immigration Policy in New South Wales and Victoria, 1840–1870, PhD thesis, University of New South Wales, 1979.

—— '"Tipperarifying the moral atmosphere": Irish Catholic Immigration and the State 1840–1860', in Sydney Labour History Group, *What Rough Beast? The State and Social Order in Australian History*, Sydney, 1982.

—— 'No Irish need apply': Aspects of the Employer–Employee Relationship in Australian Domestic Service 1860–1900, Working Papers in Australian Studies, London, 1985.

—— 'Irish Women Immigrants in the Nineteenth Century', in James Jupp (ed.), *The Australian People: An Encyclopedia of the Nation, Its People and Their Origins*, Sydney, 1988.

Hamilton, P., and J. Gothard, ' "The other half?" Sources on British Female Emigration at the Fawcett Library, with Special Reference to Australia', *Women's Studies International Forum*, vol. 10, no. 3, 1987.

Hammerton, A. James, ' "Without natural protectors": Female Immigration to Australia, 1832–1836', *Historical Studies*, vol. 16, October 1975.

—— 'Feminism and Female Emigration, 1861–1886', in Martha Vicinus (ed.), *A Widening Sphere: Changing Roles of Victorian Women*, Bloomington and London, 1977.

—— *Emigrant Gentlewomen: Genteel Poverty and Female Emigration 1830–1914*, London, 1979.

Harrison, Brian, 'Philanthropy and the Victorians', *Victorian Studies*, vol. 9, part 4, June 1966.

—— 'For Church, Queen and Family: The Girls' Friendly Society 1874–1920', *Past and Present*, no. 61, November 1973.

Hassam, Andrew, *Sailing to Australia: Shipboard Diaries by Nineteenth-century British Emigrants*, Melbourne, 1995.

Hayden, Albert A., 'The Anti-immigration Movement, 1877–1893', *Royal Australian Historical Society Journal*, vol. 48, part 1, March 1962.

Heath Stubbs, Mary, *Friendship's Highway, Being the History of the Girls' Friendly Society, 1875–1925*, London, 1926.

Hicks, Neville, *'This Sin and Scandal': Australia's Population Debate 1891–1911*, Canberra, 1978.

Hill, Ernestine, *The Territory*, Sydney, 1963.

Hoban, Mary, *Fifty-one Pieces of Wedding Cake: A Biography of Caroline Chisholm*, Kilmore, 1973.

Hume, Bertram (ed.), *A Victorian Engagement: Letters and Journals of Walter Hume and Anna Kate Fowler during the 1860s*, St Lucia, 1975.

Humphrey, Kim, 'A New Era of Existence: Convict Transportation and the Authority of the Surgeon in Colonial Australia', *Labour History*, no. 59, November 1990.

Inglis, K. S., *Churches and the Working Classes in Victorian England*, London, 1963.

International Migration Review. Special Issue: Women in Migration, vol. 18, no. 4, Winter 1984.

Jackel, Susan (ed.), *A Flannel Shirt and Liberty: British Emigrant Gentlewomen in the Canadian West 1880–1914*, Vancouver and London, 1982.

Jackson, Pauline, 'Women in 19th Century Irish Migration', *International Migration Review. Special Issue: Women in Migration*, vol. 18, no. 4, Winter 1984.

Johnson, Peter, *G.F.S. Its Story: A History of the Girls' Friendly Society in Australia*, Melbourne, 1975.

Jones, Helen, *In Her Own Name: Women in South Australian History*, Netley, 1986.

Jupp, James (ed.), *The Australian People: An Encyclopedia of the Nation, Its People and Their Origins*, Sydney, 1988.

Kiddle, Margaret, *Caroline Chisholm*, Melbourne, 1950.

Kingston, Beverley, *My Wife, My Daughter and Poor Mary Ann: Women and Work in Australia*, Melbourne, 1975.

Kitteringham, Jennie, *Country Girls in Nineteenth Century England*, History Workshop Pamphlet no. 11, 1973.

Kleinig, Margrette, 'Independent Women: South Australia's Assisted Immigrants 1872–1939', in Eric Richards (ed.), *Visible Women. Female Immigrants in Colonial Australia. Visible Immigrants: Four*, Canberra, 1995.

Lake, Marilyn, 'The Politics of Respectability: Identifying the Masculinist Context', in Susan Magarey, Sue Rowley, Susan Sheridan, *Debutante Nation: Feminism Contests the 1890s*, Sydney, 1993.

Lansbury, Coral, *Arcady in Australia: The Evocation of Australia in Nineteenth-Century English Literature*, Melbourne, 1970.

L'Esperance, Jean Lawrence, 'Woman's Mission to Woman: Explorations in the Operation of the Double Standard and Female Solidarity in Nineteenth Century England', *Histoire Sociale/Social History*, vol. 12, no. 24, November 1979.

London Feminist History Group, *The Sexual Dynamics of History: Men's Power, Women's Resistance*, London, 1983.

Lyons, F. S. L., *Ireland since the Famine: 1850 to the Present*, London, 1971.

McBride, Theresa M., *The Domestic Revolution: The Modernisation of Household Service in England and France 1820–1920*, London, 1976.

McConville, Chris, *Croppies, Celts and Catholics: The Irish in Australia*, Melbourne, 1987.

MacDonagh, Oliver (ed.), *Emigration in the Victorian Age: Debates on the Issue from 19th Century Critical Journals*, London, 1973.

Macdonald, Charlotte, 'Ellen Silk and Her Sisters: Female Emigration to the New World', in London Feminist History Group, *The Sexual Dynamics of History*, London, 1983.

—— Single Women as Immigrant Settlers in New Zealand, 1853–1871, PhD thesis, University of Auckland, 1986.

—— 'The "social evil": Prostitutes and the Passage of the Contagious Diseases Act (1869)', in Barbara Brookes, Charlotte Macdonald, Margaret Tennant, *Women in History: Essays on European Women in New Zealand*, Wellington, 1986.

—— *A Woman of Good Character: Single Women as Immigrant Settlers in Nineteenth-Century New Zealand*, Wellington, 1990.

MacGinley, Mary Rosa, A Study of Irish Migration to, and Settlement in Queensland 1885–1912, MA thesis, University of Queensland, 1972.

—— 'Irish Migration to Queensland, 1885–1912', *Queensland Heritage*, vol. 3, no. 1, November 1974.

Macintyre, S., and R. Mitchell (eds), *Foundations of Arbitration: The Origins and Effects of State Compulsory Arbitration 1890–1914*, Melbourne, 1989.

McLaughlin, Trevor, *Barefoot and Pregnant? Irish Famine Orphans in Australia*, Melbourne, 1991.

McLennan, Nicole, 'Glimpses of Unassisted English Women Arriving in Victoria, 1860–1900', in Eric Richards (ed.), *Visible Women. Female Immigrants in Colonial Australia. Visible Immigrants: Four*, Canberra, 1995.

Madgwick, R. B., *Immigration into Eastern Australia 1788–1851*, Sydney, 1969, first published 1937.

Magarey, Susan, *Unbridling the Tongues of Women: A Biography of Catherine Helen Spence*, Sydney, 1985.

Mander-Jones, P., *Manuscripts in the British Isles Relating to Australia, New Zealand and the Pacific*, Canberra, 1972.

Milton, Norma J., 'Essential Servants: Immigrant Domestics on the Canadian Prairies, 1885–1930', in Susan Armitage and Elizabeth Jameson (eds), *The Women's West*, Norman and London, 1987.

Money, Agnes L., *The Story of the Girls' Friendly Society*, London, 1913.

Monk, Una, *New Horizons: A Hundred Years of Women's Migration*, London, 1963.

Murnane, Mary, and Kay Daniels, 'Prostitutes as "Purveyors of Disease": Venereal Disease Legislation in Tasmania, 1868–1945', *Hecate*, vol. 5, no. 1, 1979.

Niall, Brenda and Ian Britain, *Oxford Book of Australian Schooldays*, Melbourne, 1997.

O'Farrell, Patrick, *Letters from Irish Australia 1825–1929*, Sydney and Belfast, 1984.

—— *The Irish in Australia*, Sydney, 1986.

Orton, Diana, *Made of Gold: A Biography of Angela Burdett Coutts*, London, 1980.

Oxley, Deborah, *Convict Maids: The Forced Migration of Women to Australia*, Cambridge, 1996.

Perrott, Monica, *A Tolerable Good Success: Economic Opportunities for Women in New South Wales 1788–1830*, Sydney, 1983.

Phizacklea, Annie (ed.), *One Way Ticket: Migration and Female Labour*, London, 1983.

Plant, G. F., *S.O.S.B.W.: A Survey of Voluntary Effort in Women's Empire Migration*, London, 1950.

—— *Oversea Settlement: Migration from the United Kingdom to the Dominions*, London, 1951.

Prentis, Malcolm D., *The Scots in Australia: A Study of New South Wales, Victoria and Queensland, 1788–1900*, Sydney, 1983.

Prochaska, F. K., *Women and Philanthropy in Nineteenth-Century England*, Oxford, 1980.

—— 'Female Philanthropy and Domestic Service in Victorian England', *Bulletin of the Institute of Historical Research*, vol. 54, no. 129, May 1981.

Quinlan, Michael, '"Pre-arbitral" Labour Legislation in Australia and Its Implications for the Introduction of Compulsory Arbitration', in S. Macintyre and R. Mitchell (eds), *Foundations of Arbitration: The Origins and Effects of State Compulsory Arbitration 1890–1914*, Melbourne, 1989.

Rayner, Keith, 'The Queensland Immigration Society', *Journal of the Royal Historical Society of Queensland*, vol. 4, no. 3, December 1950.

Redford, Arthur, *Labour Migration in England 1800–1850*, third edition, Manchester, 1976, first published 1926.

Richards, E., 'Annals of the Australian Immigrant', in E. Richards, R. Reid, D. Fitzpatrick, *Visible Immigrants: Neglected Sources for the History of Australian Immigration*, Canberra, 1989.

Richards, Eric, Richard Reid and David Fitzpatrick, *Visible Immigrants: Neglected Sources for the History of Australian Immigration*, Canberra, 1989.

Richards, Eric (ed.), *Poor Australian Immigrants in the Nineteenth Century. Visible Immigrants: Two*, Canberra, 1991.

—— *Visible Women. Female Immigrants in Colonial Australia. Visible Immigrants: Four*, Canberra, 1995.

Robinson, Portia, *The Hatch and Brood of Time: A Study of the First Generation of Native-born White Australians 1788–1828*, Melbourne, 1985.

Ryan, Edna, and Anne Conlon, *Gentle Invaders: Australian Women at Work, 1788–1974*, Melbourne, 1975.

Rudd, Joy, 'Invisible Exports: The Emigration of Irish Women this Century', *Women's Studies International Forum*, vol. 11, no. 4, 1988.

Seller, M. S., *Immigrant Women*, Temple, 1981.

Sharpe, Pamela, 'Female Emigration Schemes to Australia in the 1830s', *Essex Journal*, Spring 1994.

Shaw, A. G. L. (ed.), *Great Britain and the Colonies 1815–1865*, London, 1970.

Sherington, Geoffrey, *Australia's Immigrants 1788–1978*, Sydney, 1980.

Shultz, R. J., 'Immigration into Eastern Australia, 1788–1851', *Historical Studies*, vol. 14, no. 54, April 1970.

Sinclair, W. A., 'Women at Work in Melbourne and Adelaide since 1871', *Economic Record*, vol. 57, no. 159, December 1981.

—— 'Women and Economic Change in Melbourne 1871–1921', *Historical Studies*, vol. 20, no. 79, October 1982.

Slater, Michael, *Dickens and Women*, Stanford, 1983.

Snowden, Dianne, The Irish Female Arsonists, unpublished paper, 2000.

Spain, Daphne, *Gendered Spaces*, Chapel Hill and London, 1992.

Spearritt, Katie, 'The Market for Marriage in Colonial Queensland', *Hecate*, vol. 16, nos. i/ii, 1990.

Stanley, Liz (ed.), *The Diaries of Hannah Cullwick, Victorian Maidservant*, London, 1984.

Stedman Jones, Gareth, *Outcast London: A Study in the Relationship between Classes in Victorian Society*, Harmondsworth, 1984, first published 1971.

Strachey, Ray, *The Cause: A Short History of the Women's Movement in Great Britain*, London, 1928.

Summers, Anne, *Damned Whores and God's Police: The Colonization of Women in Australia*, Melbourne, 1975.

Susman, M. P., 'Lucy Osburn and Her Five Nightingale Nurses', *The Medical Journal of Australia*, vol. 1, no. 18, May 1965.

Thane, Pat, 'Women and the Poor Law in Victorian and Edwardian England', *History Workshop*, no. 6, Autumn 1978.

Thomas, Brinley, *Migration and Economic Growth: A Study of Great Britain and the Atlantic Economy*, Cambridge, 1954.

Thompson, Flora, *Lark Rise to Candleford: A Trilogy*, London, 1948.

Townsley, W. A., 'Tasmania and the Great Economic Depression, 1858–1872', *Tasmanian Historical Research Association: Papers and Proceedings*, vol. 4, no. 2, July 1955.

Trollope, Joanna, *Britannia's Daughters: Women of the British Empire*, London, 1983.

van den Driesen, I. H., 'Convicts and Migrants in Western Australia 1850–1868: Their Number, Nature and Ethnic Origins', *Journal of the Royal Australian Historical Society*, June 1986.

Van-Helten, Jean Jacques and Keith Williams, ' "The crying need of South Africa": The Emigration of Single British Women to the Transvaal, 1901–10', *Journal of Southern African Studies*, vol. 10, no. 1, October 1983.

Vaughan Jones, Elizabeth, *1875–1975: One Hundred Years of the Girls' Friendly Society*, London, 1975.

Vellacott, Helen (ed.), *A Girl at Government House: An English Girl's Reminiscences: 'Below Stairs' in Colonial Australia*, Melbourne, 1982, first published 1932.

Vicinus, Martha, *Suffer and Be Still: Women in the Victorian Age*, London, 1980, first published Indiana, 1972.

—— *Independent Women: Work and Community for Single Women 1850–1920*, London, 1985.

—— (ed.), *A Widening Sphere: Changing Roles of Victorian Women*, Bloomington and London, 1977.

Wagner, Gillian, *Children of the Empire*, London, 1982.

Willett Cunnington, C., *Feminine Attitudes in the Nineteenth Century*, London and Toronto, 1935.

Wilson, Elizabeth, *Women and the Welfare State*, London, 1977.

Woolcock, Helen R., *Rights of Passage: Emigration to Australia in the Nineteenth Century*, London and New York, 1986.

Wrigley, E. A. (ed.), *An Introduction to English Historical Demography from the Sixteenth to the Nineteenth Century*, London, 1966.

—— *Nineteenth Century Society: Essays in the Use of Quantitative Methods for the Study of Social Data*, Cambridge, 1972.

[Young Women's Christian Association,] *The Golden Milestone 1880–1930*, Sydney, 1930.

—— *Our Eighty Years: Historical Sketches of the Y.W.C.A. of Great Britain*, London, 1935.

General Index

For single female immigrants, ships, shipboard matrons and surgeons-superintendent, see separate **Name Index**.

Name Index

Single Female Immigrants

Adge, Frances, 39
Andrews, H., 148
Apted, Emma, 110, 130
Atkins, Dorothy (Dot), 157
Baker, Kate, 40
Barratt, Nellie (and father), 122–3
Barrett, Selina, 169
Bland, Eliza (Elizabeth), 127–8
Blanks, Martha, 169
Brown, Annie, 154
Brown, Kate, 197
Butler, Ellen
Cannaughan, Bridget (Biddy), 142–3
Carrow (or Nuncarrow), Mary Ann, 33–4
Casey, Catherine, 39
Casey, Mary, 70
Clarke, Louisa and Annie, 145
Clinch, Sarah, 195–6
'Clouton, Kate', 147, 159–60
Collins, Anastatia, 19–20, 24
Copeland, Martha, 145
Corbett, Mary, 208
Curry, Lizzie, 169
Daly, Mary, 116

Davis, Fanny, 100
Domney, Fanny ('Cockney Fan') and Emily, 205–6
Donnelly, M., 148
Door, Ellen, 18
Doyle, Annie, 66
Dransfield, Edith, 169
Dryden, Elizabeth, 175
Duggan, Margaret, 19
Dunn, Bessie, 39
Dunn, Emily, 208
Edwards, Annie Jane, 145
Egan, Minnie, 169
Elmslie, F., 148
Fitzgerald, Mary, 19
Gardner, Lilly, 84
Gilbert, Rose, 23
Grattan, Annie, 119–20
Hall, Beatrice, 154, 157
Hall, Carrie (Caroline), 197–201
Hamilton, Alice, 81
Hawkins, D., 148
Heather, Ellen, 40
Hennessy, Catherine, 39, 41
Heywood, Ellen, 23
Higgins, Jane, 19
Hill, Alice, 147
Hill, Maria, 127
Hodgkinson, Esther, 169

Ships

Shipboard Matrons

Surgeons-superintendent